THE CHANGING MIDDLE EAST

THE
CHANGING
MIDDLE
EAST

EMIL LENGYEL

THE JOHN DAY COMPANY

NEW YORK

56191

ACKNOWLEDGMENT

The author expresses his heartfelt thanks to Catherine Logan Camhy for the generous help she extended to him in the preparation of this book.

The author wishes also to thank M. H. Kessel, publisher, and Milton Elson, editor, of the Oxford Book Company, for permission to use the title The Changing Middle East, *which is also the title of an Oxford Social Studies Pamphlet, written by the author. It is only the title which the present book and the pamphlet have in common.*

PREFACE

THIS book deals mainly with Middle Eastern events in the agitated decade 1950–60. Since, however, historic events do not sprint from a sharply designated white line—as track athletes do —the mid-century mark serves merely as an approximate beginning. Occasionally, a short passage of background is provided when the history of today is in close organic relation with that of yesterday.

The Middle East covered in this book extends from Libya to Iran. There is no authoritative and generally accepted designation of the region, so that every author has to define it for his purpose. No distinction is made in this book between the Near East and the Middle East—the two terms are interchangeable.

As to the transliteration of Arabic names, the only rule is an attempt at consistency. Arab names can be transliterated into Latin script in at least half a dozen ways, as, for instance, Kassem, Kassim, Qasim, etc. Transliterations are approximations of the Arabic sounds.

The reader will notice that more chapters deal with the Arab countries than with the others. This is so because more Arab history has been packed into this decade as a result of a large number of revolutions, near-revolutions and coups.

CONTENTS

THE CHANGING MIDDLE EAST

INTRODUCTION

America's Role in the Middle East

AMERICA'S past role in the Middle East was peripheral—confined mainly to missionary and other cultural work. No special doctrine or consistent policy defined the attitude of the United States toward the region extending from the Eastern Mediterranean to Aden. If this lack is set against the dynamism of American foreign policy in other regions, its significance becomes more manifest.

Early in the nation's life the Western Hemisphere was placed under the protection of the Monroe Doctrine. "You may be unable to help waging your wars and encroaching upon other continents," the United States seemed to admonish Europe, "but the Western Hemisphere will be shielded from you and your eternal quarrels." The bold words of the Monroe Doctrine were buttressed by the forces of nature and the British navy, for it was in Britain's own interest that Latin America should not relapse into Iberia's gravitational field, with its antiquated restrictive practices of mercantilism, which would work havoc with Britain's dynamic trade. Also, the potential aggressor, Spain, was convulsed by endemic disorder and further weakened by the traditionalist tendencies of a regime that was uncommonly obscurantist even for its age. But, above all, it was the Atlantic and the Pacific that lent their strength to the implementation of the Doctrine.

In the Far East, too, a clear-cut policy was America's response

13

to the challenge of the vast land mass. Equal opportunity to all seekers of trade influence was the hallmark of the Far Eastern Open Door, because it was upon a balance of power that America's position there depended. This American policy was the projection of the "manifest destiny" creed in fulfillment of which America had swept across the continent—only to reach the ocean-girt ultimate frontier. The momentum of the westward march and the energies released by it were so torrential that the United States could not halt on the continental coast. Across the ocean new trade frontiers beckoned. America's bold approach had opened Japan, but how much more profitable would be the Chinese market than trade on the constricted Japanese islands? The mainland door, therefore, must be kept open.

Vis-à-vis Europe, America's unstated policy was misunderstood sometimes by its very makers, let alone outsiders. Assuming that America could be insulated from Europe's problems, the New World attempted to turn its back on the problems of the Old World. It was not realized, evidently, that no one particular area of the global human mansion could be fireproofed. In reality, isolation from Europe was a fair-weather attitude, because with the rise of an emergency on the continent, America's protective forces were released. In such instances the foreign policy of the United States usually ran parallel with that of Great Britain. Should Britain be imperiled, the United States must act, for a débâcle involving England would also entail disaster for America. This was demonstrated in the First World War no less than during the Second. When Britain, the first line of defense, was endangered, the United States had to act.

Britain's Peace

"The law of nations is anarchy"—but this is so only on the surface. "The sovereign equality of all nations is the rule of international law"—again, superficially only. The law of nations, in normal times, is the tacit acceptance of a balance. There was

14

classical Rome and *Pax Romana.* After several later attempts to re-create conditions of peace, including that of the Holy Roman Empire, there was a return to the balance of power operated by other nations—Spain, briefly; the Hapsburgs, futilely; and *Pax Gallica,* spasmodically. The world, eventually, turned to the Britannic peace, supervised by a small power less subject to corrosive jealousy. Isolated from the continental battlefield, Britain had certain advantages—comparative immunity to attack, sturdy national traits, the ability to rule the waves because of her maritime location and unmatched navy. She was a global police power.

The other countries were free to enjoy their "sovereign equality" except when they attempted to dominate the continent, thereby upsetting the European balance. This policy was given its classic formulation in the famous Foreign Office memorandum of Sir Eyre Crowe in 1907 that Britain will "throw her weight now in this scale and now in that, but ever on the side opposed to political dictatorship of the strongest single state or group at a given time."

It was in the interest of other powers, too, to prevent a dynamic force from monopolizing power on the continent, and these "peace-loving" nations made up Britain's "constituency" in the foreign field. France under Napoleon the Great was a menace to the balance, as was Germany under Kaiser Wilhelm II and Adolf Hitler's Third Reich. Against them Britain mobilized the protective forces of Europe. The nature of this arrangement was illustrated by its nineteenth-century name—the European concert. The conductor was Britain, and other powers, such as France, the Austrian monarchy, Italy, and even Germany, were the players.

During this time, the "constituency" of British foreign policy was limited. Members of the concert were European nations, some of which had colonies. The people of these colonies that formed the majority of mankind did not count. What counted was "quality," not quantity. With the world's largest population, China

15

counted only as a passive body, not an active participant. She was an amorphous body in search of a national soul. India was a few hundred British officials and her hundreds of millions of people were weightless in diplomacy.

Today Britain is no longer the conductor and Britannic peace belongs to the past. We live in the age of *Pax Americana,* which faces an entirely different world. The previous distinction between "quality" and "quantity" is being effaced. The "masses" of Asia and Africa have become people, no longer passive objects but active forces. America's constituency is different from that of Britain. The majority are people of color who are losing their feeling of inferiority toward the white-skinned people. At the conferences of Asian-African peoples, first at Bandung, Indonesia, in 1955, then in Cairo, Accra, and other cities, one could detect a new "revolt of the masses," the revolt of "color." Indians, Arabs, Berbers—whom the anthropologists classify as "whites"— have proudly proclaimed their affinity with the nonwhites. "There are more human beings who are colored; therefore it is more human to be a man of color."

At this point the American peace meets the American dilemma. We are proud of America's achievements in race relations but the nonwhite world is less easy to satisfy. Where are our colored Supreme Court Justices or members of the Cabinet? How will the American dilemma and the American peace get together?

The Terrible Oversimplifiers

The French sociologist, Ernest Renan, saw great danger for the world in the work of *les terribles simplificateurs.* Diplomacy may be based upon a few accepted axioms but its techniques are highly involved, requiring infinite patience, deliberation, and readiness to compromise. "American democracy," said Count Alexis de Tocqueville in his classic *Democracy in America,* "is ill-fitted to conduct foreign policy. Fortunately, it has none." But these words were written more than a century ago. Now America must have

16

a foreign policy or face the extinction not only of her own national existence but of the world. Democracy does not distinguish itself by its patience, deliberation, and spirit of compromise in the conduct of foreign relations. The old maxim: "Right or wrong, my country," has been changed to: "My country cannot be wrong." The "mass man," timorous as an individual, becomes intrepid when he strikes a heroic pose as the citizen of his country. Also he finds security within the bosom of a supposedly invincible community. His greatest admiration is evoked by an intransigent attitude, irrespective of the consequences. Great Britain, in the days of the Empire, had a democracy, too, but she had inherited the *noblesse oblige* attitude of another age. No great power conceived in the spirit of democracy has ever framed a successful foreign policy. The United States could be the first—if people learned that there can be no foreign policy without calculated risks, that in foreign relations the pursuit of absolute truth is a chimera which is the admission of unwillingness to compromise, and that compromise is the very lifeblood of democracy. All white and all black have never been the colors of international relations.

Bulls in the Arena

The American system of government was framed before the United States was a great power. How difficult it is to conduct foreign relations under this system! One of its special features is the division of power, the system of checks and balances. But in order to be truly successful, a foreign policy must be unified, consistent. In Washington the steering wheel is in the hands of the President, while the brakes are controlled by Congress. The President proposes, Congress disposes—or the other way around. The President nominates an ambassador to represent the majesty of his country, but before he can do so he is subjected to a humiliating senatorial third degree. How majestic will be the majesty he represents? An international treaty submitted by the President for the confirmation of the Senate is like a bull sent into the arena

17

—few of them come out alive. So the President employs various devices—will exaggerate the importance of the pact, will describe it as essential for national survival when it is only for convenience. Or else he gives it the silent treatment, as an "executive agreement," and will keep it from Congress.

The late Secretary of State John Foster Dulles spoke about the ultimate need of a parliamentary type of government for the successful conduct of America's foreign relations. Under such a system the executive and the legislative perform integrated, not rival, functions, working together instead of at cross purposes. The Cabinet and the House of Commons form a harmonious unit. When the nation elects the members of Parliament, it also chooses the executive branch, which carries out the will of the majority with due regard to the will of the minority as well. Under such a system there are no "blood feuds" between the various branches of government checking and balancing one another—there are no wasteful jurisdictional disputes.

Nations are devoted to their traditional institutions, which they consider superior to those of all others. The United States is no exception. America has not been long enough at the head of an international coalition to be able to appraise the restrictive effects on dynamic leadership of the strained relations between the two branches of government, especially if they belong to two parties. But the effects are very obvious when one surveys America's relations in the Middle East, where partisanship plays an important role. The time must come when stock-taking will be in order about co-ordinating the foreign-policy functions of the executive and legislative branches of government.

These are some of the basic factors in the "American dilemma" which have deep significance as the United States ventures into the field where its experiences have been even more limited than in others—the Middle East.

The Middle East and the surrounding area.

CHAPTER 1

Looking Backward

The "Dry War" in the Middle East

DURING the Britannic peace the Middle East was a "power vacuum," inadequately occupied by the flabby and amorphous body of the Ottoman Empire, which had lost the flexibility and resiliency of a Great Power and was unable to defend itself against international rapacity. Thus, it occupied the position of a satellite, for the region was important to Britain as the fulcrum of a global imperial system, which flanked strategic highways—the Dardanelles, the Suez Canal—along British lifelines leading to India, the pivot of Britain's global realm.

By the end of the eighteenth century Britain's Middle Eastern policy had been given its classical formulation by William Pitt the Younger: "In the aggrandisement of Russia and the depression of Turkey our commercial and political interests are both concerned." More than a century later an even more self-confident Britain spoke through Lord Lansdowne, her Secretary of State for Foreign Affairs: ". . . We should regard the establishment of a naval base or a fortified port in the [Persian] Gulf by any other power as a very great menace to British interests, and we should certainly resist it by all means at our disposal."

A list of great Britishers who have been involved in Middle Eastern affairs makes an impressive roster, attesting the importance of the region to the empire: Lord Kitchener of Khartoum; Gordon Pasha of Sudan fame; more recently Lord Allenby; the fantastic T. E. Lawrence of Arabia, a leader of the revolt in the desert during World War I; and the contemporary Sir John Bagot Glubb, better known as "Glubb Pasha" of the Arab Legion of Transjordan, the later Hashemite Kingdom of the Jordan.* Interest in the Middle East is also evidenced by a long line of British writers who have dealt with the region. Charles Montagu Doughty's *Travels in Arabia Deserta* is an exotic nineteenth-century classic in Chaucerian language. David George Hogarth, archaeologist and keeper of the Ashmolean Museum at Oxford, is the author of other classics of Arabia: *A Wandering Scholar* and *Ancient East*. Then there are the writings of Harry St. John Bridger Philby, author of *Heart of Arabia* and many other books; the notable women explorers, Gertrude Margaret Lowthian Bell, author of *The Desert and the Sown,* Freya Madeline Stark, author of *The Southern Gates of Arabia,* and others. No less important than the soldiers and authors were the notable colonial administrators, anonymous heroes, some of them active even today in the Persian Gulf region.

The Bear That Walks Like a Man

"Constantinople is very far from you," Czar Alexander I told the Marquis de Caulaincourt, Ambassador of Napoleon the Great. ". . . I have an idea, so that this should create no difficulties. Let's turn it into a free city."

Other Russian rulers had ideas of this nature. As they saw it, Constantinople was very far from Paris, London and Vienna but was close to St. Petersburg, Petrograd and Leningrad. "Constantinople is worth half an empire," Napoleon had said. Russia had grown huge and she had everything—a large population, vast spaces and natural resources—but she lacked the ability to employ all this wealth to best advantage in foreign relations. "A mansion

* Further references will be made to "Glubb Pasha."

with a thousand windows but no gate," Russia had a surplus of frozen waters but no warm-water exit to the great commercial sea routes.

The search for warm-water outlets began early in Russian history and was inherited in the twentieth century by the Soviet Union. No other great power shared this utterly anomalous position. The country had grown to enormous proportions by expanding in regions where she encountered no great power resistance— these powers having concentrated their energies in South Asia —or local opposition. Russia's line of march took her into the vastnesses of northern latitudes, sparsely settled by the fragments of Mongol power. Moscow's heavy hand fell on one Mongol khanate after another; Kazan and Sibir in the east; Astrakhan in the south; and the theocratic despotisms of places like Samarkand and Bokhara in Central Asia. In the west the Russians swept into the Baltic countries and Poland. As these fragments were woven into one connected land surface, the world's largest under the rule of one nation, it seemed that no force could slacken this titanic march.

During the centuries of expansion and absorption, Russia had one advantage over the more advanced nations—her people felt themselves participants in a cause, a kind of crusade. They were unlike any other nation in that they were soldiers of Christ, exalted warriors of the Christian creed. This belief might have resulted from the fact that most of the time they were combating "pagans" like the Mongols, the Tartar Khans and, later, the Muslim Ottoman Turks. They believed themselves to be impregnated with the spirit of the Holy Ghost and they described the sanctified condition of their congregation as *sobornost*. Their country's capital was not merely a city but the New Rome of Christendom. They were the chosen people; their country, Holy Russia.

So, in an inspired massive eastward march, they won mastery of all of the top of Asia and Eastern Europe. But in spite of its millions of square miles, their country had a flaw. Bicontinental and, for a time (with American Alaska) tricontinental, though they were, they had no important warm-water outlets.

With their victory over the Khanate of the Krim, the Russians touched the edge of the Middle East when they reached the Black Sea in 1783. But the sea was closed to them. Even more intolerable, it was locked in their faces by the Ottoman Turks, the despised "pagans," despoilers of the most sacred sanctuary of eastern Christendom, the Holy Church of Aja Sophia in the town of Constantine on the Golden Horn. That city, again, was not like any other metropolis but was hallowed ground, the holy place from which they had received their creed—their second Rome. Having reached the Black Sea, the Russians had encountered their great frustration.

The Ottoman Empire itself had been a global force, situated as it was at the junction of three continents, along the world's most important trade routes. It had been a global menace, too—dark Asia's threat to Christendom. Few more appalling forces had been encountered than the Turks, who moved with concentrated fury, inexorably toward their distant goal. Their march toward the west was like that of fiery lava on the slopes of an erupting volcano.

Like the Russians, they too were spurred by a religious fervor to conquer, not the "pagan," but the "infidel." But in the end, the Ottoman realm became too vast, too dependent on armed might, too arrogant. Its life forces spent, it was not able even to defend its own original lands, and thus a power vacuum was created in the Middle Eastern hub. And so it was a static Turkey that faced a dynamic Russia across the Black Sea and here was the root of the evil. With Ottoman power in the decline the Czars of all the Russias nourished the thought of redeeming Constantinople the Holy City, which the Russians called the City of the Czars, Czarigrad.

"We have a sick man on our hands," history records Czar Nicholas I as saying in 1853 to Sir George Hamilton Seymour, the British Ambassador. "It will be a great misfortune if he slips

24

through our hands one of these days, especially before the necessary arrangements are made." *

To the Western countries the Russians recalled that, centuries before, Christian leaders had launched a holy war against the Muslim pagans in the Holy Land, and now, again, Christian soldiers would be marching against Islam's heartland. Great was Russia's dismay when the Western world failed to heed the Christian call to arms. Instead, the proposed crusade moved in reverse, and Christians made common cause with Muslims as Britain and Turkey marched against "Holy Russia."

It was the age of British peace and it was Britain that objected to Christian replacing Muslim on the Golden Horn. The English suspected that what the Russians really craved was not the triumph of the cross, but an outlet on the Mediterranean, and that, London decided, was to be denied. In this region, as in Europe and the Far East, Britain pursued the policy of the balance of power, shoring up tottering regimes as counterweights in vital locations, setting the weak against the strong. Russia appeared fantastically strong (there was the testimony of the map showing millions upon millions of Russian square miles) and Britain was apprehensive that, should the Czar's massive force grind its inexorable way to the Mediterranean, Britain's slender imperial lifeline linking London with Calcutta would be snapped. The policy was firmly formulated in London that Russia was to be contained by confining it to her mansion of a million windows but not a single gate. It was Prince Khristofor Lieven, Czarist Ambassador to Berlin and later London, who noted in an official dispatch in October 1825: "All Europe looks with a shudder at this Russian colossus whose giant strength is only waiting for a signal to start in motion against it. Europe's interest is therefore to protect the Turkish power, this natural foe of our realm."

* "The sick man of Europe," the designation of the Turk, remained. There is warrant for the assumption that the Czar used the Russian-oriented phrase "dead bear" which the British Ambassador translated from the French into English as the "sick man." Whether the enemy was a sick man or a dead bear, the Russians wanted to lead a crusade against the Turks.

25

Rudyard Kipling expressed these thoughts in a verse:

> Beware the embrace of Adam-ze
> The bear that walks like a man.

This is the philosophy of the problem today, too, in the age of the "American peace."

Young America and the "Pyrates"

Looking backward at America's role in the Middle East, we do not find it occupying many pages of history. The few contacts of the United States were not of an overwhelming importance. There was the case of the Barbary pirates at the beginning of the last century. In the search for markets, enterprising Yankees had not overlooked the Mediterranean. A report of Secretary of State Thomas Jefferson to Congress in 1790 spoke of about a hundred small ships venturing into these perilous seas, infested by "pyrates." The aggregate tonnage was some twenty thousand, navigated by about twelve hundred seamen. Mediterranean ports took about one-sixth of the wheat and flour exported from America. Then the "pyrates" began to interfere. They had their way along the Barbary (Berber) Coast of North Africa as the attention of the British "policeman of the seas" was engaged elsewhere. At first America did not think it worth while to fight the sea robbers and, for a time, bought a measure of immunity from Moroccan piratical raids for a paltry $10,000 in 1787. Secretary of State John Jay viewed this degrading situation with a curious satisfaction. "If the Barbary corsairs could only cause deep enough humiliation, the American people might be shamed into strengthening their national government to meet the foreign peril." When Jay heard of a reported declaration of war upon the United States by Algiers, he was pleased. "This war," he wrote, "does not strike me as a great evil. The more we are ill-treated abroad the more we shall unite and consolidate at home." Jay's hope was fulfilled in 1789 when the United States abandoned the inadequate articles of Confederation and adopted the present federal Constitution. . . .*

This policy encouraged the lawless elements of the adjacent coasts: Algeria, Tunisia and Tripolitania. In October 1800, the Dey (Viceroy) of Algeria—which was nominally under Ottoman rule—ordered the S.S. *George Washington* to haul down her banner and hoist the flag of the Algerian outlaws. Then he ordered Commodore William Bainbridge to sail to Constantinople, carrying tribute to the Sultan. When the Commodore remonstrated, the Dey replied: "You have become my slave, because you pay me tribute. I have the right to order you as I think proper." Peace, on America's terms, was eventually forced on the pirates in Algerian and Tripolitanian waters. The hero of the War with the Barbary Pirates was Stephen Decatur and it was battles in these waters that prompted him to propose the celebrated toast which enriched the English vocabulary with another winged phrase: "Our country! In her intercourse with foreign nations may she always be in the right; but our country, right or wrong!"

By that time American farm surplus, which was to plague the economic life of this country, was already playing a role in foreign relations. President Andrew Jackson dispatched special agents to the Ottoman Empire to negotiate the sale of such surplus. While not much business was transacted with the Turks, a treaty of extraterritoriality was negotiated under which American citizens were to be subject to their own consular courts in the Empire, just as the nationals of European Great Powers.

It was a *cause célèbre* that first involved the United States in Middle Eastern history and its name was the "Koszta Affair." Márton Koszta was a Hungarian who appears to have fought the Hapsburgs in his country's notable war of independence in 1848-1849. When the Hungarians were defeated, he fled the country and, after adventurous peregrinations, found his way to the United States, where he declared his intention of becoming a

* Thomas A. Bailey, *A Diplomatic History of the American People.* New York: F. S. Crofts & Co. 1942, p. 52.

citizen and obtained his first papers. Before becoming a full-fledged American citizen, however, he went to the city of Smyrna on a business trip. This was in 1853. In Smyrna he got into very serious trouble.

The Ottoman Empire was so weakened by that time that it was not able to control the activities of the agents of Great Powers on its soil. It is possible that the Austrian representatives stationed at this Turkish port knew about Koszta's past, but it is also possible that the events of which he became the center were all due to mistaken identity. In any case, he was kidnaped on the Smyrna waterfront and taken in chains aboard the Austrian brig *Hussar*, then at anchor in Smyrna bay. Before his disappearance he had made his presence known to the Consul of the United States.

At that particular time, the American sloop of war *St. Louis*, Duncan Nathaniel Ingraham, U.S.N., commanding, sailed into Smyrna harbor. Commander Ingraham, having been promptly informed about the kidnaping, dispatched an ultimatum to the Austrian vessel to release Koszta. The Ottoman authorities took no action in matters where foreign powers were involved and it was thus left to the captains of the American and Austrian war vessels to settle this matter. The Austrian commander replied that his prisoner was not a United States citizen and did not even claim citizenship rights. He was an Austrian subject, to be dealt with according to Austrian laws. Ingraham knew that Koszta was in possession only of American first papers but that was enough for him to claim that he was under the protection of the United States. At his own responsibility he took further action. He had the muzzles of his cannons bared and trained on the Austrian ship and repeated his ultimatum. Koszta was promptly released and conveyed to the American ship.

The Austrian chargé in Washington, Chevalier Hülsemann, protested against Ingraham's action to Secretary of State William L. Marcy, who, however, returned a vigorous reply. Marcy desired the Democratic presidential nomination and aimed at appealing to the large immigrant vote. The case received much publicity in the United States, and Ingraham a hero's welcome.

The rest of the story is largely anticlimactic. Koszta failed to make his mark in the United States and vanished into Central America, where he appears to have fallen the victim of foul play. Commander Ingraham fought on the side of the Southern Confederacy during the Civil War and became commander of the naval forces on the coast of South Carolina.

The significance of the incident is noted in an echo of the Koszta affair, a comment by a very famous correspondent of the New York *Tribune:* "Americans have abstracted another Hungarian from the claws of the Austrian eagle. It is cheering to see the American intervention in Europe beginning with just the eastern question."

The correspondent of the American newspaper was Karl Marx.

The Middle East, Karl Marx and America

In his correspondence to the *Tribune,* Marx paid close attention to the connection of the United States with the Middle East. Writing in the summer of 1853 he noted that although the United States was not considered a leading power in the Middle East, it could no longer accept the "humble position assigned to it in the past," having "sprung up to the most exalted degree of wealth, civilization, and power."

He recorded diplomatic grapevine and European press comments. It is of interest to recall that as far back as 1840, if Marx's reporting can be trusted, the administration in Washington sought to gain a Mediterranean naval base. The United States government, according to a diplomatic *on dit,* which had been leaked to the Italian newspaper *Il Parlamento,* had approached the King of Two Sicilies to grant it the temporary use of Syracuse in Sicily. The title of this story was *"La Politica Americana in Europa."* If such an attempt was ever made, it was abortive.

29

Marx also recorded press notices in Germany about a "secret treaty pretended to have been concluded between the United States and Turkey, according to which the latter would receive money and maritime support, the former the harbor of Enos in Rumelia, which would afford a sure and convenient place for a commercial and military station of the American Republic on the Mediterranean."

Enos (classical Ainos and today's Enez) is on the Aegean, at the mouth of the Maritsa (Ergenez) River, at the present Greek-Turkish frontier. If the United States really ever wanted its small harbor, it surely could not have been for the purposes of a naval base. While all of this may not have been more than diplomatic gossip, it is of interest to note that Europe, evidently, expected the United States to take a hand in Mediterranean affairs fully a century before the establishment of the Sixth Fleet of the United States in Mediterranean waters.

Marx also called attention to the Isthmus of Suez which, in his opinion, would be important to the United States as well as to Europe. He questioned whether America should not exercise vigilance with regard to the neutrality of the Isthmus, especially in view of the possibility of the dissolution of the Ottoman Empire and the control of Egypt and Syria by some first-rate power. It seems, then, that the celebrated founder of Marxist socialism much preferred the United States to Russia, and American capitalism to Czarist feudalism.

The American Civil War and Egyptian Cotton

The Middle East, especially Egypt, played a small role in the American Civil War in a rather roundabout way. The American South believed that the Western European Powers, especially those with important cotton industries, would support the Southern cause because of their dependence on Southern cotton. "The cards are in our hands," exulted the Charleston *Mercury* in a typical Southern comment on this issue, "and we play them out to the bankruptcy of every cotton factory in Great Britain and France, or the acknowledgment of our independence."

However, events did not take the course anticipated by the Confederacy. Southern cotton no longer had a monopoly in the markets of the world. There were now the "Pasha Cotton" of Egypt and the "Maharajah Cotton" of India to replace the "King Cotton" of the American South. Western Europe was not forced to its knees by the threatened withdrawal of Southern cotton. It was largely as a result of the American Civil War that Egypt's cotton production increased vastly, the revenue multiplying five-fold, from £5 million to £25 million, during approximately that period.

Americans appeared briefly on the Egyptian scene during the regime of the reckless Ismail Pasha, Khedive of Egypt, who in 1875 was compelled to sell those famous Suez Canal shares to Britain's Disraeli for £3,976,582, and thus deliver to the British government a controlling interest in the Canal company. Khedive Ismail followed an expansionist policy, moving into the Sudan's remote regions and trying also to move into Ethiopia. For his military adventures he needed a more effective army. It needed thorough training but the Khedive did not wish to bring British, French or other European officers into his country, apprehensive lest once they were there they would want to stay there. Instead, he invited a group of forty-eight American officers under General C. P. Stone to reorganize his army. However, venality and intrigue were so rampant in Egypt that the American training officers had to withdraw, their mission unaccomplished.

The flag of the United States appeared in the harbor of Alexandria, in the company of the banners of other major powers. In 1882 a revolution broke out in Egypt against the government, the Turks, and foreign influence, under the leadership of Ahmad Arabi al-Misri. Many European lives were lost in the rioting. Warships of leading powers appeared in Alexandria for the protection of their nationals, and one of those vessels represented the United States. Eventually, the British took Alexandria and placed Egypt under their military occupation, which lasted for three-quarters of a century.

Missionaries and Printing Presses

America's main concern with the Middle East in the nineteenth century was missionary and cultural. The first American missionaries arrived in the region about 1820, and fourteen years later they set up an Arabic press in Lebanon, which was the main entrance gate of the West to the coast of the Levant. In 1866, an Amherst graduate American missionary, Daniel Bliss, founded the Syrian Protestant College (now the American University) of Beirut. Situated on the beautiful St. George Bay, in the shadow of the mountains of Lebanon, it became one of the most distinguished schools of higher learning in the Middle East, with a roster of graduates that contains well-known names. Bliss himself served as president of the college and devoted forty years to work in Syria.

Bebek Seminary was established in Turkey in 1863 by another missionary, Cyrus Hamlin. Eight years later it was transferred to Constantinople and renamed Robert College, after C. R. Robert of New York, who provided its initial funds. Hamlin opened a workshop where young Turks could train and test their manual skills. This was an important beginning, because manual labor was held in low esteem in the Ottoman realm and was one of the causes of its technical backwardness.

Religion and nationality were as one in the Muslim Middle East, and relinquishing one's creed was tantamount to forswearing one's country—disloyal, even treasonous. Direct missionary activity was thus hampered but, luckily for the few converts, the authorities were often as indolent as they were venal. Arts and sciences, however, were not under the ban even though taught by missionaries. Much of the missionary activity was therefore directed toward those fields. The Society of Arts and Sciences and the Syrian Scientific Society were the by-products of missionary work. In a variety of ways the standards of morality, education and material well-being were raised. "Directly or indirectly," a United States consul at Smyrna said about the missionaries, "every phase of their work is rapidly paving the way for American trade."

Americans were also engaged in significant Biblical and archaeological work. Edward Robinson is considered the "pioneer and father of Biblical geography." A professor of Biblical literature at Union Theological Seminary, he left America for three years of study in Palestine and Germany in 1838, and he initiated an important program of historical exploration, the fruits of which were his famous *Biblical Researches* and *Physical Geography of the Holy Land*. He was aided by Eli Smith, a distinguished scholar in the field of Oriental studies and an ardent missionary.

Less fruitful were some of the enterprises which Americans sought to launch before the discovery of oil in the Middle East. The beginning of the twentieth century was the age of the great railway rush, and in many parts of the world Americans promoted building projects. Commander Arthur Chester, son of Rear Admiral Colby Mitchell Chester, foresaw great opportunities in a railway line which was to link the Mesopotamian hinterland with the Mediterranean port of Alexandretta (Iskenderon), part of the Ottoman Empire then. At the outset, he felt encouraged concerning the "Chester Project" by influential circles in Constantinople, and he established the Ottoman-American Development Company. No sooner had he settled down to business when British, French and German competitors began to wage a bitter war on him. The American diplomatic representatives in the Ottoman Empire and the State Department supported Chester completely. However, the business representatives of other nations were more strongly entrenched. The Sublime Porte * in Constantinople was not so sublime that *baksheesh*—graft—was not accepted in court

---

* The Sublime Porte in Turkey, the name once given to the government, derived from the high gate giving access to the building in Constantinople where the officers of the principal state departments were situated.

circles as an insurance of favor toward a particular firm. The authorities failed to approve the Chester plan and it collapsed. After the First World War, when stakes in the Middle East became enormous, Americans recalled this experience.

The Ottoman Empire Goes to War

The Ottoman Empire, in which theocracy and secular power were fused, was headed by the Caliph, who claimed to be the successor of Mohammed and of his exalted seed. In Islamic theocracy the world consists of two parts, the regime of peace, the world of Islam—and the regime of war, the other worlds. This was far more a theory than diplomatic practice. In the past the Sublime Porte was dependent on the help of non-Muslims, particularly the British. In the Crimean War, in the middle of the nineteenth century, the regimes of peace and regimes of war went to war together against the Turks' most hated foes, the Muscovites. The First World War broke out in 1914 and this time the Ottoman Empire was not making common cause with the British, which had despoiled the Porte of Egypt and was waging war on the Germans in the company of the Russians. The enemies of the Russians were bound to be the friends of the Turks; and the Germans were now the Russians' foes. Another reason for this change may have been the result of the reappraisal of the world situation by the Turks. The Sublime Porte had probably reached the conclusion that in the twentieth century the past belonged to London, the future to Berlin.

It was therefore on the side of the Central European Powers, Germany and Austria-Hungary, that the Ottoman Empire marched to war against Britain and the other members of the Triple Entente. The Germans were non-Muslims, of course, and the times were such that now even in the East the alliance with them had to be explained to the Turkish "man in the street." The explanation was provided to the Sultan's subjects that the Germans had let themselves be converted to the Prophet's true faith and had become Muslims. Incontrovertible proof was provided in the form of photographs of Germany's devastated Christian churches, which the Islamic Germans themselves were said to have wrecked. These pictures were disseminated all over the Ottoman Empire. Nor was this entirely an invention of the Turks. The Christian churches had, indeed, been destroyed by the Germans—only they belonged to the French.

By the time the United States entered the war, the Ottoman Empire already was disintegrating under British hammer blows. This was not a nation in the modern sense of the word, but a country consisting of disparate elements held together by the *mystique* of a dynasty and the assumption that it had strength. The ethnic Turks occupied only the core of the realm, the Anatolian plateau. In the larger cities, the "minorities"—Greeks, Armenians, Jews—taken together often formed the majorities. Outside Anatolia, the inhabitants of the empire were largely Arabs, mixed with Kurds and other nationalities. This situation, plus the defeat of the Central European Powers, seemed to call for the extinction of the "sick man of Europe." It was taken for granted that the separate parts of the Ottoman Empire would be distributed among the victors of the war. Various "secret" treaties to this effect were no longer secret, having been made public by the newly established Soviet government. The fate of Poland—distributed among her neighbors in the late eighteenth century—would most likely befall the Ottoman Empire in the twentieth century.

The government of the United States, however, dissented. It had not broken relations with the Ottoman Empire when it went to war against the Central Powers. "Self-determination of the nations" was an important tenet of the American creed and the capstone of the world of perpetual peace that was to dawn upon mankind in the wake of an apocalyptic war.

The Twelfth Point

Wilson's peace message to the world was his Fourteen Points, the twelfth of which dealt with the fate of the Ottoman realm:

The Turkish portions of the present Ottoman Empire should be assured a secured sovereignty, but the other nationalities which are under Turkish rule should be assured an undoubted security of life and an absolutely unmolested opportunity of autonomous development, and the Dardanelles should be permanently opened as a free passage to the ships and commerce of all nations under international guarantees.

There was also an official commentary of the Fourteen Points, approved by President Wilson. It was prepared by Walter Lippmann, young secretary of the organization, who collected data for the peace conference, directed by the President's adviser, E. M. House. These commentaries went into greater detail than the Points themselves. The one on the Twelfth Point recommended that in dealing with the Ottoman Empire the Turks should be assigned that portion of the realm in which they formed the majority: Anatolia. The Armenians in the Ottoman Empire were to obtain a country of their own, with access to a port on the Mediterranean. The capital of the empire, Constantinople, was to be placed under international control. Parts of the Empire inhabited by non-Turks—largely Arabs—were to be placed under a new kind of regime, "mandates," in which the mandatory, or governing, power was to train the people under its control for eventual self-government.

"A Sacred Trust"

The "mandate" was a new concept in international relations. The system was created by Article 22 of the Covenant of the League of Nations, forming part of the Treaty of Versailles. In the language of the Covenant, this tutelage was to be entrusted

36

to "advanced nations who by reason of their resources, their experience or their geographical position can best undertake this responsibility, and who are willing to accept it, and that this tutelage should be exercised by them as mandatories on behalf of the League."

The term applied to territories designated by the treaties for the administration of non-Turkish possessions of the Ottoman Empire and the overseas possessions of the German Reich. The area detached from the Ottoman Empire was inhabited mainly by Arabs and was to be turned into several mandated territories.

In the distribution of the Arab regions, France received Syria and Lebanon, whose people did not consider themselves backward or in need of a training period. Lebanon, particularly, had long been exposed to Western influence. The former Mesopotamia was renamed Iraq and placed under the tutelage of Britain, as was Palestine, which eventually was bisected into Palestine proper and Transjordan. Russia had been promised Constantinople and the Straits during the war, but the 1917 Revolution and the subsequent separate peace which the Soviet government had made with the Central Powers had, so far as the Allies were concerned, canceled the obligation. Besides, fear of the "Bolshevik menace" had already set in and the West was as determined to keep the U.S.S.R. from access to the Mediterranean as it had been with the old Russian Empire.

In general, the mandatory idea found little favor in Arab eyes. Meeting in Damascus on July 2, 1919, the General Syrian Congress protested: ". . . We protest against Article 22 of the Covenant of the League of Nations, placing us among the nations in their middle stage of development which stand in need of a mandatory power." The Arabs inhabiting the Syrian area, the protest stated further, were not naturally less gifted than the Bulgarians, Rumanians, Serbians and Greeks had been at the beginning of their independence.

President Wilson sought to ascertain the wishes of the communities that were to come under mandatory rule, and with that

37

end in view he attempted to prevail upon Britain, France and Italy to establish an international committee on mandates in the Middle East; but the plan was rejected. The three nations had already made their arrangements through their wartime pacts. Consequently, a fact-finding committee, headed by Dr. H. C. King and Charles R. Crane, was deputized only by President Wilson. They visited Syria and found that the population rejected the idea of the French mandate. Nevertheless, it was decided upon in accordance with the agreement between Britain and France.

The United States was urged by David Lloyd George and Georges Clemenceau, Prime Ministers of Britain and France, to accept a mandate for a re-created Armenia. Under Turkish rule the Armenians had been the victims of a campaign of race extermination, and there was much sympathy for their cause in the United States. The mandate was to assure the Armenians an "undoubted security of life and absolutely unmolested opportunity of autonomous development." But the offer to the United States was not seriously considered, let alone accepted. It did not help much that at the Paris Peace Conference in 1919 the Armenian delegates demanded a "Great Armenia" extending from sea to sea. The United States Senate broke with President Wilson and kept the country out of the League, which, under its Covenant, was largely an American creation. The idea of an independent or even an autonomous Armenia was dropped. Eventually, the Armenian Soviet Socialist Republic, a component of the Soviet Union, came into being to speak in the name of that much-tried community.

The Voice of Silence

Between the two World Wars the diplomatic role of the United States in the Middle East was extremely limited. This was the classical age of isolation which reveled in the assumption that regarding foreign relations, the United States was not part of the globe. Many Americans assumed that international problems, if

38

ignored, ceased to exist. The administration in Washington went so far as to refuse even to acknowledge receipt of communications of the League. America had withdrawn to her side of the great ocean, closing her eyes to the situation on the other shore.

A notable exception to this indifference was the disarmament conference in Washington, late in 1921 and early 1922. The diplomatic problems of the Far East, with which it was partly concerned, stood much closer to America's heart than did those of the Middle East. Besides, the limitation of certain types of naval armaments, the main issue under discussion, was considered a matter of domestic interest.

In the Middle East, meanwhile, attempts were being made to regulate shipping in the Turkish Straits, a perennial problem. Then, as for generations before, the narrow three-part waterway— Dardanelles, Sea of Marmora and the Bosporus—was an anomaly to the Russians, for they were still at the mercy of the Turks, who had retained control of Constantinople and the Straits. The United States, as one of the world's most important maritime powers, was expected to participate in the solution of the problem of the Straits. But America remained aloof from that too, and was not even a signatory of the 1923 Convention Relating to the Straits, which provided for the demilitarization of the waterway, nor of the Lausanne Treaty, which terminated the long-drawn-out war with Turkey. A seat on the International Straits Commission, which was to supervise the execution of the Convention, was offered to the United States but not accepted. Neither was the United States a signatory to the Montreux Convention of 1936, which regulated traffic in the waterway anew and provided for the remilitarization of the Straits by Turkey.

"A National Home for the Jewish People"

There was one Middle Eastern issue, however, in which the United States took an interest—the proposed establishment of a national home for the Jewish people in Palestine.

39

On November 2, 1917, Britain's Secretary of State for Foreign Affairs, Arthur James Balfour (later Lord Balfour), had made a basic policy declaration on behalf of his government:

His Majesty's government view with favour the establishment in Palestine of a national home for the Jewish people, and will use their best endeavours to facilitate the achievement of that object, it being understood that nothing shall be done which may prejudice the civil and religious rights of the existing non-Jewish communities in Palestine or the rights and political status enjoyed by Jews in any other country.

At the time, the British were pushing the Turks out of the Levant and it was assumed that soon the Allies would be victorious over the decrepit realm. It was anticipated that the Ottoman Empire's collapse would create a vacuum, and measures were taken to fill the void.

The thought of a homeland for the Jews was not new in the United States. John Adams, second President of America, wrote to Major Mordecai Manuel Noah, pioneer American "Zionist," in 1818: "I really wish the Jews again in Judaea and an independent nation." Then, in 1891, the Rev. William E. Blackstone, prominent Protestant clergyman, presented a memorial to President Benjamin Harrison and Secretary of State James G. Blaine, urging the convening of an international conference to promote the Jewish claim to Palestine. The petition, signed by prominent Americans, began: "Why not give Palestine back to them [the Jews]? According to God's distribution of nations, it is their home. . . ."

President Wilson endorsed the Balfour Declaration on August 31, 1918: "I welcome the opportunity to express the satisfaction I have felt in the progress of the Zionist movement in the United States and in the Allied countries since the declaration by Mr. Balfour, on behalf of the British government. . . ."

Congress also went on record in favor of the Balfour Declaration. Unanimously it resolved on June 30, 1922, that "the United

40

States of America favors the establishment in Palestine of a national home for the Jewish people." This stand was reiterated several times in the ensuing years, as for instance, in 1944:

Resolved, that the United States shall use its good offices and take appropriate measures to the end that the doors of Palestine shall be opened to the free entry of Jews into that country, and that there shall be free opportunity for colonization, so that the Jewish people may ultimately reconstitute Palestine as a free and democratic Jewish commonwealth.

Since the United States had not been a signatory to the treaties liquidating the Ottoman Empire, and since Palestine was a British mandate, these declarations had weight only as briefs of *amicus Britanniae.* But resolutions of this nature could be presumed to express the American people's wishes and it was within the purview of the British government to consider their importance in the two countries' relations.

Besides the Palestinian question, the Arab countries' good will also had to be considered, especially during World War II when the Middle East played a crucial part as a staging area for allied forces and a vitally important territory for the shipping of goods to the Soviets. The Arab nations' attitude was also important in American calculations of postwar developments. Middle Eastern oil was to play an increasingly important part among the power resources of the world. Hence, the attitude of the American government toward the Arab countries had to be assayed.

The attitude of the Arab countries toward the possibility of a "Jewish homeland in Palestine" was one of unmitigated hostility. President Franklin D. Roosevelt, a master in diplomacy, had to reconcile the traditionally friendly attitude of the United States toward a Jewish homeland in Palestine with the exigencies of a policy that demanded friendly relations with countries possessing vast oil reserves in which leading American corporations had invested—and were to invest—huge sums. The most important Arab oil-producing country in those days was Saudi Arabia, ruled over by King Ibn Saud, one of the leading figures in the Arab world.* It was with him and King Farouk of Egypt that President Roosevelt and Prime Minister Winston Churchill of Great Britain met on April 5, 1945, when the war was approaching its end. "Your Majesty will recall," President Roosevelt told the Saudi Arabian King, "that on previous occasions I communicated to you the attitude of the American government toward Palestine and made clear our desire that no decision be taken with respect to the basic situation in that country without consultation with both Arabs and Jews. . . ."

Nothing more enhanced the economic value of the Middle East than the discovery that it was sitting on top of the world's most fabulous petroleum find. Suddenly that region which previously had been merely a means to the achievement of ultimate objectives (such as the exploitation of the "treasures" of India) became a goal in itself, and a very important goal at that. The "oil rush" in the Middle East was very different from the gold rush of California a century before. The prospectors in the Middle East were multibillion-dollar corporations and it was expected that its natural wealth would last for long. American companies, new to the region after the First World War, slowly but relentlessly overcame the resistance of the pioneer British, Dutch and French oil companies. In this connection the State Department in Washington broke its silence, because isolation could no longer be maintained in a region where oil erupted in fantastic gushers. However, this is a special chapter in the story of America and the Middle East, to which references will be made in their proper places.

The Voice of Thunder

The Second World War demonstrated the strategic importance of the Middle East, a true global hub, the real heartland. From

* His real name was King Abdul-Aziz, or, to give him his full name: Abdul-Aziz ibn Abdur-Rahman al-Faisal Al Sa'ud.

the West the German juggernaut lumbered into the region and approached its coreland along the Nile. From the East the Japanese moved westward with ponderous agility. The two forces might have met somewhere in this heartland. However, the Allies still retained the whiphand in Egypt, Palestine, Transjordan, Iraq and Iran. American arms were being supplied to the Middle East command in Egypt and the logistics control of the area was directed by the Middle East supply center.

The Axis momentum was broken in the western desert of Egypt at El Alamein. In the Soviet Union the Germans had overextended themselves, ran up against the incredible cruelties of weather and the Russians' fanatic love of the motherland, whether Czar or commissar, and the inevitable consequence of the Allies' superior ability to supply themselves with arms, ammunition, oil and other supplies. The juggernaut in the West had hit full stride, and victory was within reach.

The Yalta Conference, February 1945, was to tackle the problems of the expected post-victory age. It dealt with a very large variety of difficult problems, some of which involved the Middle East, especially Iran. British and Russian troops had kept the trans-Iranian "lifeline," from United States supply depots to the Soviet front. However, the Western Allies did not want the Russians to tarry in the country of their Persian neighbors. It was decided in the Tripartite Pact among Britain, the Soviets and Iran and now reiterated at Yalta, that the Allied troops were to evacuate Iran not later than six months after the termination of the hostilities. However, the Russians wanted the petroleum in Iran's five northern provinces. The concession in the southwest was held by the Anglo-Iranian Oil Company. The Soviets thought that in the intoxication of Allied victory it would be difficult for the wartime friends to say no. The Western allies were not "intoxicated" to the extent of being blind to the Russian scheme. Upon their advice, the Tehran government pressed home the point that negotiations about the northern oil fields should be suspended until after the cessation of hostilities. With the war over and a degree of normality restored, a refusal would no longer trouble vital Allied contacts. And, indeed, after the end of the war, the Soviets were given a categorical no.

The Voice of Discord

After the Second World War a basic change in America's relationship to the rest of the world took place. Renouncing isolationism, seemingly forever, America assumed the role of leader in world affairs. Proud Albion had been humbled, not by defeat, but by the price of victory. Fighting for humanity's common cause, she had dissipated much of her abundant strength. Britannic peace no longer prevailed and with the end of Britain as a world power a vacuum was created, to be filled by the United States. The Middle Eastern problems of Whitehall were inherited by the White House.

A few years before the outbreak of the war the United States had refused to participate in the negotiations that led to the signing of the Montreux Agreement for the regulation of traffic in the Black Sea and the Straits. Now the Straits question was raised again by the Soviets. It was their perennial problem, their great frustration. In the wake of victory the time appeared opportune to them to make another and perhaps final attempt to reach their ardently coveted warm-water goal.

Turkey was the keeper of the Straits under the Montreux Agreement. The Soviets now charged that Turkish neutrality during the war was a farce. This was then the time to see to it that the Turks did not slam the gates at the Straits in Russia's face.

At the Potsdam Conference, which began on July 17, 1945, it was agreed that the interested powers were to submit their proposals about possible changes in the existing regime of the Straits. A year later the Soviet Union and the United States did that, besides Britain and Turkey. The Kremlin's program consisted of five points. The Straits should be open to all merchant vessels at all times; also to the warships of the Black Sea powers; the warships of other powers would be kept out, with specified exceptions; the regime of the Straits should be in the hands of Turkey and the Black Sea powers; the defense of the Straits should be organized by the Soviets and Turkey.

This meant control of the Straits by the Soviets, as the dominant power in the Turkey-Russia combination. This time it was the United States that replied for the non-Communist world. Washington accepted the first three points of the Russian proposal but rejected the last two, under which the U.S.S.R. would have realized the age-old Russian ambition of obtaining control of the Straits.

America and Palestine

Another old question, that of Palestine, became the concern of American diplomacy. Millions of Jews had been killed in the charnel house of the "New Order" of the Nazis and many of the survivors turned to Palestine, which they considered their ancestral homeland where they might live out their lives among their kin. However, the British government still had mandatory rights in Palestine and the gates of the region were all but closed to the Jews. The government of the United States took much interest in this problem.

The British government convened an Anglo-American Committee of Inquiry regarding the problems of European Jewry and Palestine which proposed in April 1946 that the mandate, as it was then, should be transformed into a United Nations Trust Territory and that, meanwhile, a hundred thousand Jews should be allowed to immigrate there immediately instead of the monthly quota of fifteen hundred permitted under the prevailing British policy. The British government rejected this proposal. The American government, speaking through President Harry S. Truman, urged Britain on October 4, 1946, to admit a hundred thousand Jews into Palestine.

In April 1947, a session of the General Assembly of the United

45

Nations established UNSCOP (The United Nations Special Committee on Palestine), which stayed six weeks there and a month in Geneva. In August UNSCOP reported a plan to divide Palestine into a Jewish state, an Arab state, and a small international enclave with its center in Jerusalem. The Jewish state was to comprise eastern Galilee, the central coast and the Negev, in the south. The Arab state was to include the rest of Galilee, nearly all the central inland territory and the southern coast. Led by the United States, the General Assembly adopted the recommendations. The Jewish leaders accepted the plan, the Arabs rejected it.

Then, in March 1948 the United States withdrew its support of the partition plan and the American representative on the Security Council of the UN formally proposed that it should instruct UNSCOP to suspend its efforts and that a temporary trusteeship for Palestine be established under the Trusteeship Council of the United Nations. The UN manifested no enthusiasm for the "Draft Trusteeship Agreement for Palestine" and, instead, instructed UNSCOP to terminate its work, and established the office of the United States Mediator for Palestine, headed by Count Folke Bernadotte, Swedish internationalist and nephew of King Gustavus V.

What was the reason for the American *volte face?* In his memoirs, *Years of Trial and Hope,* former President Truman revealed a little-known feature of America's Middle East policy. "Like most of the British diplomats," Truman wrote, "some of our diplomats also thought that the Arabs, on account of their numbers and because of the fact that they controlled such immense oil resources, should be appeased. I am sorry to say that there were some among them who were inclined to be anti-Semitic." Under date of October 21, 1948, Secretary of Defense James V. Forrestal noted in his diary that, actually, our Palestine policy had been for "squalid political purposes" and he hoped some day to make the issue clear. That day never came but it may be that the vacillations of American policy on the Palestine issue were due to conflicting currents in the Cabinet.

The British reached the conclusion that the best thing for them was to withdraw from Palestine. This they did and there appeared to be some danger that by creating a vacuum so suddenly a state of anarchy would ensue. However, the Jews of Palestine were not unprepared. They were ready to assume the responsibilities of government. At midnight on May 4, 1948, the independence of Israel—the name given to the new country—was proclaimed. Thus the place of Palestine was to be taken by *Medinat Israel*—the state of Israel. Acting without delay, the government of the United States recognized the new state *de facto* within a few hours.*

The Birth of Pax Americana

In an area directly adjacent to the Middle East an important American postwar foreign policy decision was made. After the cessation of hostilities civil war had erupted in Greece. While the country had been under Axis occupation, a guerrilla front, on which the local Communists played an important role, was opened in the mountains. The war over, the Communists presented their claim to participate in the government of their country. Because of her maritime location, Greece was traditionally close to Britain and British forces had borne the brunt of battle to expel the Axis forces. At the same time, they were also involved in a conflict with the Communists, who had a well-protected sanctuary in the adjacent Iron Curtain countries of Yugoslavia, Bulgaria and Albania.

The British felt that on the outcome of the struggle in this key area the fate of the Balkans might depend. They appear to have interpreted the conflict as the continuation of the traditional Russian policy of reaching southern warm waters. For generations it had been Britain's policy to contain the Russians; for, once in the eastern Mediterranean, they would find the Straits within easy

---

* However, the Soviet Union preceded the United States on May 17 with its *de jure* recognition.

striking distance. From the strategic location of Greece they would have had the best chance to realize their historic ambition.

Great Britain was no longer in a position to continue this policy of containment when she called upon the United States for help. The response was quick. On March 12, 1947, President Truman spoke and his words made history. The Truman Doctrine was born and has served since then as the foundation of American foreign policy, to fill up power voids, not only in the Middle East but in Europe, southeast Asia and the Far East.

Thus was born *Pax Americana,* successor to the Britannic peace. An epoch ended and another historic age began.

CHAPTER 2

Egypt and Arab Unity

A Synthetic People

EGYPT has been described as the least Arabic of all Arab countries, and yet it is Egypt which has been trying to create a United Arabia. If anthropology and ethnography could employ the methods of archaeology layers upon layers of ethnic groups could be found along the Nile. The deepest discernible stratum would be Pharaonic Egypt, a racial cocktail with Hamitic overtones, in which were mixed all the people who were attracted by the "miracle of the Nile" from all parts of that world, up and down the river, from east and west, Nilotic and Semitic people, colored people too, from the deep south. Superimposed upon that basic layer would be the remnants of victors and vanquished, people whom Egypt of the Pharaohs had conquered and those by whom they were conquered. Not all the Jewish people of Moses left the "fleshpots" of Europe. We would find layers of Hittites, Persians, Scythians, Abyssinians, Assyrians, Babylonians, and then, in the topmost layers would be Macedonians, Hellenes, Romans, all mixtures themselves, who had drawn upon the ethnic groups of other parts of the world—people from all over Europe, the Levant, attracted to this fabulous land where the black humus was deeper than anywhere else.

In the struggle for supremacy, one of these groups would assert itself for a time, only to be swamped by another ethnic group, which would try to dominate the others, each finally yielding to a new superior force, a hungry arrogance. Then, in the Byzantine period, a cataclysmic event occurred that altered the basic ethnic composition of this amazing land. Fanatic people from the dusty deserts of the East, the Arabs swept in during the first half of the seventh century. Something happened in Egypt which had never taken place before and would never happen again. The penetrating power of these lean desert people was so strong that all previous layers were drowned in the Arab flood. There remained small pockets of the past, as for instance Christians, who resisted Islam and whose descendants are today members of the Coptic Church. Arab institutions were superimposed upon their predecessors.

It is necessary to visualize these developments in order to comprehend Egypt's role today. The most important Arab country, it aims to be the leader of the Arab world, with the largest population among all the Arab nations—larger indeed than that of all the other Middle Eastern Arab countries combined, from Libya to Yemen. The largest and most important Arab cities are in Egypt—Cairo and Alexandria, and Cairo's Al Azhar University is the most outstanding in the Arab world, everything that Bologna, the Sorbonne, Oxford and Harvard mean to the West. The libraries, museums and mosques of Egypt's large cities are also among the most important in the Arab regions. The chief newspapers of the Arabic-speaking world are Egyptian and Radio Cairo is the Voice of the Arabs. Cairo is the headquarters of the League of Arab States (Arab League) which was established to co-ordinate Arab efforts in the political, social and economic fields and, from the beginning, Egyptians have served in its highest posts.

Egypt's claim to leadership of the Arab world does not go uncontested, although its critics seldom get a hearing because, these days, criticizing Egypt comes close to sacrilege in certain quarters. Large is the number of the critics—some are radicals,

50

but there are also the hyperorthodox who consider Egypt an intruder, least Arabic among the Muslim states. The Hejaz, in Saudi Arabia, is considered the most truly Arab portion of their world because there are the hallowed towns of Mecca and Medina. Also, Baghdad in Iraq and Damascus in Syria were the seats of the great medieval dynasties, Ummayads and Abbassides. Egypt is considered too much a mixture of the Levant, where Greeks, Italians, Maltese and Albanians have played an inordinately large role. Even the dynasty which until recently ruled over Egypt was not Arabic, but of Albanian descent.

This critical attitude was most pungently expressed by the former leader of the Arab Legion of the Hashimite Kingdom of the Jordan, Glubb Pasha, who spoke from the experience of a lifetime spent among the Arabs:

The Egyptians, indeed, were not regarded as Arabs, nor did they consider themselves as such. The great majority of the Egyptians who gave the subject any thought at all looked upon Egypt as a separate nation, the heir of the Pharaohs and one of the most ancient civilizations of the world. They considered the Arabs to be a backward and ignorant race. The inclusion of Egypt in the list of Arab states was profoundly to modify the position of the Arabs in subsequent times.

A Look at the Past

The past is part of the present in the lives of nations. This is true particularly in countries like Egypt where the past casts enormous shadows on the pages of history. Today Egypt is considered a dynamic country, and this dynamism draws nourishment especially from one recent period of the country's life. During the first half of the nineteenth century the Albanian soldier of fortune, Mohammed Ali, known to his contemporaries as "the Great," ruled over Egypt for forty-four years. He started as the Turkish Governor and was recognized as the hereditary Vizir of Egypt, Governor of Nubia, Sennar, Kordofan and Darfur. The nominal suzerain was the Ottoman Sultan whose realm was still considered a world power but of whose weakness Mohammed Ali was aware. With the aid of French officers in Napoleon's army—veterans of those immortal battles in the shadow of the pyramids—he created a force superior to that of his nominal masters. Under the command of Ibrahim Pasha his army overran Syria, Palestine and parts of Asia Minor. As it approached Constantinople, it seemed that the ruler of Egypt would become the overlord of the Ottoman Empire. But Europe frustrated Mohammed Ali's designs, for the Great Powers preferred the static Turks to the dynamic Egyptian. This demonstration of her dependence upon the final word of European powers was a traumatic experience for Egypt—a humiliation which Egyptian history recalls.

The supreme indignity came, however, after the opening of the Suez Canal in 1869. Now it was across Egyptian territory that Britain's sensitive lifeline ran, from London to the very ends of the globe, via India, the South China Sea, Australia. With the resultant increase of the importance of Egypt's location, her ruler was unable to maintain himself against Great Power interference. In 1882 Britain moved into Egypt and, at the outbreak of World War I, declared her a protectorate. This was another great humiliation.

After the war the national self-determination of people was to prevail. The Western idea of a virulent type of modern nationalism penetrated into Egypt through her great metropolitan areas, and the National Party—Wafd (Delegation)—under Saad Zaghlul Pasha became its standard-bearer. Fuad I, who played at being King, was titular ruler of Egypt at this time. Nominal independence for Egypt was established by a series of pacts, the most significant of which was signed on May 10, 1936, to provide for the withdrawal of most of the British troops, except for those stationed in the vicinity of the Canal. Under the treaty, Britain retained the right to use Alexandria as a naval base, and in case of war the contracting parties were to extend assistance to each other. In war and under the threat of war Britain had the right to move her troops in all Egypt. This improvement was just enough to prompt supercilious Egyptians to quote the adage: *plus ça change, plus c'est la même chose.*

In April 1936 King Fuad died and was succeeded by his sixteen-year-old son, Farouk I.

Egypt as the Hub

During the Second World War Egypt's strategic importance was demonstrated anew. There the *Afrika Korps* of the "desert fox" Erwin Rommel sought to force one of the war's greatest decisions—to reach the Nile and the Suez Canal, throttle the Allies' supply centers, strike out for the Middle Eastern oil fields, fill up Axis tanks and planes to the brim, and prevent American war material from reaching the Russians via Iran. Had the Germans' designs succeeded the Allies' resistance would have been crushed. Near an Egyptian outpost, El Alamein, the decisive battle was fought and the Axis powers were routed. As had happened so many times in the past, the challengers' failure to win this crucial region of the Middle East resulted in their ultimate defeat.

When the war was over, the map of the Middle East had changed. Syria and Lebanon, which had belonged to France as mandates, were now independent. Farther east, India was set free by the Labour government in London. Egypt considered herself as far advanced as Syria or Lebanon. The significance of Egypt for Great Britain was, after all, in her relationship to India—the route through the Canal. Once India was independent could freedom for Egypt be far behind?

Yet, Britain held on to Egypt. What was the explanation? The Suez Canal "lifeline" was not only a maritime and strategic reality to Britain but also a symbol. What would the United States do rather than relinquish her hold on the Panama Canal? Holding on to the Suez Canal, Britain was still a power to be reckoned with in the Middle East. That region meant much to the British,

53

who opened it up to the Western world, kept it open, pioneered in oil exploration, got out the petroleum. Great Britain was now an ally of the United States. In the relations of nations sentiments count for little, hard facts count for much. Should Britain let her hold in the Middle East go, what would she have left? She was ready to play a subordinate role as an ally but was unwilling to be relegated to the part of a satellite.

Enters the Sudan

The British ruled not only in Egypt but also in the large amorphous region to the south—known as the Anglo-Egyptian Sudan. The authority of the Egyptians was purely nominal, that of the British real. Egypt and the Sudan were different in many respects but they were interdependent because of the Nile which traversed both of them from end to end. The waters of the Nile were needed by Egypt and the Sudan—agreements had to be entered into about their use.

In the nineteenth century the Egyptians extended their rule into the Sudan, but were ousted by the British. Now that the pressure was on to have the British relinquish their hold on Egypt, Cairo increased the pressure to relinquish England's hold also on the Sudan. A connection was established between the evacuation of British troops from Egypt and the relinquishing of London's hold on the Anglo-Egyptian Sudan.

Finally, Egypt's Premier Ismail Sidqi Pasha and Britain's Minister of Foreign Affairs Ernest Bevin drew up a treaty which provided for the withdrawal of British troops from the Canal zone and contained a formula about the Sudan. The British were to withdraw from the Canal as a protective power but would conclude a defense arrangement with Egypt under which they would retain certain workshops and installations ready to be turned over to the British army in case of war. The formula for the Sudan was full of double-talk:

The policy which the high contracting parties undertake to follow in the Sudan within the framework of the unity between the Sudan and Egypt under the common crown of Egypt will have for its essential objectives to assure the well-being of the Sudanese, the development of their interests, and their active participation for self-government and consequently the exercise of the right to choose the future status of the Sudan.

Sidqi Pasha seems to have concentrated on the first part of this long sentence where reference was made to the unity between the Sudan and Egypt under the common crown of Egypt. On the basis of this interpretation, he announced unity for the two countries under the Egyptian crown. Mr. Bevin, on the other hand, concentrated on the numerous reservations in the latter part of the sentence which qualified the first part. When the Ansar tribesmen of the Sudan learned about this disappointing misinterpretation they created a disturbance in the late autumn of 1946. The British withdrew from the agreement and Sidqi Pasha resigned.

A Traumatic Experience

Probably nobody, and least of all the government of Egypt, knew how weak was the country until the war with Israel broke out in mid-May 1948. The Egyptians marched into war with the expectation that they alone would tear "Jewish resistance" to bits. Israel's other Arab neighbors also marched to war. With the exception of the Arab Legion, commanded by Glubb Pasha, all the Arab armies suffered humiliating defeats at Israeli hands.*

It was denied at first by the Arab countries that they had suffered a defeat in Palestine. On its return, the defeated Egyptian army staged a "victory celebration." However, the people were not deceived. The Israeli campaign proved to have been the dividing line in the histories of the Arab world, especially Egypt, Syria and Iraq. These Arab countries gradually began to realize

* Further reference to this war will be made in the chapter on Israel.

55

that medieval system could not stand up to the spirit of the twentieth century and that they must introduce modern reform. Soon the great housecleaning in the Middle Eastern Arab world was to begin.

Four more years were to elapse, however, before the royal regime in Egypt was to fall. During that period the government of Egypt was mainly concerned with attempts to have the British ousted from Suez and the Sudan. Judging by the tone of Egyptian newspapers and the Cairo radio there seems to have been no more important question.

In the solution of these problems the government of the United States was taking a hand, sometimes under the spotlight, but more often behind the scenes. The "cold war" reached an intensity which stimulated the search for solutions to solve a problem which affected what was now not merely the lifeline of the British Empire but also of the entire Western world. To satisfy Egypt's national pride, several plans were considered. Most realistic was the plan for Britain to evacuate the Canal zone and then turn it back to Egypt, which would join a Middle East Defense Organization composed of the United States, Britain, France, Turkey and Egypt. Britain would play a leading role along the Canal again, but only as a member of the defense organization. The plan was not accepted.

Meanwhile, the preponderance of the United States in the region grew apace. The Sixth United States Naval Task Force had been strengthened into the Sixth United States Fleet, consisting of about seventy ships, and was operating between Istanbul and Gibraltar. The British had only some thirty vessels operating along this most vital lifeline. In the view of the Pentagon the eastern Mediterranean had achieved new strategic importance. In the past it had been considered a suitable defense position but the new plans saw it as the very gateway to the Soviet heartland, an offensive position. The admission of Greece and Turkey into NATO closed the link between the eastern Mediterranean and the North Atlantic nations. In the spring of 1951 George McGhee, America's Assistant Secretary of State, who specialized in Middle Eastern affairs, broached the idea to Egypt that she should join the North Atlantic Treaty Organization. Geographic incongruities no longer attracted attention since Greece and Turkey had been promoted to the status of North Atlantic powers. The American official also expressed the view that with Egypt's adherence to NATO the British could withdraw from Suez without qualm.

The royal regime in Egypt was reaching new lows. The country was buzzing with rumors about corruption in high places. The dissolute life of the King was a public scandal. Economic conditions were getting worse as a result of corrupt practices, especially in the cotton export market. The royal regime had to stage a spectacular coup in order to distract attention from its misdeeds and this was done on October 16, 1951. In a unilateral action Egypt abrogated the treaties under which Egypt maintained troops on the canal, and under which the Condominium of the Sudan was ruled. King Farouk I was solemnly proclaimed King of Egypt and of the Sudan.

The next step should have been the implementation of the proclamation. That, however, would have required a fighting force that could have stood up to the British. How could the Egyptians, who had been defeated by the Israeli, hope to destroy Britain's forces on the Canal and in the Sudan?

Since this was impossible, the Egyptian government took what appeared to be the next best step. It fostered guerrilla activities by so-called liberation forces, consisting of fanatic members of a religio-political organization, the Muslim Brotherhood, and university students searching for a cause in order to cut classes. Roadblocks were thrown up around the Canal and Egyptian workers there were induced to abandon their jobs. Violence flared up and a bitter war of attrition ensued. Still, the British refused to give up their posts under pressure.

A battalion of Egyptian auxiliary police and British troops clashed on January 25, 1952, at Ismailia, between Port Said and Port Suez, along the Canal. The casualties suffered by the police were great and soon all Cairo knew about "Bloody Friday." The grapevine worked very fast. The following day in Cairo a mysterious signal brought together a host of idlers and trouble-makers who quickly bore down upon the center of the city, looting shops and banks, and setting fire to houses, stores and hotels, including the Middle Eastern landmark, Shepheard's. "The whole center of the town was ablaze," reported Anwar El Sadat, a young officer, who was to play a role in later events. His book, *Revolt on the Nile,** tells the story. The police were sympathetic to the rioters, did nothing to stop the mob and the looting continued until, finally, the army was called up. Colonel El Sadat reported that while Cairo was in the grip of anarchy, the King was giving a banquet, the Premier was visiting his manicurist, and the Minister of Interior was moving a piece of furniture he had just acquired. This was "Black Saturday."

Le Roi Est Mort, Vive le Comité

The King, unheedful of the warning signal, continued to pursue his pleasures, surrounded by a sycophantic court camarilla that was so wrapped up in its nefarious practices that it was unaware of the ominous signs on the country's political horizon. Corruption assumed even larger proportions. Turning their inside knowledge of crop reports to account, highly placed officials and their wives made fortunes on Egypt's most important export item, cotton. King Farouk did not except himself from corrupt business deals—the initiated knew at the time that the Court had benefited greatly on shipments of defective arms to the front during the Palestinian war.

Some kind of leadership and a new political line were needed but where was it to come from? The chief political party, Wafd, was thoroughly compromised and the others were no better. The fanatic slogans of the Muslim Brotherhood carried no conviction and, besides, its terroristic methods were no substitute for policy.

* John Day, 1957.

Only the army was uncontaminated, because it was not directly involved in politics. True, it had suffered ignominious defeat in Palestine, but it had an excuse—the defective weapons and the corrupt court cabal. It was therefore the army officers who now took matters into their hands. Most active was a young lieutenant colonel, Gamal Abdul Nasser.

The secret organization of the Free Officers—*Zubat el Ahrar* —had nine members and its founder and first president was Nasser. After the burning of Cairo in January 1952 General Mohammed Naguib became the president. The Free Officers were opposed to the royal regime; they wanted to have the British ousted from Egypt and the Sudan, and Israel from the Middle East. Their attitude toward the government was summarized by Naguib: "Corruption ruled in every public office. Egypt had become the epitome of all that was wrong with the Eastern world." *

Egyptian landowners, instead of paying their taxes, bribed the civil service to accept a fraction of what they owed the government. Instead of investing their legal or illegal savings in Egyptian productive enterprises, they exported them or invested them in inflated real estate. The result was a land boom in the midst of unprecedented suffering "that an irresponsible, corrupt, and impoverished government was neither willing nor able to remedy."

The laws of economics were as perverted as the laws of men. Rising prices were accompanied by unemployment. There were few jobs open to anyone, and there were almost no jobs open in any field to the increasing numbers of young people graduating from the high schools and universities. Even worse were conditions on the countryside. The higher the price of cotton, the higher the price of the land; and the higher the price of the land, the higher the rents exacted from the tenant farmers, whose real income was shrinking with every month that passed.

If the royal regime was to fall, who was to take the reins? There was no aristocracy in Egypt except the royal family. The

* Mohammed Naguib, *Egypt's Destiny. A Personal Statement,* Garden City: Doubleday, 1955, p. 14.

rich landowners' and traders' sons enjoyed a sybaritic life and did not bother with military service. The officers' corps in consequence was largely composed of the grandsons of peasants and the sons of soldiers and civil servants. General Naguib himself was the grandson of a peasant on one side of his family and the grandson of a colonel on the other. His father was an Egyptian army captain, prison warden and district officer. His mother was a Sudanese.

The Free Officers were also very critical of the United States, which they accused of wanting to force its authority on the Islamic world, from the Caucasus to the Indian Ocean. In the words of Colonel Anwar El Sadat, editor of *El Gumhouriya,* the Egyptian government newspaper, Secretary of the Pan-Islam Congress and at one time or another Minister of State in the Egyptian government:

They [the United States] set up the State of Israel in the hope of gaining a foothold in the Middle East, astride one of the world's trade routes, where they could keep an eye on the Russian colossus. . . . The imperialist economy of the United States came to the assistance of European imperialism in Palestine, by investing an enormous capital sum in the country.*

Conditions in Egypt in the first part of 1952 revealed a serious *malaise,* a groping for a solution and an inability to find one within the existing framework. The country had no fewer than six governments in a six-month period. The King remained blind to the numerous omens and wanted to "solve" the country's problems by petty court intrigues. How long he would be protected by the myth of the sacredness of the royal person was questionable, and "sacred" was the last epithet that could be applied to him.

* Colonel Anwar El Sadat, *Revolt on the Nile,* New York: John Day, 1957, p. 103. It was common knowledge, contrary to Colonel El Sadat's statement, that Western capital was rather reticent about investing large funds in the new state of Israel. Also, El Sadat seems to have been unaware of the inner combats in the Washington administration about its attitude toward the establishment of Israel, as revealed by former President Truman. See *op. cit.*

Most of the officers engaged in the conspiracy of the Free Officers were young, unknown to the country. They needed a front man, an impressive façade, a man with a high rank and, above all, with a national reputation. These qualities were found in Major General Mohammed Naguib, a man with a good record. In the 1948 Palestine campaign he was wounded and was pronounced dead "because he had no pulse." His abandoned body was discovered by the commander of the medical service. On lifting the blanket that covered his face, and noticing that he blinked his eyes, doctors brought him to life with the help of adrenalin, blood transfusion and an oxygen tent.

He possessed another advantage in that he was part Sudanese and thus in himself embodied the "unity of the Nile." In spite of his high rank, he turned out to be manageable, of soft timber. Naguib appeared to be the ideal man for window dressing.*

Nasser Means Victory

Behind the scenes at first, the most dynamic of the Free Officers was Lieut. Col. Gamal Abdul Nasser. His official biography, prepared by the Egyptian Embassy, Washington, D.C. (and printed in *Egypt's Liberation. The Philosophy of the Revolution,* by Premier Gamal Abdul Nasser, Washington: Public Affairs Press, 1955), says that he was born in Beni Mor, a small town in Asiut Province, Upper Egypt, on January 15, 1918, the son of a middle-class family. At the age of eight, he was sent by his father to be educated in Cairo. He displayed an interest in law and the

---

* That was not, however, Naguib's view of himself. "As for the charge that I was but a figurehead, the facts are as I have stated them. I joined the Free Officers in the summer of 1949 and became their president in the spring of 1952. Abd el Nasser, who had meanwhile been promoted to the rank of lieutenant colonel, realized that a successful revolution could not be carried out by a group of junior officers unless they were led by a senior officer with special qualifications. I was that senior officer." Naguib, *op. cit.,* p. 32. Naguib says that he was known to every man in the army and could count on its support, and his personality was such as to appeal to the Egyptian people. As president of the executive committee he acted as the movement's commander in chief.

history of great men. He entered the Military College in 1937, where he was known for "his outspokenness and his rebellion against colonialism." On graduating from the Military College, he joined the Third Rifle Brigade and was transferred to Mankbad in Asiut. In 1939 he was sent to Alexandria, in 1942 to El Alamein and again back to Alexandria where he followed at close quarters the political tension which engulfed Egypt at that time.

He served as a lieutenant with the Fifth Infantry Brigade, "but could not tolerate the conditions then obtaining in the army, which he could observe but was powerless to correct," so he asked to be transferred to the Sudan. In 1942, he was also appointed a teacher at the Military College. Later, he entered the Army Staff College, graduating with honor.

Before the outbreak of the Palestine war, he tendered his resignation from the army to fight as a volunteer, despite the fact that he was the sole support of his family, but his resignation was rejected. The tragedies and scandals he witnessed during his action in Palestine filled him with wrath against the responsible authorities, especially when he realized the army's dire need for munitions and arms which were withheld from it. . . . His heroism in the Palestine war was attested to by all those who fought him; he always led his men in action, and was shot above the heart in one of the battles. He was taken to a hospital where he was expected to recover in one month, but escaped in a few months to return to Palestine.

In Palestine he met his colleagues of the Revolutionary Command Council, which succeeded that of the Free Officers. He hand-picked each with care and, having satisfied himself of their loyalty, he began to plan with them their next move and to gather information through friendly sources in the royal palace, the cabinet and the army.*

* The record says that in 1942 Nasser was transferred to El Alamein. There one of the most decisive campaigns of World War II was being prepared and fought in that year and it is to be assumed that the British would not jeopardize the success of a crucial engagement by sending there an Egyptian officer "known for his rebellion against colonialism." Also, according to the official record, Nasser in 1942 was "appointed a teacher at the Military College." It, too, was

The strength and resistance of the old order was still partly an unknown factor. After all, this was Egypt, the land of the Pharaohs. What if the people continued to see a hallowed image in the royal crown? The young officers had to tread with care. First, they won over the key regiments and then they arranged subsequent steps. The country was highly centralized and that facilitated the plotters' work. Cairo and Alexandria were the key places and once they were in revolutionary hands it was expected that the rest of the country would follow. The slogan of the officers was "Boldness and Resolution"—and their password was *Nasser* —victory!

As it turned out, the anxious preparations were not needed. The key points were seized during the night of July 23, 1952. The telephone, the telegraph, radio, military barracks, government buildings offered no resistance. Somebody made the comment: "Rotten trees yield quickly to the ax," and this tree appeared rotten to the roots. The royal crown on the head of the scape-grace had evidently ceased to be a hallowed image, its *mystique* was gone. The old order had no foundations. Members of the corrupt upper class had never coalesced into a cohesive unit. The regime probably depended on the bayonets and those were now in the hands of the revolutionary officers.

At the time, the King was in one of his palaces, Ras El-Tin, in Alexandria, the summer residence. Not one arm was raised in his defense in the streets of the towns or in the villages of the Nile. The question was what to do with him? Should he be allowed to leave the country or could he cause trouble from there, and should he be executed? According to the officers, the King had sought to establish contact with the British along the Canal. The British troops would have been more than sufficient to rout the free officers. Could the British have refused to stand by the King, the head of the Egyptian state, if he asked for their aid?

---

a highly sensitive spot during that period of the war and, furthermore, it stood under British supervision. Nasser was either a consummate artist in dissimulation or not noted for his rebellion against colonialism.

The officers took no chances and had roadblocks thrown up on the roads leading from the Canal region to the cities but no move was made by the British forces. Nor is there any authentic confirmation of the statement that the King had sent official word to the British to interfere.

Some of the revolutionary officers argued that there was no need to besmirch the coup with blood, while some favored the more radical course. In the end, the will of those prevailed who wanted the King to leave. On July 26 he was presented with an ultimatum to depart from the country before six o'clock that afternoon.

It was issued by Mohammed Naguib in the name of the officers and it was an indictment of the royal regime.

. . . Corruption has spread throughout the country as the result of your repeated violations of the Constitution and your complete disregard of the people who have lost confidence in the administration of justice, public security and honor. . . . You have damaged Egypt's reputation in other countries' eyes. . . . You have condoned the bribery and treachery revealed in consequence of our defeat in the Palestinian war.

In the name of the army "representing the people's will," General Naguib called upon Farouk to abdicate in favor of his infant son, Prince Ahmed Fuad II. If the King refused to comply with this ultimatum he was going to be held responsible for the consequences.

Enters the American Ambassador

The officers set up a government, with General Naguib as Prime Minister. There are two versions as to what happened thereafter, one by Naguib and the other by Colonel El Sadat. According to Naguib, Farouk became panicky and established contact with the United States Embassy to ask that Ambassador Jefferson Caffery, with whom he was on good terms, come to see him. At 10:30 A.M. on the day Farouk was to leave Egypt, the First Secretary of the American Embassy, Joseph S. Sparks, visited Naguib and transmitted a message from the Secretary of State in Washington to the effect that the government of the United States was prepared to regard the *coup d'état* as an internal matter and therefore of direct concern only to Egyptians. At the same time, however, the government of the United States hoped that the situation would not be allowed to get out of hand and, the message continued, Ambassador Caffery would welcome some assurance from Naguib that no harm would befall the King or his family and that they would be permitted to leave Egypt with honor. The General told Sparks that so long as the King "behaved himself," neither he nor any member of his family would be harmed.

During this conversation, Naguib received a call from one of his officers doing duty at Ras El-Tin palace. The American Ambassador's personal secretary, Robert Simpson, determined to see the King, had been stopped while trying to force his way through the cordon of troops surrounding the palace. Naguib ordered the officer in charge to let him pass. A report on what then transpired was later given to the General.

"Come in, come in," said Farouk. "I have never been so glad to see anyone in my life. . . . I have just this to tell your Ambassador. Ask him if he will do what he can to save my life. If he does, will he come to say good-by?"

According to the version provided by Colonel El Sadat, it was Ambassador Caffery himself who made the visit to the palace. The King begged the Ambassador to let him escape aboard an American ship but Caffery dissuaded him, arguing that it would be unworthy of him to flee the country in such a way. At the same time El Sadat saw the American military attaché who told him that Washington "demanded" a guarantee of the safety of the King's person.

Farouk seems to have been thinking of his personal comfort during all this time and he asked permission to go into exile on

65

board the resplendent royal yacht *Mahroussa*. Evidently reassured that no harm would be done to him, he appeared at the appointed time in his gala white uniform of an Egyptian admiral. He was surrounded by a tremendous number of traveling cases. Only a few close relatives, palace domestics and officers came to see him off. Present also were Prime Minister Naguib, Ambassador Caffery and Mr. Simpson. Unlamented by his people, Farouk went off into exile.

The dynasty was to continue, according to the original plans of the *junta*. However, so great appeared to be Egypt's joy at the ousting of the King that the officers in power had a second thought about the continuation of the monarchy. The memory of the royal reign was so bitter that Egypt seemed to be ready to turn to another kind of rule. Thus on June 13, 1953, Farouk's infant son Ahmed Fuad also lost his throne and Egypt was proclaimed a republic. The age of the Pharaohs was over.

General Naguib, who was considered Egypt's providential savior, became President and Prime Minister. So great was the affection of the *fellahin* for this man that, on more than one occasion he would have been trampled or torn to pieces by his admirers had his protective guard yielded. Here was a new "father image," no longer a Pharaoh but the President of a Republic.

The Republic and Its Children

Within the revolutionary *junta* there was a clash of personalities and, above all, of ambitions. Naguib, an older man, was quiet and easygoing, and favored a serene life. The great housecleaning would come in time, but let us not be hasty or too zealous. He was averse to bold ideas, adventurous solutions and excitement. Nasser, however, was by nature a gambler—impatient, eager to transform the country quickly, according to his specifications. He played the leading role in the council of Free Officers, renamed the Revolutionary Command Council, which designation indicated its bold program.

66

The Council began to criticize Naguib who did not seem to grasp the significance of the change of the times. The younger officers spoke of him as too settled in his way, too old. Also, there appeared to be an ideological split which some artifice on the part of the younger men transformed into a gap, and then into an abyss. It was claimed that Naguib wanted to continue governing the country with the political parties, especially the Wafd, by far the most important of them. This would have meant the continuation of Egypt's system of "parliament," never more than a façade, to make the people believe that they were at the helm. It is true that General Naguib eventually dissolved the political parties, confiscated their funds and announced a three-year transitional period to precede the restoration of parliamentary government, but the young officers asserted that he did this under pressure. They, and particularly Nasser, contended that Egypt's parliament was a farce, a mere garment for the naked lust of the political parties, and the parties themselves merely lobbies to protect the interests of the feudal lords. The revolution now began to devour its children.

There were rumors that President Naguib was aiming at a personal dictatorship and even that he was plotting with people of the old regime against the republic. Word spread in Egypt that the real leader of the revolution had been Nasser, not Naguib, who had been called in at the last moment to serve merely as a "front." On February 25, 1954, it was announced that General Naguib had resigned from his offices as President and Premier after disagreement with other *junta* members. However, this resignation was followed by symptoms of trouble in the making. Cavalry officers in Cairo were said to be on Naguib's side and ready to come forward on his behalf. The capital gave the impression of an armed camp, as troops patroled the streets. The Sudan always considered Naguib one of her own and she, too, showed signs of restlessness as a result of the treatment accorded to the General in Cairo. Egyptians were anxious to have the Sudan join their country, and Naguib's personality was a connecting link.

On February 27, Naguib was restored as President "of a parliamentary republic" but he was no longer Prime Minister nor head of the *junta*. These two posts were transferred to Colonel Nasser. It was announced now that national elections would take place in June. On March 8, Naguib again became Prime Minister, with Nasser his deputy. Nasser was now also Military Governor of Egypt, replacing Naguib. An early return to parliamentary government was promised. On April 17, Naguib resigned the office of Prime Minister, but remained President. Nasser now went to work on the friends of Naguib. Senior army officers believed to be close to the President were withdrawn on the ground that they were plotting to overthrow the Council of the Revolution. President Naguib was said to be in league with the plotters. The press was placed directly under Nasser's control, and the organization of journalists and newspaper owners, the Press Syndicate, was dissolved. The radio and the press now turned against Naguib and represented Nasser as the hero of the revolution. Naguib's career ended, apparently, on November 14 when he was stripped of the office of presidency and placed under house arrest. Nasser became the new public hero of the revolution.

Again the Suez Canal

The Suez Canal had become a symbol to Egypt. British troops along it denoted "imperialism," absence of them meant freedom. For years now the governments of Great Britain and Egypt had been working on this problem. The government of the United States had been offering suggestions for the solution of the problem and was now working with the two governments "on the diplomatic level," not exposed to public view and criticism. We have seen that the government of King Farouk had denounced the treaties dealing with the Suez Canal and the Anglo-Egyptian Sudan but was not able to implement it. The only way this could have been done would have been with armed forces and Egypt was in no position to use them against the United Kingdom.

The government of Prime Minister Nasser placed much emphasis on the solution of this problem. "Prestige," "national honor," "glory" were important in the life of a new regime which was not yet firmly established. On July 27, 1954, an agreement was reached between Britain and Egypt, which put the relations of the two countries on "a new basis of mutual understanding and firm friendship." British troops were to evacuate the Canal zone within twenty months. However, substantial parts of the British base were to be maintained. The United Kingdom was to be entitled to reoccupy the base in the event of an attack upon Egypt, any of the members of the Arab League or upon Turkey. The final treaty about the Suez Canal zone was signed in Cairo on October 19. The President of the United States expressed pleasure at the agreement and so did heads of states of other countries. The Prime Minister of Israel, Moshe Sharett, expressed his government's concern at the possibility that the withdrawal of British troops from the Canal zone might lead to an Egyptian attack on Israeli territory. British troops in the zone had served as a "buffer."

"An Islamic Arab State"

Before the stipulated time, the British evacuated their Canal base and Nasser's government hailed this as a signal victory. The time had come now to present to Egypt the new order. A constitution was framed which the people of Egypt were to confirm with a plebiscite. At the same time they were to give their approval to Prime Minister Nasser who was to be the President. He was the only "candidate."

The constitution proclaimed Egypt to be "an Islamic Arab State under a republican and democratic form of government." It reiterated the basic points of the revolution: liberation from imperialism, from feudalism, from monopolies, and from capitalistic influences over the government; a strong army, social justice, and a democratic society.

Egypt was proclaimed part of a greater Arab unity.

69

"We, the Egyptian people, realize that we form an organic part of a greater Arab entity, and are aware of our responsibilities and obligations toward a common Arab struggle for the glory and honor of the Arab nation." Here was the statement of the ultimate Arab aim, the expression of the dream for the integration of the entire Arab people in a larger "entity."

The new constitution provided for the establishment of the *Majlis al-Ummah*—Council of the People. Nominated by it, the presidential candidate was chosen by popular referendum for a six-year term in office. Political parties were prohibited, as there was only one "National Union" in the country—a Liberation Front. Members of the Council of the Union were hand-picked by President Nasser. As a result it became a debating society and, at best, an advisory body—a mere rubber stamp. In a dual plebiscite on June 23, 1956, voters elected Colonel Nasser the nation's first President under the new constitution and adopted that basic instrument by 99.9% of the total votes.*

Eventually, the National Union became an all-purpose political, social and economic organization. Every village was to elect a council, replacing its appointed mayor. A group of five villages was to establish a social center, with educational and economic branches. The council works with the government farm experts, implements the land reform and soil improvement program: irrigation, seed supplies, cooperative marketing.

Two members of each village council were elected to the provincial council which was to elect the thousand or so members of the National Union. It was this National Union which was to elect a three hundred member parliament. This legislative body

* The significance of this 99.9 per cent vote does not have to be stressed. The constitution of Egypt typifies what seems to be a need and a trend in many of the underdeveloped countries. The need is to emphasize the "democratic" nature of the institutions set up by the constitution, including a legislature which, in this case, pays homage to the "people"—"Council of the People." Hypocrisy in such matters is a compliment autocracy pays to democracy. The trend is to concentrate authority in a pair of presumably strong hands because of the assumption that the "masses" are not really capable of governing themselves.

was designed to be merely an advisory branch, divested of the power to force the resignation of a government. However, it was to have the right to express its lack of confidence in individual cabinet members.

"The Victorious One"

In the Muslim world one often encounters names beginning with Abdul—Arabic for the "servant of . . ." followed by one of the ninety-nine attributes of Allah. Abdul Nasser means "servant of the Victorious One." Gamal Abdul Nasser was now on the way to victory. Was he to become "Mr. Arabia" or even "Mr. Middle East"?

The Middle Eastern Muslim world has produced few internationally famous constructive statesmen. Turkey's Mustapha Kemal Atatürk was one. A bold innovator, he was the first to introduce the West into the East. His fame transcended the boundaries of his country, but his fellow statesmen of the Muslim faith were not of his caliber. Iran's Reza Khan Pahlevi, founder of a royal line and champion of Westernization, relapsed into tyranny after an auspicious start. Nuri es-Said Pasha was the leading statesman of Iraq for a generation but he aroused deep hostility because he was the spokesman of an atavistic feudal class and was considered a "stooge of the imperialists." King Abdullah of the Hashemite Kingdom of the Jordan could not keep his ambition under a bushel and aroused much hatred in other parts of the Arab world. The King of Saudi Arabia, Ibn Saud, was known to the world as an exceptionally colorful personality, rather than as a man of dynamic achievements. He created "law and order" in the desert, keeping the poor from robbing the rich, so that the rich could rob the poor with greater ease. In Egypt, the political leaders, Saad Zaghlul Pasha and Mustapha al-Nahas Pasha had internationally known names but they did little to solve the tremendous problems of their country.

In the post-World War II Arab Middle East, Nasser is the first and only statesman to arouse universal attention. He has been filmed, televised, interviewed and written about more than any of the Arab leaders of this century. In the Arab world he has achieved a spectacular and unprecedented fame. In this he has been helped by the Egyptian radio, which dominates the world of the Arabs.

One of Nasser's great advantages over many of his contemporaries is his lack of inhibition and his sense of historic mission. "Believe in yourself and people will believe in you."

His speeches are self-confident.

"We shall do whatever we like. . . ."

"We have taken this decision to restore the glories of the past and to safeguard our national dignity. . . ."

"We shall show them. . . ."

"We shall fling them [the Israeli] into the sea. . . ."

"We shall do to them what our glorious ancestors did to the Crusaders. . . ."

The *pluralis majestatis* in these sentences obviously refers to himself.

Something new in the land of the Nile, Nasser appeared to be much concerned with the little man. His predecessors spasmodically had introduced minor reforms but had always lost interest and, under their regimes, living standards in Egypt had continued to decline—contrary to Western trends. Nasser, according to his friends, has been aware of the people's problems from the very outset and is devoted to their relief.

Far more was heard, however, about Nasser's plans for Arab unity. His "philosophy of the revolution" and his public speeches stressed this part of his program over all others. In his view, the definite solution of Egypt's problem—and that of the other Arab countries, too—hinged on the unity of the Arabs and a joint effort to overcome the common troubles. Why should there be a dozen Arab countries—Egypt, Syria, Iraq, Jordan and all the others—and why not only one? Only through such unity could the affluent aid the poor; could the "Arab nation" derive the economic benefits of common production, a common market, a currency union, and

72

then ultimately the political and diplomatic benefits of amounting to something in the community of nations. By presenting Egypt as the unifier of the Arabs, Nasser, the incarnation of the will of Egypt, presented himself as an Arab Bolívar, a kind of Middle Eastern George Washington.

And the Arabs seemed to love it. A mercurial and emotional people, they found a "universal remedy" in Nasser, a kind of global witch doctor. Whenever he appeared, he became an object of adulation: *"Ya, Nasser!*—Thou Victorious One!" Pride, dignity, greatness, were to be the share of the Arab fellah. Can pride and dignity produce greatness and fill empty stomachs? Perhaps not, but Nasser's words about the nation's prestige continued to elicit frenzied exultation. He could do no wrong, as far as the common people were concerned. From the outset he invested them with a sense of their identification with the coming greatness of Egypt and the Arab world. As members of that great Arab community they, the fellahin, would grow in stature. People did not seem to recall that at one time the frenzied admiration of the people almost crushed General Naguib. "The god that fails to deliver life-giving rain is god no more."

And what about the obverse of the coin? If there were grumblings within Egypt they were drowned by the shrieking hallelujahs. Outside of the country, enthusiasm was not so widespread. Western diplomatic opinion wanted to await more substantial results. *Sotto voce* it agreed that Nasser was a charmer, who probably believed the things he said at the time he uttered them. However, he was "not solid," perhaps a good politician and a "sloganeer." "Nasser can unleash, but can he stop?" "He can promise, but can he perform?" "He is a good tactician, but not a strategist." "He wins battles, but will he win the war?" "He has been helped by his enemies." "He is a Cairene Machiavelli." "He is delightfully frank and sincere in appearance, but he is always telling lies"— this testimony from Glubb Pasha.

"A Role in Search of a Hero"

To learn more about him, we can turn directly to Nasser. He committed to paper his philosophy of the revolution and of himself, the embodiment of that revolution.* Though the book has been compared with Hitler's *Mein Kampf*, it lacks the diabolic drive of that work. Described as "jejune" and "immature," nevertheless, it should be taken seriously as the earnest expression of the aspirations of an important man in the Arab world.

"A Role in Search of a Hero" is the title of the key chapter in this book. "I do not know why I recall," Nasser writes, "whenever I reach this point in my recollections as I meditate alone in my room, a famous tale by a great Italian poet, Luigi Pirandello— *Six Characters in Search of an Author.*" † Then he continues:

The pages of history are full of heroes who created for themselves roles of glorious valor which they played at decisive moments. Likewise the pages of history are full of heroic and glorious roles which never found heroes to perform them. For some reason it seems to me that within the Arab circle there is a role wandering aimlessly in search of a hero.‡

This role, exhausted by its wandering, settled down near the borders of Egypt and is beckoning to her to take up its lines, to put on its costume, since no one else was qualified to play it.

According to Nasser, Egypt's history took place within three concentric circles, the most important of which was the Arab circle. For centuries the Arabs had suffered together, victims of foreign intruders who imposed a "murderous, invisible siege upon the whole region." The Arabs needed to form a single entity in order to organize for the common struggle against imperialism. The Arab circle was the most important to Nasser, and the one with which the Egyptians were most closely linked. "We have

* Gamal Abdul Nasser, *Egypt's Liberation. The Philosophy of the Revolution,* Washington: Public Affairs Press, 1955.
† Pirandello was a dramatist and *Six Characters . . .* is a play.
‡ Nasser, *op. cit.,* p. 87.

suffered together, we have gone through the same crises, and when we fell beneath the hooves of the invaders' steeds, they were with us under the same hooves."

The second circle was Africa, where Egypt occupied the most strategic position along the continent's great lifeline, the Nile, and the world's lifeline, Suez. Egypt could not remain aloof from the sanguinary conflicts between the five million "whites" and some two hundred million Africans of that continent. A tragic turbulence, according to Nasser, was convulsing the "Dark Continent," which the white man, representing Europe's dominant nations, was attempting to redivide. "The people of Africa will continue to look to us, who guard their northern gate and constitute their link with the outside world. Under no circumstances will we be able to relinquish our responsibility to support, with all our might, the spread of enlightenment and civilization to the remotest depths of the jungle land."

Finally, the third and last circle was almost global in its scope, encompassing hundreds of millions of Muslims, from the Atlantic deep down into China.

When I consider the eighty million Muslims in Indonesia, and the fifty million in China, and the millions in Malaya, Siam and Burma, and the nearly hundred million in Pakistan, and the more than a hundred million in the Middle East, and the forty million in the Soviet Union, together with the other millions in far-flung parts of the world—when I consider these hundreds of millions united by a single creed, I emerge with a sense of the tremendous possibilities which we might realize through the co-operation of all these Muslims. . . .*

Within the first circle, that of the Arabs, Nasser detected three great sources of strength. The first was that all the Arabs formed a community of neighboring people linked together by material and moral ties. They possessed a distinct civilization of many traits. The second source of Arab strength was the proximity of

---

* Most of these figures seem fanciful, especially the ones relating to China and the Soviet Union.

strategic locations. Their lands embraced the crossroads of the world, the traders' thoroughfares and the armies' marching grounds. Their third great source of strength was their fabulous oil wealth. Comparing the productivity of the world's leading oil regions, Nasser found that the average daily production per petroleum well in the United States was only 11 barrels, compared with 4,000 barrels in the Arab world; and it cost 78 cents to produce a barrel of oil in the United States, while it cost no more than 10 cents in the Arab lands. "And now I go back to that wandering mission in search of a hero to play it. Here is the role. Here are the lines, and here is the stage. We alone, by virtue of our stage, can perform the part."

The Population Explosion

Egypt's great problem is production, especially of food. Mainly an agricultural country, she depends entirely on the Nile, for there is not enough rain to expand the productive surface on a large scale. A cynical Egyptian once told me: "The only solution of the Egyptian problem would be the creation of another Nile."

Each year, many more Egyptians reach working age than there are jobs to support them. "Only recently, the Minister of Industry reported that during the country's ambitious five-year industrialization program new industries will absorb 100,000 workers. But in the same period, the Egyptian labor force will increase by 900,000 workers. Of these, perhaps some 400,000 will be settled in agriculture. And 400,000 surplus workers will be left to join Egypt's unemployed." *

Here is the supreme paradox. The modern age is killing Egypt's people. When plagues swept the country and kept the population down, they had more to eat. But now we have the "miracle drugs," and though occasional plagues still visit the valley, they are far less devastating than before. As a result, the Egyptians must divide

* Robert C. Cook, "The Democratic Maelstrom," Report of the President, *Population Reference Bureau*, Annual Report, 1958, p. 6.

food among more and more people and, contrary to the prevailing trend elsewhere, the farm population's living standards are declining. If further improvements in standards ensue and unless other quick economic remedies are found, Egypt will be reduced to a charnel house where people perish not from plague but from starvation. This tragedy is best illustrated by the words of Egypt's first President, General Naguib:

In 1798, when Egypt was invaded by Napoleonic France, it was a backward Turkish colony inhabited by two and a half million people who lived precariously off the produce of some three million sparsely cultivated acres along the banks of the Nile. Today, after a hundred and fifty-six years of Western influence and seventy-two years of total or partial British occupation, Egypt is inhabited by twenty-two million people who live precariously off the produce of some six million acres of intensively cultivated area.

Indeed, only twice as much land must feed nine times as many people. Not all the available water nor the best machines and fertilizers could perform such a miracle. Though the people of Cairo and Alexandria may fare better, the former President pointed out that remaining millions "have been reduced to the lowest standard of living that the civilized world has ever seen." This tragic situation may be at the root of Nasser's policy of Arab unity. There may be no other solution of the Egyptian dilemma than dispersal over more favored lands, like Syria and Iraq. But then it would not be in the interest of these countries to have their living standards reduced.

The per capita income, on the rise in most other places, especially the West, declined in Egypt by some 45 per cent in the first half of this century. Though the population doubled in that period, income for the increased numbers went down by 20 per cent. In the Delta along the Nile, some eighteen million Egyptians live on land that has the deepest alluvial soil in the Old World. Yet, it is a tragic land, for they do makeshift "work" which could easily be dispensed with. They are marginal people who hold on to life for a while and die an early death. In 1949 ten million people depended on less than an acre per family. Since two-thirds of the land was owned by 6 per cent of the people, 85 per cent of the peasants had either no land or less than an acre. Eleven and a half million people had to subsist on $50 to $60 a year.

Egyptian "Socialism"

In Egypt, the Western economic way of life, capitalism, was equated with imperialism. "Socialism" was the label the *junta* adopted for its economic doctrines. So great was the attraction of this label that even the Pashas, during the brief period it was possible to set up political organizations, called theirs "socialistic."

In an agricultural country, land represents not only economic but also political power and this is particularly true of Egypt. The resistance of the old order had to be broken or at least weakened and since most of the land was concentrated in its hands, the method used was land reform. By law, no individual was to possess more than 200 feddans (1 feddan is 1.038 acre), no family unit more than 300. "We do not want landlords to become tenants," Nasser said, "but we want tenants to become landlords. We never did and never will destroy individual initiative."

Altogether some 566,000 feddans were distributed among two hundred thousand peasants, and the owners were encouraged to join co-operatives to learn how best to use this land. The expropriated landlords were to be compensated with ten times the annual rental value of their lands plus the value of improvements, payable in 3 per cent government bonds.

But the land reform failed to solve the country's basic economic problem. First, there was not enough land to go around; and second, the landholdings exempt from redistribution were large. There appeared to be two reasons for the lavish exemptions. The fellahin wanted land, which means security and human standards, but once they had it, many of them did not know what to do with it. Debilitated and listless, they lacked staying power and

78

initiative. The large holdings at least were cultivated properly. Too, the government did not want overly to antagonize the landowners. Money continued to have an anonymous power in Egypt, not easily identified but very real. An uneasy truce was to be maintained between the new regime and the old ruling classes.

In the past the country belonged not to the people but to a small clique of exploiters [Nasser said in a 1956 declaration]. The revolution came and declared that it was against the domination of the government by capital, not against capital itself. Capital had begun to depart from its natural duty. It ought to have directed itself to investment and the increase of production and national income. Instead, corrupt capital sought to dominate the affairs of the government. The social philosophy of the revolution must be given a chance to develop. . . .

The ideal, as Nasser saw it, was a community in which the worker co-operated with the proprietor, "a community free from monopoly, political despotism, foreign influence and social injustice."

This called for an immense amount of work. Previous regimes had placed some social laws on the statute books but there they remained, unobserved. Social conditions in Egypt were so backward it took a postrevolution labor law to provide that workers were to be paid in legal currency, at periodic intervals, at their places of employment, on workdays. A Ford Foundation study, completed late in 1957, showed that with all the revolution's reforms the average wage in the manufacturing and mining industries was only $5.60 a week, and close to one-fifth earned less than $2.80. Another one-fifth made more than $10.20. Since these figures mainly were provided by employers they were subject to discounting. Managerial and other such salaries were shrouded in secrecy, but there seemed little evidence in them of "Egyptian socialism."

The value of human life in industrial occupations was reported to be low. Accident prevention in plants was little more than a blueprint and employers seemed unconcerned about it. Laborers were found stumbling over debris in plants. They transported material on their backs, worked in hot rolling mills without shoes, and at too close a proximity to the furnaces. "The cost of human labor and the value of human life are too low," the study concluded, "to command serious attention to safety. The toll of industrial accidents, high though it is, is insignificant in comparison with the misery attributable to disease and undernourishment."

Industries to the Fore

In Egypt, as in similarly backward countries, "industry" is a magic word. High standards of living are possible in industrial civilizations where, almost miraculously, machines multiply the output of man's hands. Fields of wheat and cotton produce no arms, but steel mills do and today most countries are rated according to their ability to produce weapons. President Nasser realized that his country's success was dependent upon its ability to industrialize rapidly.

Young Egyptian bureaucrats seldom make any secret as to what country's example they would like to follow in order to raise their own living standards. Like most people in the economically backward parts of the world, they are astounded by the standard of living of the United States. If they have not been exposed to it directly they know about it—in exaggerated form—through hearsay or the films. Shangri-La is situated between the Atlantic and the Pacific, in North America. However, many of these observers, Egyptians and others, consider the "American experiment" the product of another age, the era of the robber barons. In the Soviet Union they see an immeasurably lower standard of living and a harsh world of hard labor, but the "Russian experiment" fits into their own experience, for, a generation or two ago, the Soviet Union was as backward as their own lands. Thus they feel attracted to its accomplishments, though repelled by its methods.

Egypt under her new revolutionary regime had much in common with postrevolutionary Russia in that she lacked adequate capital that could be utilized immediately for economic development. Egypt had, and still has, people of great wealth—before the revolution, Cairo and Alexandria were the largest importers of jewelry diamonds, after the United States and the United Kingdom. But domestic money went into industrial production only peripherally. As in other Arab countries, most of it went into gold hoards, jewelry and investments as well as savings accounts abroad in an effort to avoid the risks of large-scale industrial pioneering.

It was finally decided in Egypt to adopt the Soviet idea of the five-year plan and, paradoxically, an American-educated Egyptian economist, Harvard graduate Aziz Sidky, was charged with drawing it up. Formulated in 1957, it was to raise the national income by 13 per cent. Control was vested in an Economic Board which was to co-ordinate the nation's efforts in the governmental and private sectors. Partly an "Operation Bootstrap" and pay-as-you-go venture, its object was to produce more than was consumed. The plan was to draw upon whatever outside resources Egypt could obtain. The important feature was industrialization.

The projected new industries included a considerable number of plants for the processing of domestic products—textiles, chemicals, metals. Also, the accent was on industries to produce the necessities Egypt had to buy abroad. Turning out these products at home would save foreign currency as well as the extra costs of intermediaries and transportation. New fertilizer and cement plants, freight-car shops, a tire and tube factory, iron and steel plants, a battery plant and a rifle factory were also planned. Many of these factories were being built with foreign capital and technical assistance, mainly provided by the Soviet Union and satellite countries. Egypt received economic aid of $311 million from mid-1955 until the beginning of 1959.* The German Federal Republic and the German People's Republic also have extended aid. In Egypt, as in most of the Arab world, Germans are in great de-

* *The New York Times,* March 29, 1959.

mand because of their efficiency, as well as the Nazi ideology left over from Hitler.*

Nasser's strategy has been equated with Hitler's. He was impressing the Arabs with Egypt's ability to get things done and conquering their minds as well as their emotions. His object seemed to be to display to the Arab world the shining example of Egyptian progress. Hitler conquered only the emotions of his countrymen; Nasser has conquered the emotions of the people of a large area outside of his country and he has done it by exploiting Arab neuroses and frustrations. "Even as Goering used to cow Germany's neighbors with displays of the Luftwaffe, Nasser amazes and heartens his Arab brothers by showing off the economic progress Egypt has made since it shook off the yoke of Britain's 'capitalist imperialism.' " †

In the early years of the *junta* the reforming zeal was actually impressive. However, a publication of the Royal Institute of International Affairs pointed out: "Most of the internal reforms were initiated during the first few months after the *coup d'état* of July 1952 and since then there have been no major developments. The only completed reform, land re-distribution, benefited only some 8 to 10 per cent of the farm population, as against the one-third who benefited from the postwar land reforms in Japan." ‡

The Storm Over the Dam

A spectacular regime such as Nasser's naturally wanted to score a spectacular achievement, and in Egypt there is only one natural

---

* Former Nazis were in demand also in other capacities in Egypt. Oscar Dirlewanger, SS special officer in the Ukraine during World War II, who fled Germany to escape trial as a war criminal, became an adviser on guerrilla warfare to the Egyptian army; Johannes Demling, wartime Gestapo chief in the Ruhr, was entrusted with the task of reorganizing the Egyptian police; Dr. Johannes von Leers, one of the leading experts in anti-Western and anti-Semitic propaganda in the German Nazi Propaganda Ministry, became chief propaganda adviser to President Nasser; etc.

† Gilbert Burdick, "Nasser's Imperial Economics," *Fortune,* October 1958.

‡ "Nasserism and Communism," *The World Today,* October 1956, Vol. 12, No. 10, p. 393.

phenomenon, the Nile, which lends itself to such a role. A part of the river has been harnessed, but much of its water goes to waste and Egypt can ill afford to waste water. Dams had already doubled the arable surface of the country, bringing it to six million acres. An additional two million acres could be added by building a new High Dam at Aswan.

It has been said, "Every time Egypt has turned to the Nile, it has never been disappointed." Now again the country must turn to the Nile. The "population explosion" coupled with the decline in the death rate threatened tragedy if something were not done.

The Aswan High Dam project had been presented to King Farouk in 1947, but it was rejected. Now, the *junta* turned its attention to the project and had it examined by competent bodies: experts of the American Technical Assistance—"Point Four"— program; the UN's International Bank for Reconstruction and Development; and two of Egypt's own technical administration bureaus, the Ministry of Public Works and the Permanent Council of National Production.

The findings of these organizations were favorable to the plan —but with reservations. It was found that the plan was feasible both from the technical and economic points of view, yet it was also pointed out that the financing of the project would be difficult. The High Dam would give Egypt a breathing spell but would not ensure a significant rise in income. Egypt was not the type of country where any one measure, no matter how important, would ensure a rapid rise in per capita income. Since the High Dam was only part of a more extensive project, including industrial development, additional funds would be needed for that purpose too. Also, the needs of the Sudan, Egypt's neighbor to the south, had to be considered, since, by treaty, that country was entitled to a certain proportion of the waters of the Nile. Then, too, the vast artificial lake created by the Dam would cause the Nile waters to back up into the Sudan's northern province, all the way to Wadi Halfa, in the Nubian Desert region, near the Second Cataract

83

of the Nile. Compensation would be due the neighbor for land and settled areas thus submerged.

Reservations were also expressed about the desirability of putting everything into the construction of one large dam, instead of several smaller ones that might benefit more regions. The evaporation rate at the High Dam site would also be very high, with consequent loss of water. A United Nations report suggested that an integrated plan be prepared to cover all the headwaters of the Nile. Such a regional project would include not only parts of Egypt, but also parts of Ethiopia—the Tana Lake where the Blue Nile rises—and sections of Uganda, Kenya, Tanganyika and the Belgian Congo. Under this plan the Nile would be treated as a hydrological unit.

"For thousands of years," President Nasser said, "the great pyramids of Egypt were the foremost engineering marvels of the world. They insured life after death to the Pharaohs. Tomorrow, the gigantic High Dam, more significant and seventeen times greater than the greatest pyramids, will provide a higher standard of living for Egypt."

The plans were drawn up and the preliminary work got underway. A stupendous structure was to rise across the Nile. Three miles wide and 250 feet high, it would cause a man-made lake 250 miles long. Egypt's arable land would be increased by 30 per cent, to bring the country's total cultivated area to the maximum possible under present conditions. Ten billion kwh. of energy a year would be generated at a very low cost and the abundance of cheap electricity gained was to obviate the need of using fuel oil. The dam would cut down imports, boost foreign-exchange reserves, render possible the erection of a chain of industries, and increase the annual national income by a billion dollars. Against a runaway birth rate, the Aswan Dam was represented as the only hope of maintaining the standard of living. It might even raise it.

Financing the High Dam

An International Bank study, prepared largely in Washington, showed that Egypt required $1,350 million to finance the High Dam. A vast amount even for an affluent country, it was staggering for Egypt where some 80 per cent of the people were not far from hunger, and where the rich were not inclined to put their money into High Dams. Still, it was calculated that Egypt would probably be able to raise the $550 million necessary to defray the costs of local labor and material in Egyptian pounds. Also, the government would launch a bond drive, combining it with a strong patriotic appeal, to coax some $400 million out of rich Egyptians.

This left $400 million to be obtained abroad in foreign currency to pay for raw materials and technical help from the United States and other international markets. The International Bank expressed its readiness to grant a ten-year $200 million loan if Egypt fulfilled certain conditions. The Bank proposed to Nasser to cut costs on arms and social services, and for ten years to gear Egypt's government economy to harmonize with the financing of the Aswan plan.

The participation of the United States in the project was considered essential. American influence was strong in the International Bank, and much of the material needed for the project was to come from the United States. The Egyptian government was not particularly anxious to become a debtor of Western countries—it was precisely because of such debt transactions that Britain had occupied Egypt. But there was no choice. After protracted negotiations, it was agreed that the United States and Britain would offer Egypt an initial grant of $70 million, of which the United States share would be $56 million and Britain would put up $14 million in "blocked sterling." * America and Britain said they would also consider favorably additional grants and

* Money owed to Egypt by Britain for goods and services during and after World War II.

loans to help pay for the final phase of the construction. The rest of the projected expenditures would be derived from other sources.

An Agreement and a Rebuff

In September 1955, the Egyptian government concluded an arrangement with the Soviet Union to exchange cotton for arms. It was first thought to be an $80 million deal but, later, it was believed that a quarter of a billion dollars was involved. Then when Egypt, followed by Syria and Yemen, recognized Communist China the events were interpreted as a Soviet breakthrough on the Middle Eastern diplomatic front. For the first time in the twentieth century Russia had vaulted the Western defenses and found herself in the core of the Middle East.

Not long before, Nasser had been denounced by the Soviet satellite press as a "stooge of the imperialists." His "revolution" had been ridiculed. Now, suddenly, the villain became the hero. The tenor of the Soviet press changed overnight and Russian and satellite film companies descended upon Egypt, taking shots of a land of beauty, sunshine, song and happiness. One would have thought Egypt was the land of the lush grass, the fat soil and flowers. Even the desert was shown only from its most romantic angle—the pyramids and Sphinx.

This sudden change in relations between Egypt and the Soviet bloc threw the Western camp into consternation. What was Cairo's game? Was this part of a diplomatic flirtation or was Egypt committed to the Soviets? Then, word of a new deal was received from Egypt. The Soviet Union was reported to have offered Cairo money, on favorable terms, and "with no strings attached," for the building of the Aswan High Dam.

Cairo was slow in announcing acceptance of the American offer to help finance the Dam, and then lightning struck. On July 19, 1956, Secretary of State Dulles announced America's withdrawal from the offer, giving this explanation:

Developments within the succeeding seven months have not been favorable to the success of the project and the United States government has concluded that it is not feasible under the circumstances to participate in the project. Agreement by the riparian States has not been achieved, and the ability of Egypt to devote adequate resources to assure the project's success has become more uncertain than at the time the offer was made.

But was this the real reason for America's withdrawal? A new angle of the American refusal was mentioned at a congressional hearing later in the year. Egypt is an important producer of long-staple cotton which the American South also raises. According to this interpretation, the "cotton lobby" in Washington had a hand in the American withdrawal. The Aswan High Dam would have enabled Egypt to produce more long-staple cotton.

Another cause of America's change of policy was discussed in diplomatic circles—the State Department wanted to flush out the Russians, since word had come from Cairo about the Soviet offer to help finance the Dam. In withdrawing American support and leaving the way open for a Soviet grand gesture, Mr. Dulles was sure that the Soviets would not respond and thus would be discredited in Middle Eastern eyes. Only later did it become known that the Soviets had made no offer and that Cairo's announcement had only intended to stimulate Washington to action.

The actual reason for America's refusal to have a hand in the financing of the High Dam was probably much simpler. In the view of the State Department, Cairo had become too deeply committed to Moscow with the arms deals and the recognition of the Communist Chinese regime, and by financing the Dam, the United States would be indirectly financing the Kremlin.

Though the United States' share in the $1,350 million project would have been nominal, it played a decisive role in the chain of events that followed. Great Britain withdrew from the venture and, more important, so did the International Bank for Reconstruction and Development. With these three sources of outside funds gone, it appeared, for the moment at least, that Nasser's dream to feed more Egyptians was at an end.

The Consequences of the Rebuff

To Nasser, Secretary of State Dulles' strictures about Egypt's ability to finance the Aswan structure had added insult to injury by reflecting on the country's credit standing. Now invested with dictatorial powers, Egypt's "man of destiny" could not tolerate any denigration of his regime. Five days later he reacted to the statement of Mr. Dulles and his emotion-laden words echoed in the entire Middle East.

"If rumor in Washington tries to insinuate that the Egyptian economy is not strong enough to warrant America's aid," he said on July 24, "then I tell them: Choke with rage but you will never order us about because we know our path which is that of freedom, honor and dignity. . . . Publish your bulletins in Washington and then think of this: if they are sincere but due to misinformation, that is too bad, but if they are lies to deceive public opinion, that is more unfortunate for a World Power which has constituted itself the champion of liberty. We Egyptians will never allow any colonizer or other despot to dominate us politically, economically or militarily. We will yield neither to force nor to your dollar!"

Denouncing the "cabal" contrived between the United States and the International Bank, Nasser accused these of tricking Egypt into making plans to build the Dam in order to impose conditions which would affect the country's independence and integrity. However, this was only the beginning. Neither the State Department nor the International Bank had anticipated Nasser's reaction. The financing of the Aswan Dam was, after all, a business transaction which should have no relation to any other issue. But not in Nasser's view—he would have his Dam, and the Western Powers would pay for it. On July 26 he announced the nationalization of the Suez Canal Company. With the revenue Egypt would derive from its operation he would build the Aswan High Dam.

Not long before, Nasser had come into conflict with the British over the evacuation of their Suez Canal bases. This new action affected the British in a different manner. The government of the United Kingdom was the largest single stockholder of the Canal Company, Compagnie Universelle du Canal Maritime de Suez, a private corporation with a special status, operating under French and Egyptian laws. "We shall build the High Dam," Nasser ranted, "on the skulls of the 120,000 workmen who died building the Suez Canal. We shall industrialize Egypt and compete with the West. With the revenue from the Canal we shall not look to Britain and the United States for their grant. . . ."

The income from the Canal, a hundred million dollars a year, he said, would be used to build the Dam. This figure was based on the previous year's gross income from the Canal, $97,596,000. However, the net income in that year was only $45 million. The Canal Company was engaged in a $54-million, five-year expansion program, begun in 1954, to increase the maximum draft of the vessels using the Canal from 35 to 37 feet, and to enlarge the capacity of the Canal from forty to fifty ships a day. In addition, $8 million a year was spent on routine improvements. The remaining sum was still very far from the hundred million dollars a year to be used for the building of the Aswan High Dam.

Secretary Dulles was convinced there was no connection between the nationalization of the Canal and the High Dam. "Indeed, President Nasser did not and does not attempt to justify his action on the ground of the withdrawal of the aid to the Aswan Dam. He justifies it as a step in his program of developing the influence of Egypt, what he calls its 'grandeur' and as part of his program of moving 'from triumph to triumph.'"

A *"Murky Ditch"*

The Suez Canal, one of the world's great engineering achievements, shortened shipping routes by thousands of miles. An oil tanker from the Middle Eastern petroleum fields took forty-eight days to reach New York by way of Suez, instead of the sixty-six days required to round the Cape.

Tonnage figures bear out the importance of the Canal. Net tonnage increased from 55,081,056 in 1948 to 115,756,000 by the year of the nationalization. The average tonnage through Suez was three times that of the Panama Canal. The tonnage increased at such a fast rate, and so profitable was the enterprise, that passenger tolls were eliminated after 1950, and dues were reduced to 97½ cents per Suez net ton for laden ships, and 44½ cents a ton for vessels in ballast.

To many countries, however, the Canal was far more than a great convenience. To the French it was the reflection of the national *gloire,* the work of a French genius, the projection of the grandeur of France into the Middle East. To the English it was the lifeline of an empire—now the Commonwealth of equal partners—a global hub and, above all, a symbol of greatness. The indispensability of the Canal had been demonstrated in the two World Wars. During the first one, the British had chased German raiders from the eastern seas with the aid of Suez. The role of Suez in the Second World War was even greater. Through it, the Allies were able to maintain a line of global communication, even when the Mediterranean was closed by their enemies. Without Suez they might have lost the war.

The cold-war role of Suez was also important. Western shipping used the Canal far more than the Soviet bloc. Since the NATO countries obtained 80 per cent of their vitally needed oil from the Middle East, the Suez Canal was their most important petroleum tanker route.

The Sound of Distant Thunder

The operation of the Suez Canal was subject to international regulation—the Constantinople Convention of 1888. The signatories were the Ottoman, Russian, Austro-Hungarian, German and British empires, the kingdoms of Spain, Italy and the Netherlands, and the Republic of France. Egypt inherited the rights and obligations of the Ottoman Empire under the Convention.

"The Suez Maritime Canal shall always be free and open, in time of war as in time of peace, to every vessel of commerce or of war, without distinction of flag," states Article I of the Convention. In Article IV the high contracting parties agreed that no right of war, no act of hostility, nor any act having for its object the obstruction of the free navigation of the Canal, should be committed in it. However, Article X stipulates that the provisions of the Convention are not to interfere with the measures that the riparian state [Egypt] might find necessary to take for securing its own defense and the maintenance of public order. But Article XI of the Constantinople Convention categorically rules out Articles IX and X on which Egypt bases its case, and it reads: "The measures taken in cases provided for by Articles IX and X of the present treaty shall not interfere with the free use of the Canal."

Nasser asserted that his nationalization of the Canal was not in derogation of the rights of the international community in the Canal, because the Constantinople Convention would be scrupulously observed under Egyptian management. The nationalization of industries, mines and banks, Nasser pointed out, was common practice in both Great Britain and France, and Egypt would even reimburse the stockholders. In the Egyptian President's emphatic view, the nationalization of the Canal abridged no foreign rights.

The Western Powers, particularly Britain, France and the United States, took issue with the Egyptian government. The British and French treasuries took measures to freeze Egyptian accounts. The United States government froze Egyptian government and Suez Canal assets. France's Minister of Foreign Affairs,

91

Christian Pineau, recalled that the Canal had been financed by stocks issued in several international markets; that the waterway itself had been built according to rules laid down by an international scientific commission, that it had always been managed by an international board of directors and that, therefore, the company always enjoyed a special status which the Egyptian government itself had recognized by negotiating some hundred contracts with the company regarding customs duties, foreign exchange and employee rights, among many other items. The Minister pointed out that Egyptian courts had recognized the international character of the company, which had not been placed under the Egyptian tariff laws and was not subject to certain Egyptian corporation laws. "While the company has Egyptian nationality," Egyptian courts had said, "it also has universal character."

As the battle raged on the diplomatic front public opinion was crystallizing in the countries involved. The French had recently sustained a crushing defeat in Indochina, had lost the protectorates of Tunisia and Morocco, and were engaged in a bloody battle in Algeria. Under the circumstances they felt they could not yield on still another front. They knew Nasser was aiding the Algerian rebels. Should he win in the Canal crisis, further encroachments might follow in French Equatorial and West Africa. The French appeared determined to take a stand on the Suez issue. "Strike off the Egyptian hydra's head," the popular press clamored.

Britain had lost far more than France through the independence of her colonies, but a line had to be drawn somewhere, and this was the line. To many Britishers Nasser appeared very much like Hitler. Let there be no appeasement, they admonished the government. Prime Minister Anthony Eden was not in the habit of appeasing dictators and besides, the Suez group, an influential faction within his Conservative party, was getting restless. Both the French and the British governments began to take military measures.

92

The Crisis and the Solutions

"When on July 26 the Universal Suez Canal Company was abruptly seized by the Egyptian government," the American Secretary of State said, "all the world felt that a crisis of momentous proportions had been precipitated."

While the diplomats debated, the old directorate of the Suez Canal Company acted and, with the approval of the French and British governments, called upon the Canal pilots to leave their posts, offering them substitute positions as compensations. Navigation in the Suez Canal was described in the Western press as an extremely difficult operation—sudden winds in the desert could play tricks on the pilots and knowledge of the whims of the Canal and of the desert land required long periods of training. Withdrawing the pilots, therefore, was thought to be tantamount to paralyzing the Canal.

About half of the entire staff did leave, but Nasser, in turn, issued a call for seafaring men to fill the abandoned posts in return for good pay, and the responses came from many parts of the world—Germany, the United States, the Soviet Union and its satellites. After only a short training period the new pilots took over and operations continued without a hitch—no more mishaps than under the old management. The Suez Canal Company was now under the management of Mahmoud Younes, an Egyptian, and in his opinion the smooth operation was due to the fact that now the Canal was managed on the spot and not by remote control from Paris. The success of the Canal under Egyptian management was a national triumph for Egypt and the Arab world.

Diplomatic Moves

A conference of those countries mainly concerned with the Canal met in London on August 16, 1956, remaining in session until the twenty-third. Of the twenty-four nations scheduled to attend, eight had been signatories of the Constantinople Convention. The rest were important Canal users. Egypt and Greece declined to attend, the latter because of the conflict with Great Britain about the island of Cyprus. Thus, there were twenty-two participants at the London conference.

A majority plan was produced by eighteen nations, calling for the establishment of an international organization to operate the Canal—the Suez Canal Board. Nasser alone was not to be entrusted with the operation, but his nationalization of the Canal was not to be undone. The minority report was endorsed by the Soviet Union, India, Indonesia and Ceylon. Under their plan, the Canal was to remain under Egyptian management but with an advisory board of international user representatives.

The majority plan was presented to Nasser by the Australian Prime Minister, Robert Gordon Menzies. Nasser took the stand that it was Egypt's sovereign right to nationalize the Canal. He declared his readiness to observe the Convention of 1888, and to negotiate on such matters as dues and technical advice, but he rejected the plan. By defying the West, he had become the hero of Egypt, the Arab world, and other countries formerly under European rule. By accepting the plan he would have disestablished himself in their eyes.

One of the chief aims of the main user powers was to "insulate" the Suez Canal from Egypt's politics.* Upon the failure of the first plan a second conference was called which met in London during September 19-21. Fifteen countries, headed by the United States, Britain and France, now decided to form the Suez Canal Users' Association, which would employ its own pilots, collect the tolls, and pay Egypt appropriate fees. It was to cooperate with Egypt but should she refuse the passage of ships, the powers would be free to "take such further steps," in Prime Minister Eden's words, "as seem required either through the

---

* Egypt had discriminated against Israeli shipping. It was feared that in an emergency situation she might close the Canal to Western countries and try to keep it open to the Eastern bloc.

United Nations or by other means, for the assertion of their rights."

Even before the Association was established, Nasser announced his policy: "We shall not allow the Western-proposed Canal Users' Association to function. . . . We Egyptians will run the Canal efficiently and if, in spite of all this, the Canal Users' Association forces its way through the Suez Canal, then it would mean aggression and be treated as such." Here was another checkmate.

On September 23 Britain and France asked the Security Council of the United Nations to consider the "situation created by the unilateral action of the Egyptian government in bringing to an end the system of international operation of the Canal. . . ."

The Security Council adopted six basic principles for the operation of the Canal: transit through it was to be free and open without any overt or covert political or technical discrimination; Egypt's sovereignty was to be respected; the operation of the Canal was to be insulated from the politics of any country; the tolls were to be determined by agreement between Egypt and the users; a fair proportion of the dues was to be allotted to the development of the Canal; and disputes were to be submitted to arbitration.

These were sufficiently innocuous to be accepted unanimously, but the draft agreement submitted by Britain and France, under which Egypt would agree to co-operate with the Users' Association pending definitive settlement of the issues, proved objectionable to Nasser, and succumbed to a Soviet veto.

At this point the Suez controversy became linked with the conflict between Israel and Egypt. In time, two seemingly unrelated cases of hostilities erupted: between Israel and Egypt, on the one hand; and Britain, in league with France against Egypt, on the other. Eventually these conflicts merged. Since the two strands of history cannot be separated without damaging the fabric of events, we must turn our attention to the conflict between Egypt and Israel, which was to end not far from the banks of the Canal.

95

"The Second Round"

We have seen that many of the initial reforms in Egypt were introduced during the first months of the coup staged by the officers' *junta*. Egypt was not the type of country in which sudden increases in living standards could occur. But Nasser was a "miracle man" and when strong men can't give people bread they divert them with a circus; and, if one ring is not enough, they provide two or more.

Israel had been the whipping boy of the Arabs for whom Nasser presumed to speak. In February 1949, Egypt and Israel had concluded a general armistice agreement under the auspices of the United Nations. Actual warfare between the two countries had come to an end.

However, on February 6, 1950, the Egyptian government promulgated a "Decree on the Procedure of Ships and Airplane Searches and of Seizure of Contraband Goods in Connexion with the Palestine War," in which a large number of Israel-bound goods were listed as contraband and subject to confiscation. The list included drugs, chemicals, fuel, machinery and parts, many raw materials, in addition to arms and ammunition.

Israel cited the Constantinople Convention when it took the case to the Security Council of the United Nations. Egypt argued that Israel was a belligerent and Article X of the Convention in regard to self-defense covered the case. The Security Council found that neither party could reasonably assert that it was actively a belligerent. The Council resolution, passed on September 1, 1951, called upon Egypt "to terminate the restrictions on the passage of international commercial shipping and goods through the Suez Canal wherever bound and to cease all interference with such shipping beyond that essential to the safety of shipping in the Canal itself and to the observance of the international conventions in force."

Egypt refused to abide by the resolution of the United Nations. On the contrary, on November 30, 1953, it tightened the restric-

96

tions and added to the list "foodstuffs and all other commodities which are likely to strengthen the war potential of the Zionists in Palestine in any way whatever." The list now included even such commodities as cloth and bicycles.

Subsequently, the Egyptian authorities drew up a black list of ships carrying certain materials to Israel and imposed penalties upon those vessels when they passed through the Canal, denying them water, fuel and repair facilities. Also the Egyptian authorities confiscated, from time to time, Israel-bound cargo aboard neutral ships in the Suez Canal. Israel ships were barred from the Canal by the Egyptian blockade.

Again Israel took the case to the Security Council—on February 5, 1954. This time it was the New Zealand delegate, Sir Leslie Munro, who introduced a draft resolution calling upon the Egyptian government to comply with the previous decision of the United Nations and with the Constantinople Convention. "The Security Council notes with grave concern," the resolution said, "that Egypt has not complied with that [1951] resolution; calls upon Egypt, in accordance with its obligations under the Charter to comply therewith." On March 29 the vote was taken in the Security Council. It was vetoed by the Soviet Union.

The Fedayin Attack

The radio stations of Arab countries kept on threatening Israel with being flung into the sea, as the Christian Crusaders had been in the Middle Ages. Before that, however, there were premonitory steps, preparations, attacks by commandos that revealed reconnaissance activities. The *fedayin,* rangers, took off from the Sinai peninsula or from the Gaza Strip, which had belonged to Palestine and was now under Egyptian occupation. These fedayin attacked stealthily, often in the protective penumbra of dry river courses, wadis, when the moon hid its countenance. Nothing was sacred to the nocturnal prowlers, Israel complained, and their terror was naked. Two-thirds of the casualties sustained by Israel were civilians. The Israeli intelligence reports were grim. Preparations for larger-scale action were unmistakable under the protection of sand and stone. The confirmation came after the Suez campaign had broken out. There were the words of the Egyptian staff officer, Liwa (Major General) Ahmed Salem, in Directive No. 2, marked "Very Secret" and that it was, indeed. Its date was most important, a peacetime day, but there was no peace: February 15, 1956. "From C.O. Egyptian District, Palestine," it read, "to the C.O. Reinforced 5th Infantry Brigade," and it referred to earlier directives to commanders operating close to Israel, including the Gaza Strip. The names of the places it mentioned brought back memories of the Bible: Gaza itself, with all its memories; El Arish, also famous in Napoleon's Middle Eastern campaign; Rafah and Khan Junis.

The directive came to the point in its introduction:

> Every commander must prepare himself and his soldiers for the important battle with Israel in which we are fully immersed, with the aim of realizing our lofty tradition, i.e., to overpower and destroy Israel in the shortest possible time and with the greatest brutality and bestiality in battle.*

Then there were the training instructions for the administrative units, year 1956-57, in which Bikbashi (Lt. Col.) Mahmus Anis Ismail, 3rd Infantry Division, issued a document marked "Most Secret" and in which he wrote: "The basic purpose of training this year is transition from defensive to an offensive position. The administrative units must co-operate with the other units and prepare their men for these operations."

An earlier document, dated July 10, 1955, from Headquarters, Military Forces in Sinai—Intelligence—to the Head of Operations Division, signed by the Egyptian staff officer, commander of the military forces in Sinai, Lt. Col. Ahmed Salem, containing

---

* "Brutality" and "bestiality" in battle were terms which the German Nazis had used, and attention was called to the fact that former Nazi officers played part in training Egyptian forces.

such interesting information as this: "These volunteers were recruited for service in the National Guard, and not in the regular forces, by the Chief of Intelligence in Palestine, and most of them have a criminal past and they have but one desire: to wreak vengeance on Israel and to steal there."

The document continued: "The action of the volunteers was taken in accordance with the proposal of the above-mentioned Chief of Intelligence to the Commanding General of the Armed Forces who approved it on the condition that the volunteers constitute a part of the Egyptian National Guard. The approval was given during a visit of the commanding general to the front."

From the Kingdom of Jordan came these words: "This is to testify that the Palestinian fedayin who arrived in Jordan after accomplishing acts of revenge inside Israel during the period April 8-15 have handed over their arms and supplies to the Egyptian Embassy at Amman. A Committee has been established in Gaza to register these supplies and arms. The lists have been passed on to the Eastern Command." This document was signed by Major Mohammed Fathi Mahmoud, Assistant Director, Field Military Intelligence.

Glubb Pasha's Indictment

The commander in chief of Jordan's Arab Legion, Glubb Pasha, who was vehemently opposed to Israel, confirmed this documentation of Egyptian aggressive acts. Israel had the longest frontier with Jordan, he pointed out, some 160 miles long, cutting across wild country, boulder-strewn mountains, dry river beds, a zigzagging border where infiltration was easier than from the Sinai and Gaza deserts. According to Glubb, the Egyptians operated in many instances from Amman, capital of Jordan. Ample funds were at the disposal of the Egyptian Embassy there to finance the raids into Israel. Glubb mentioned a particularly daring instance when a group of saboteurs in Egyptian pay hired a taxi in Damascus, the Syrian capital, cut across Jordan, drove straight into Israel, blew up a target, rushed back to Jordan and continued to Damascus. Such Egyptian-staged acts increased after 1954, when, according to Glubb, "Nasser's domestic revolution had petered out."

There had been blows and counterblows, infiltration into Israel across her meandering frontiers, across the hills of Judaea and Samaria; on the plains where the Philistines had dwelt; from the Gaza Strip along the Mediterranean. The counterblows were against fedayin encampments in Gaza and elsewhere. Attacks were made upon Israeli farms sizzling under the subtropical sun, water pipes were blown up; many attacks were made in the dead of the night. Then there were the reprisals—an eye for an eye, sometimes two. The attitude of Israel was this: the initiative always came from the opposite side and the little nation needed the peace of undisturbed work to build reality upon a dream.

At the height of the Suez Canal controversy there were diplomatic apprehensions that Israel was contemplating drastic action to discourage Egyptian attacks. At the same time, in France, the upholders of the national *gloire* in Egypt seemed to have obtained the upper hand and, in Britain, the vocal Suez group which maintained that the line had to be drawn somewhere and that this was the line, was chafing under new restraints. The United States, sensitive to trouble, cautioned restraint all around, and President Eisenhower transmitted a message to Prime Minister David Ben-Gurion, warning against armed action. But what went on behind the diplomatic curtain of silence in Paris, London and Jerusalem remained a mystery. On October 29, 1956, the government of Israel announced that it was striking out to wipe out the fedayin bases. During the ensuing days, events were telescoped in such a way that years will be required to disentangle them. The object of this chapter cannot be to chronicle the events of that fateful period. It may be a long time before the dark recesses of the diplomatic jungle are cleared and the proper view obtained. Here the author will seek some of the motives, recording some of the results. The few dates he mentions are meant only as landmarks for the reader's orientation.

When Egypt and the other Arab countries were at war with Israel in 1948 it was the ineffective King Farouk who held the reins. Colonel Nasser had blamed him and his camarilla for the Arab armies' crushing defeat. The soldiers were deficient in arms, their weapons were of inferior quality, they were poorly trained and inadequately fed. Now, however, the Cairo *junta* had been in power for years and had received large arms shipments from Russia and her satellites. "The Egyptian army is able today to liberate every foot of Arab land from the invaders' defilement," General Amer, commander in chief of the Egyptian army, had said on January 22, 1956. He was even more emphatic on June 11: "There is no longer any importance to the Israeli danger and the Egyptian army is now able to return blow for blow and wipe out Israel within forty-eight hours."

Israel moved swiftly into Egypt's Suez peninsula and slashed into Nasser's forces as the "knife cuts through the butter." This "exodus in reverse" took as many days as the original took decades. The Egyptian forces were incapacitated at each encounter, and large numbers of men surrendered forthwith. "Over 50 per cent of the Egyptian officers ran away from their units," reported the Israeli chief of staff, Rav Aluf Dayan. "An army may be forced to retreat," he commented, "an army may be taken prisoner but an army whose officers are the first to flee is not one that fights. Among the 5,000 Egyptian war prisoners taken not more than 200 were officers."

In a few hours Egypt had lost about 85 per cent of her jet aircraft, which had been obtained from the Soviet bloc countries. Israeli jokesters suggested that a monument be erected to the "Unknown Soviet Benefactor" who had enabled their country to obtain so much war material. "I hope," said Israel's Prime Minister, Ben-Gurion, in the Jerusalem legislature (Knesset), his white waving hair framing his lined face like a prophet of the past, "that . . . in the future the Egyptian dictator will not compel us to violate the injunction never to return to Egypt, which was imposed upon us when we left that country 3,300 years ago."

Two Pivots

President Nasser's foreign policy had been based on two pivots: the belief that the Egyptian army was an effective fighting force and that several Arab countries would rally to his cause. He seems to have expected two types of aid: direct military attack on Israel, and fedayin work. The only military movements consisted of the unconfirmed advance of Iraqi, Syrian and Saudi Arabian units into Jordan, and their size was anybody's guess. That they could not have been large may be seen from the fact that the entire army of Saudi Arabia, the largest and most populous of these nations, even though the most backward one, was believed to be 13,000 men. The trumpets were sounded afar but action failed to follow. As to the commando operations, everyday routine was observed. Eight Israeli civilians were killed by them.

Moving rapidly eastward and southward, the Israeli found a region bristling with Egyptian arms. Large advance ammunition depots at the desert outposts of El Arish, El Midan and Abu Awgeila were discovered, along with other supply depots in the process of construction at Jebel Lebini. Fuel storage tanks had been set up at Bir Rodsalim and El Arish, supply of arms and spare part depots at Abu Awgeila and Nahal Rafa—all but a short distance from the Israeli frontier. The quantities of arms, equipment and ammunition stored in these installations were enough to sustain an all-out attack on Israel by all the existing units of the Egyptian armed forces, and they included also large amounts of ammunition for guns of heavy tanks of the Stalin and Centurion types, indicating that they were intended for attack. In Sinai and Gaza the Israeli found that the Egyptian military dispositions were clearly of an offensive, and not defensive, nature.

The Israeli destroyed these arms bases, together with the Egyptian fortifications blockading the Gulf of Aqaba. This approach to the Israeli port of Eilat at the southern apex of the Negev had been controlled by the Egyptian base at Sharm-el-Sheikh, near the southernmost point of the Sinai peninsula, near towering Mount Sinai. The islands of Tiran and Sanafir, off the coast, were also taken. Egypt had interfered with navigation to Elath through these straits. These quick actions produced two major results: they put an end to the commando campaigns and opened the port of Eilat.

Britain and France Step In

At this point the Sinai campaign became part of a larger conflict. On October 30 Britain and France dispatched joint ultimatums to Egypt and Israel, demanding that they cease fighting and withdraw their forces to positions ten miles east of the Suez Canal, deep in Egyptian territory and about 150 miles from the Israeli border. In order to safeguard these operations, the two countries called on Egypt to accept the temporary occupation of Port Said, Ismailia, Suez and other key points along the Canal. Prime Minister Eden announced in the name of the two allies that unless the ultimatum was complied with in twelve hours their armed forces would intervene. Israel accepted the ultimatum; Egypt rejected it. At 6:30 A.M. on October 31, the ultimatum expired and Cyprus-based Anglo-French aircraft began the bombardment of Cairo, Alexandria, Port Said, Ismailia and Suez. "Aerial bombarding will continue," the commander in chief of the Anglo-French forces declared at Nicosia. "The length of operations depends on how quickly Egypt accepts our terms."

This action of the British and French was justified as a step to end the Israeli-Egyptian war. The real reasons were different. The two countries wanted to restore international control over the Suez Canal and to humiliate and, if possible, help overthrow President Nasser. The British saw him as a danger to the power balance they wanted to maintain in the Middle East.* The French were also fighting for Algeria when combating Nasser.

British and French actions in Egypt were motivated by their

---

* It has been suggested that they also wanted to weaken American influence there.

spokesmen before the General Assembly of the United Nations on November 1.

"Egypt stands today in open defiance of the UN," [said the delegate of the United Kingdom, Sir Pierson Dixon]. "It has deliberately maintained the exercise of belligerent rights against Israel and has refused to afford free passage to Israeli ships and cargoes through the Suez Canal, thereby flouting the express injunctions of the Security Council. . . . So grave indeed is the present situation that it would be wrong for this Assembly to turn a blind eye on the malevolent activities of a country, outside the area, which are no less pernicious for being practically concealed. The Soviet Union bears a heavy responsibility for the present situation. . . . Our overriding purposes are: the safeguarding of the Suez Canal and the restoration of peaceful conditions in the Middle East. . . ."

France spoke through her delegate, Louis de Guiringaud:

"If the French government was impelled to take measures which at first sight might appear to be out of line with its traditions, it was not for lack of grave reasons. . . . Who can conscientiously question the fact that ten years of United Nations deliberations, resolutions without number of the General Assembly, the Security Council, and even the very able efforts of our Secretary General were powerless not only to eliminate the danger of war in the Middle East but even to prevent that danger from growing to the point where it became a menace to the peace of the world? . . .

"These [Egyptian] ambitions are as unmeasured as those which, twenty years ago were harbored by another dictator whose megalomania ultimately led to the deaths of more than 25 million human beings. . . . Is there any need to recall that, on the eve of what is now called Israeli aggression, a number of Egyptian commandos had carried out incursions deep into Israeli territory, claiming numerous casualties among the civilian population? . . ."

In the name of Egypt delegate Omar Loutfi spoke:

"The bad faith of the aggressors needs hardly to be proved further. . . . We thought that the United Nations Charter had put an end

104

to the reign of force and that the epoch of ultimatums and *diktats,* which brings to mind sad memories, had come to an end. . . . Egypt is being invaded; its sovereignty is being jeopardized. . . . The question is in your hands: condemn the aggressors. Put an end to aggression!"

The Soviet Union Intervenes

The Sinai campaign coincided with the revolution in Hungary against her Communist rulers and the ruthless intervention of the Soviets to crush the Magyar freedom fighters. Public opinion the world over was aroused, as it had not been since the end of the war. The war in Egypt was a windfall to the Soviets to divert attention from their misdeeds in Hungary, to let them appear as the protectors of "law and order," pose as the friends of the Arabs and as the ardent antagonists of "imperialists." Soviet Premier N. A. Bulganin informed Prime Minister Ben-Gurion that the U.S.S.R. was taking steps to "put an end to the war and restrain the aggressors." A veritable paroxysm of praise for Egypt convulsed the Soviet press in the days to come. The Egyptian Ambassador to the Soviets revealed over Radio Moscow: "Every day the Egyptian Embassy here receives numerous telegrams and letters from the Soviet people. The telephone rings continuously. We have many callers. They speak of their readiness to come to our country and to defend it from the aggressors, shoulder to shoulder with the people of Egypt." *Pravda* wrote about the "wrathful indignation of the Soviet people against the aggressors." But the most ominous news was released by the official Soviet news agency, Tass, that if Britain, France and Israel failed to withdraw their forces from Egypt, then the "appropriate authorities of the U.S.S.R. will not hinder the departure of Soviet citizens as volunteers to take part in the Egyptian people's struggle for their independence." The world knew from previous experiences in the Far East what "volunteers" meant in the Soviet language.

105

The British and the French landed armed forces on November 5 at the northern end of the Suez Canal, overcame the commando-type resistance, and occupied Port Said and Port Fuad. Then they moved southward along the Canal to El Cap, 22 miles south of Port Said. As they moved on, the United Nations, spurred on by the United States, began to act quickly. The Kremlin now proposed joint action with Washington against the "aggressors" in the form of naval and air demonstration, but the White House rejected the Russian proposal out of hand. Pocketing the rebuff, the Kremlin then proposed to the Security Council that the United Nations authorize a joint United States–Soviet "police action" in Egypt. This proposal was also rejected forthwith.

The Security Council called an emergency session of the General Assembly of the United Nations on October 31 to make recommendations on the "actions undertaken against Egypt." The United States proposed a cease-fire and it was approved by a vote of 64 to 5; Britain, France, Israel, Australia and New Zealand in the opposition. Four days later, however, London and Paris announced that they were ready to comply with the United Nations resolution on the condition that Israel and Egypt accepted a UN force to preserve peace between them and that the force was to be maintained until Israel and the Arab countries agreed on a peaceful settlement and until satisfactory arrangements were made about the Canal. On November 5, an international United Nations command force was established under Major General E. L. M. Burns of Canada to supervise the cessation of fighting. It was on that same day that British and French forces invaded Egypt by air, but two days later they halted the advance of their forces against the Egyptian troops in the zone of the Suez Canal. Thus the "Suez Crisis" came to a halt. The United Nations Emergency Force was recruited from small countries and was to be stationed in the Gaza Strip and the southern tip of Sinai.

Why the Hurry?

Had the United States acted with less dispatch through the United Nations, the British, French and Israeli forces, at the rate they had been advancing, would have swept down the Suez Canal zone and Nasser's defeat would have been manifest. In that case, mercurial public opinion in Egypt might have turned against the hero of yesterday. However, Washington felt that the delay would increase the danger of the Soviet Union taking a direct hand in the crisis. In addition, the action of Britain and France looked to the State Department very much like old-fashioned "gunboat" diplomacy and these two countries were no longer supposed to engage in such practice. There was also hope that, by appearing as the "knight in shining armor," the United States would regain lost ground in the Middle East. On the surface, the cease-fire was a victory for the United Nations but it could have accomplished little had it not been for America's intervention and the Soviet threat.

Thousands of Egyptian war prisoners were eye-witnesses of the Nasser regime's shame, and upon returning to their villages in the Delta and on the river banks they would have spread word about his fiasco. Paradoxically, Nasser appears to have been saved from this shameful fate by the Franco-British intervention. Though he was defeated by Israel in a few hours, the action of France and Britain provided him with a foolproof alibi. How could Egypt stand up against the onslaught of two of the world's Great Powers? Thus Nasser, defeated on the battlefield, became victor at the diplomatic table.

What force had stopped the Middle Eastern war? Was it the moral force of the United Nations—since it lacked physical strength—or was it the United States pursuing its aims through the United Nations? Was it the United States alone or in league with the Afro-Asian group—a massive anticolonial club? Could it have been the threat of Russian "volunteers"? Had the war been

107

stopped because of the oppositon of an influential segment of British public opinion? No such opposition had existed in France where the Communists alone combated the policy of the Quai d'Orsay. Or had the Egyptian expedition been stopped by the vacillations of Downing Street? Or was it a combination of two or more of these factors that changed history's course? Could the world have been faced with a hitherto unknown force, a factor "x," something basic, such as had turned the individual lawlessness of the Middle Ages into the national lawlessness of modern times? To say that only history will provide the answer is merely repeating a tired phrase. History is often no more than the mouthing of national publicity slogans.

"The only new element that had come in," said the United States Ambassador to France at that time, A. C. Douglas Dillon, in a radio interview on CBS, on December 11, 1956, "was those Soviet threats, which were very, very strongly phrased." The Ambassador did not think that France and Britain had called off the campaign because of moral suasion. They had gone ahead with their Suez plans despite sharp criticism in the United Nations and the United States. Nor, he added, was it the pressure of dwindling oil supplies from the Middle East because "that had not had time to make itself felt."

A few days later the newspapers reported that State Department spokesmen had expressed annoyance with Ambassador Dillon's statement because it would cause Arabs to see in the U.S.S.R. and not in the U.S., Egypt's savior against the Franco-British attack.

However, similar views were expressed by other observers, most pungently perhaps in the *Bulletin of the Atomic Scientists* * by its editor, Eugene Rabinowitch:

The year 1956 could be called A.D. I—the first year of deterrence. A few days after the Anglo-French ultimatum to Egypt, Britain and France were presented with a virtual ultimatum threatening, by clear

* January 1957. "The First Year of Deterrence."

implication, the air-atomic destruction of both countries if they failed to call off the Suez expedition.

This demonstration of the power of air-atomic deterrence is a turning-point in history, and we should not be distracted from recognizing its significance by incidental events, such as the diplomatic pressure of the United States . . . or the speeches given, and the resolutions passed in the United Nations.

These latter consequences the leaders of Britain and France had discounted, anyway. They were confident that their rapid military success and the Nasser regime's downfall would be followed by the acceptance of the *fait accompli*. "What England and France did *not* anticipate was the readiness of the Soviet leaders to unleash all-out atomic war in response to a local conflict so far from their borders."

On the other hand, Drew Middleton reported in *The New York Times* on January 31, 1957, that the British now conceded that the most important of the many factors that had influenced London to agree to a cease-fire was the American attitude. Unless the British ended fighting, the United States would not be ready to help Western Europe with oil supplies or to stem the weakening of the pound sterling. Other factors were the Commonwealth nations, particularly Canada, and the state of public opinion in Britain. There was ample evidence that the "Cabinet was not moved either by Soviet threats that 'volunteers' would be sent to the Middle East or that the Soviet Union might direct rocket bombs on London and Paris."

President Eisenhower and Secretary of State Dulles thought at first that military measures against Nasser might be necessary, according to the Memoirs of Anthony Eden, published in *The Times* (London), early in 1960, but later changed their minds, thinking of the Panama Canal, and let Britain "hold the bag."

And the Consequences?

The Middle Eastern conflict did temporary damage to Britain's national finances. It all but wrecked the Western grand alliance by causing deep dissension among former friends. It sharpened political conflict in Britain. The Suez Canal itself was in a sad condition and it appeared that months would be needed before its operations could be resumed. Britain learned that her power of initiative in the diplomatic field was more limited than she had assumed and that she could not go counter to the policies of the United States. As a result of the Middle East fiasco, Prime Minister Eden's political reputation became tarnished and, pleading ill health, he resigned. He was followed by Harold Macmillan. France, the specialist in government crises, saw its cabinet remain in the saddle for a time at least. But the reputation of the Fourth French Republic was further corroded. Not much later the forces erupted that led to its downfall and to the sudden emergence of the Fifth Republic under General Charles de Gaulle.

The significance of Suez was not the evidence it supplied of Britain's military and diplomatic vulnerability [wrote Peregrine Worsthorne, leader writer of the (London) *Daily Telegraph*]. This, after all, was well known. What was not well known was the grave condition of Britain's body politic. The fruits of ten years of social revolution were revealed: a faltering government, an inefficient armed force, a confused public opinion and a younger generation whose most articulate members clearly felt a profound contempt for the country of their birth. . . . Both left and right, looking at contemporary Britain, can only see reflected a caricature of their respective social images.

Meanwhile, however, a near-miraculous transformation appears to have taken place in Nasser's fate. The Israeli believed that in spite of his braggadocio, the Egyptian president had suffered a major political reverse. They pointed out that after the 1948 Egyptian débâcle in Palestine it had taken considerable time before the lesson of the defeat began to sink into people's minds. This second débâcle was even more disastrous and its true nature was bound to be revealed in Egypt, too. Instead of that, the defeated dictator saw his prestige rise to the zenith in the Arab world. It was he, a strong, monolithic leader of men, who dic-

110

tated to the victors. He Egyptianized Franco-Egyptian concerns and expelled many Egyptian citizens of the Jewish faith, whose ancestors had lived there since times immemorial.

The war of a "hundred hours" taught mankind a few lessons about the United Nations and the United States. It showed that the UN could act forcefully on major international issues only under certain conditions. It could act effectively in 1950, at the time of the Korean invasion, when the Soviet Union was absent; and again it acted effectively at the end of 1956 when the two World Powers, the United States and the Soviet Union, agreed on the solution of a problem, even though for different reasons.

In spite of the apparent success of American diplomacy in the Suez crisis, it showed up weak elements in American leadership and revealed the way to the future. Throughout the Suez crisis the Western allies felt that Washington lacked a clear-cut policy, was hesitating, wanted to please too many people with divergent interests. When the conflict sharpened between the Anglo-French alliance and Egypt, American diplomacy was still standing in the middle of the road. But in an age of fast transportation the middle of the road is a dangerous spot. On the one hand, there was America's concern with Middle Eastern oil and the strategic value of the region. On the other hand, there was America's traditional friendship with France and common interests with England. In the past it was Britain that sought to appease the Arabs because of the area's importance to world strategy. Now it was the United States' turn to appear in the mantle of the Arabs' protector. Britain disliked this change of roles.

And the lesson was this. The Middle East had acquired such vital importance in the affairs of the world that a "local" conflict there was bound to assume global implications. Still another lesson was learned in this "hit and run" war. The secrets of many government archives would have to be revealed before mankind would know the full implications of the events of the week that shook the world.

Again the Canal

During the hostilities, Canal barges filled with concrete were sunk and railway spans wrecked by the Egyptians in order to render the Canal unnavigable. The Cairo government authorized salvage operations only after arrangements had been completed for Israel to evacuate Sinai and the Gaza Strip, and so, early in 1957, Lt. General Raymond Wheeler, of the United States, working under the auspices of the United Nations, began clearing the Canal. By the time this work was completed, the Egyptian Canal Company was in full operation without the aid of a users' association or advisory body. Though the United States still insisted that the Canal was affected with international interest and was therefore subject to international control, there was question as to what form such control should take. There was no assurance that Egypt would comply with another United Nations resolution, and force was not practicable—the United States itself had called off a punitive measure, and besides, Egypt seemed to be immune to it. The only effective measure would be a boycott of the Canal, but the Western powers needed it as much as ever and through a boycott would only spite themselves. The Canal was a monopoly and Nasser well knew that the final decision was in his hands.

Thus, despite his defeat by Israel, it was a victorious Nasser who spoke on the matter of the Canal. He reiterated his previous statement that Egypt would abide by the Constantinople Convention while the world wondered how seriously to take his assurance. Egypt had flouted the Convention even when the waterway had been in the hands of the "universal" Canal Company. Though Israel as a nation had the right to send her ships through the Canal, Israeli shipping had been fettered.

Nasser's official statement was made to Secretary General Dag Hammarskjold in March 1957. Tolls, according to the statement, were to be paid to the autonomous Suez Canal authority. "Disputes arising out of the Canal's management could be referred to arbitration." Nothing was said about the Security Council's "six

112

principles" about the operation of the Canal. The West attempted to apply a degree of diplomatic pressure to regularize the status of the Canal but it was impotent to act since the Egyptian government felt it was now in the driver's seat, as the Western allies had neutralized one another. Since an "international instrument," a kind of charter of operations, was needed for the Suez Canal, it was provided on April 24. However, it bore only one signature, that of President Nasser, and was thus not a multilateral agreement but a one-sided declaration. The Egyptian government affirmed its respect for the Constantinople Convention of 1888, which guaranteed freedom of passage to ships of all nations, but excluded Israel from this declaration. It announced that 25 per cent of the Canal revenue would be set aside for maintenance and improvement, and agreed to accept arbitration in certain disputes. Of the dues collected by the authority 5 per cent would be paid to the Egyptian government as a royalty. Ships not willing to pay tolls to the authority would not be allowed to pass through the Canal. The Egyptian government rejected international control for the Canal but would welcome the co-operation of the nations using the Canal.

The representatives of several countries objected to the declaration as a purely unilateral act, contrary to the Constantinople Convention. Others, too, felt that the Egyptian position "remained to be completed." Speaking for the United States, chief UN delegate Henry Cabot Lodge advised that the proposed regime should be afforded a chance. A short time later, Britain advised owners of ships chartered under her flag that, while they might use the Canal, the government in London reserved the right to say the final word regarding tolls. French boats began to use the waterway in June. On the first anniversary of the nationalization of the Canal, it was operating at full capacity. Commenting upon a year of trial and tribulation, a London newspaper entitled its leading article: "A Lesson in Futility."

The storm over Suez had blown the world to the verge of a serious conflict. Had the United States acted more slowly and the

Soviets more quickly—had the Russian volunteers actually descended upon the Canal, almost anything could have happened. It appeared that now was the strategic time for the United States to extend its security system into the heartland of the Middle East.

America Takes the Lead

This, then, was the time for the United States to make a basic policy declaration, connected possibly with a new defense system in the Middle East—to set up a fence around it, to make it out of bounds for the Soviets. A limited policy declaration in regard to a part of the Middle East had been made by the United States early in 1947, in the Truman Doctrine, through which the government extended the American defense perimeter to the part of the eastern Mediterranean region adjacent to the Soviet Union— Greece and Turkey. With this act the United States gripped the baton in the international relay race—*Pax Americana* replaced *Pax Britannica*. Now, however, the Soviets had vaulted above these defenses into the Middle East and were established in Egypt. In addition, Soviet policy had succeeded in convincing several Arab key countries that Moscow was the protector of their interests. A bold new policy was needed, something like a regional Truman Doctrine to put the rest of the Middle East out of bounds for the Soviets. The question was the form the new policy should take. Somehow, the conflicting interests of the Arab countries might be reconciled. President Nasser was bent on organizing as many Arab countries as he could into a Pan-Arabian union and success would mean he could extend the Soviet influence into all of the Arab Middle East, if it suited his interests.

Prior to the Suez crisis several policy declarations about the Middle East had been made by the United States, but they referred to specific issues and lacked the solemnity which important Great Power declarations elicit.

Back in 1950, on May 25, the United States, Britain and France had signed a tripartite declaration which expressed their

114

desire to promote the establishment and maintenance of peace and stability in the Middle East. By this they pledged themselves to take action within and outside the United Nations to forestall frontier violations by Israel and her Arab neighbors. No operative clause to establish machinery for its enforcement was contained in this declaration, however; nothing more than an expression of intent and it was not invoked even during the Suez crisis.

In the autumn of 1950 President Truman dispatched a state document to King Ibn Saud in which he expressed the deep interest of the United States in the continued independence of Saudi Arabia. But this was prompted by America's interest in the Dhahran airfield on the Persian Gulf coast of Saudi Arabia—the largest and most convenient civil and military air base in that part of the world.

Five years elapsed before Washington again declared its position in connection with the Middle East. This time it was Secretary of State Dulles who spoke. At the Council of Foreign Relations in New York on August 26, 1955, Secretary Dulles offered help in solving some of the urgent problems in Israeli-Arab relations. Working on the assumption that these relations formed the pivotal problem of the international situation in the Middle East, he offered American guidance in fixing the definitive boundaries between Israel and her neighbors, international participation in guaranteeing those frontiers and financial aid in the resettlement of the Arab refugees from Palestine. This offer floundered, largely because of the attitude of the Arab countries toward the refugee problem. Settling it would mean recognition of the existence of Israel and would have counteracted the bitterness against the new state in their midst.

These pacts, declarations and speeches failed to fill the Middle Eastern void but the United States was ready to take more determined action. The Western European power vacuum presumably had been filled by the North Atlantic Treaty Organization. Attempts had been made to establish such an organization before the Suez crisis. At the time America recognized that Great Britain had special interests in the Middle East, and that she was an "expert" in the region.

Great Britain was the representative of the West in the organization which was to strengthen the "northern tier" of the Middle East and which extended the defense perimeter of the "free world" beyond Turkey, into Iran and Pakistan (neither of which had free, representative political systems). One Arab country, adjacent to the northern tier but not part of it—Iraq—was also a member and because it was in her capital that the basic pact was signed, the organization was that of the Baghdad Pact, which came into existence in 1955. While the United States had a hand in its creation, it was not a member.*

From time to time the government of the United States issued warnings and gave notices in regard to its interest in the stability of the Middle East. This happened again on April 9, 1956, when President Dwight D. Eisenhower felt impelled to declare that the United States would oppose aggression in the Middle East "within constitutional means" and would support any nation that might be subject to aggression. The Soviet Union had established friendly contacts with Egypt and there were evidences of Communist infiltration into Syria. The Egyptian fedayin were perpetrating acts of aggression in Israel and the government of Prime Minister Ben-Gurion appeared to be getting restless. The President's warning may have been apropos of any or all of these incidents.

At the time of the Suez crisis the United States spoke again, declaring that any threat to the territorial integrity and political independence of the Baghdad Pact countries in the Middle East—Turkey, Iraq, Iran and Pakistan—would be viewed by Washington with the utmost gravity, and reiterated the readiness of the United States to assist in measures to strengthen the security of the nations in question.

All of these diplomatic moves of the United States conveyed

* The story of the Baghdad Pact is told in the section about Iraq.

the impression of being unco-ordinated and forming no basic foreign policy pattern. Obviously, the United States was not coming
to grips with the reality of the Middle East crisis. Negative factors
in diplomacy are seldom—if ever—explained and the observer
was thrown upon his devices to explain a strange reticence.

By this time it was a commonplace that the Middle East was
a crucial area. The very term "power vacuum" applied to the
region had become generally known. In all other vulnerable areas
of the world American leadership had established protective
shields against the Soviet Union. Why not in the Middle East
where the Russians were "naked," ungirded by satellites, adjacent
to them east and west?

The United States had to tread with extreme caution in the
Middle East. Most reliable and strongest ally of America was
Great Britain, the one stout friend whose loyalty was not in doubt.
Great Britain had had vital interests in the Middle East for generations. She had also important investments, especially in oil. Retaining a hand in the Middle East was a matter of prestige, too,
for London. As long as the United Kingdom retained a foothold
in the region, its status as a great power was not in doubt. London
wanted to remain an ally of Washington, not a subordinate, and
ceding the Middle East to the United States would have entailed
the cession of its great-power position. The United States, too,
did not wish to wound British susceptibilities and this it would
have done, had it organized a Middle Eastern defense organization, as it had organized NATO.

Then there was the problem of the Arab countries—problems
within problems. Throughout the existence of these nations since
the end of the Second World War a strong polarization had taken
place among them. One of the poles was Cairo, the other one was
Iraq, each of them trying to rally the other Arab countries to the
cause of a supranational unification.* Most of the Arab countries

---

* While King Abdullah of Jordan was alive, he attempted to create another
pivot. His "Fertile Crescent" schemes were to enhance the significance of his
country and render it viable.

117

had a very strong prejudice against the Western nations. Great Britain and France, former mandatories in the region, were the "imperialists" par excellence and any diplomatic combination with them was scorned. The United States was frowned upon for two reasons, partly because of its close association with France and the United Kingdom—"guilt through association"—and partly because of its espousal of the cause of Israel.

The Arab countries did not recognize the state of Israel. Small though that country was, it occupied perhaps the most strategic area within the Middle East. It barred the way between Egypt and the other Middle Eastern Arab countries.

The normal procedure for the United States would have been to follow the NATO precedent—multilateral mutual assistance pacts among all the countries of the region—an "armed attack against one or more of them" would be considered an attack against them all, and if such an armed attack occurred, each of them would assist the party or parties so attacked. This solution, however, was not open because of the special conditions prevailing in the Middle East.

Steeped in the ideology of the cold war, the United States carried away one impression from the Suez crisis: the threat of Soviet "volunteers." In a country such as the Soviet Union, a volunteer is under government control. The presence of Soviet fighters would have introduced the U.S.S.R. directly into the Middle East. This was to be prevented by all means. The Suez crisis stimulated Washington to search for a formula to bar the road into the Middle East to the Soviets—this time it was not merely a promise to help maintain existing borders, but an all-inclusive "barn-barring" operation—and the "barn" was to be closed only to the Kremlin. A presidential message to Congress on January 5, 1957, signaled the beginning of what some observers called a new era in American diplomacy in the Middle East.

The Eisenhower Doctrine

"The Middle East has abruptly reached a new and critical stage in its long and important history," President Eisenhower said in his message. He reiterated the oft-repeated phrases: This region has always been the crossroads of the continents of the Eastern Hemisphere. . . . The Middle East provides a gateway between Eurasia and Africa. . . . The reason for Russia's interest in the Middle East is solely that of power politics.

"The action which I propose would have the following features," the President continued. "It would, first of all, authorize the United States to co-operate with and assist any nation or group of nations in the general area of the Middle East in the development of economic strength dedicated to the maintenance of national independence. It would, in the second place, authorize the executive to undertake in the same region programs of military assistance and co-operation with any nation or group of nations which desires such aid. It would, in the third place, authorize such assistance and co-operation to include the employment of the armed forces of the United States to secure and protect the territorial integrity and political independence of such nations requesting such aid against overt armed aggression from any nation controlled by international communism."

Also, the proposal would authorize the President to employ, for economic and defensive military purposes, sums available under the Mutual Security Act, without regard to existing limitations.

The importance of this presidential message was promptly recognized. The President of the United States is authorized by the Constitution to conduct foreign relations and when he goes to Congress with a message on basic policy, asking for its approval (which he does not need) it is because he wants to have it recognized as a standing national policy. The Monroe Doctrine, too, had its origin in a presidential message.

The presidential message was discussed in and out of Congress, in and outside of the United States. Secretary of State Dulles followed it up with the statement that, unless Congress acted promptly, the Middle East would be lost in a "great and maximum disaster." Former Secretary of State Dean Acheson expressed himself strongly against the message at a congressional hearing. He described it not as a statement of policy but an invitation to devise one. He saw in it the possibility of unilateral action which would be disliked by our allies. "This is reckless talk. Vague phrases which suggest that we might respond to any but the most vital danger by nuclear retaliation carry a vicious risk, whether believed or not believed, and may cause fatal miscalculation. There can be no bluff here."

Former President Harry S. Truman condemned the message as "too little and too late," after having at first welcomed it. The boldness and uniqueness of this approach was evidently recognized by Congress—and it was something to be thought over very carefully. Many legislators were of the view that applauding key passages of the President's message might be interpreted as implied commitment, and newspapers reported that Eisenhower got a really "big hand" when he declared that the Middle East was the birthplace of three great religions. A senator explained the ardent congressional reaction to this statement: "We all have Jewish and Christian voters and you may never know when a Muslim may turn up in your district."

There were serious questions, too. Did the procedure proposed by the President jeopardize the congressional prerogative to declare war? What President Eisenhower asked for was a blank check. And what if one of the countries ruled by the landlords represents itself to the naïve United States as being endangered by "international communism" and involves Washington in a domestic issue? Was "legitimacy" in any form to be endorsed by the United States? Was this a new Holy Alliance in the Middle East? And what about the feelings of the British and the French, former mandatories in the region? There was some grumbling in congressional smoking rooms—as conveyed to the public by newspapers—about the "scare-talk" tactics of the Secretary of

State. Vexation was expressed at the executive's treatment of the legislators as if they were retarded children to be goaded into action with horror stories.

The first reaction of the House Foreign Affairs Committee was not too favorable since it inclined to the view that Mr. Dulles had failed to produce evidence about the imminence of Communist aggression. This initial reticence was transformed into grumbling acquiescence on the part of several lawmakers. They felt that "something had to be done in the Middle East" and this was the only course open to them. This appeared to be the "line of action" and many legislators felt they could not afford to be marked with the stamp of "do-nothing." Linked in the minds of the people with Middle Eastern events was the recent Hungarian revolution. If the Soviets had their chance to penetrate into the Middle East would they imitate their Hungarian performance?

The Senate passed the "Joint Resolution" recommended by President Eisenhower with a vote of 72 against 19 and the House representatives with 350 to 60. Congressional action was completed on March 7 and the key presidential recommendation was rephrased to read that "if the President determines the necessity thereof, the United States is prepared to use armed forces to assist any [Middle Eastern] nation or group of nations requesting assistance against armed aggression from any country controlled by international communism . . ."

This Joint Resolution of Congress became known as the "Eisenhower Doctrine"—on the pattern, no doubt, of the "Monroe Doctrine" and the "Truman Doctrine."

Reaction to the Doctrine

This was a policy declaration of the United States and not a treaty. The reaction of the Arab countries was particularly important. Iraq, which was already part of the Western system of alliances, hailed it. The three other Asian members of the Baghdad Pact also "noted with satisfaction" that President Eisenhower's

121

plan for the Middle East recognized the threat both by Communist aggression and subversion. They declared their full support for the measures outlined in the plan as best designed to maintain peace in the area and to advance the economic well-being of the peoples.

The reaction of the other Arab countries was far more mixed. Lebanon gave it her unconditional approval, and her foreign minister, Charles Malik, termed it a "good and timely move." A little over a year later, however, the small republic withdrew its approval after a period of bitter civil strife. On many things the remaining Arab countries did not see eye to eye but most of them agreed on being critical of the Eisenhower Doctrine. Their strictures were numerous and emphatic. They disagreed with the premise of the Doctrine that the Middle East was a "power vacuum." They agreed that even if it had been one, the task of filling it out would have been incumbent not on outsiders but on the countries within the area. They saw a refurbished version of "imperialism" in the doctrine. Since it was directed only against "international communism," they asked what would happen if the aggressor was an international capitalist, such as the United States or, for that matter, Britain or France? The solution of the Middle Eastern problem, as they saw it, was integral Arab nationalism.

The Soviet Union attacked the doctrine with vehemence. Nikita S. Khrushchev, First Secretary of the Communist Party of the U.S.S.R., declared that the Eisenhower Doctrine would end on the "garbage heap of history." The officially inspired Soviet press attacked the United States for wishing to replace the imperial influence of Britain and France and for threatening the independence of the Arab states.

Elsewhere, too, the Eisenhower Doctrine met with criticism. Prime Minister Jawaharlal Nehru was of the opinion that if there were a power vacuum in the Middle East it would have to be filled through the internal strength and unity of the countries in the region. Even in many respectable organs of the friendly West it was pointed out that the doctrine did not protect the area from

122

the real danger of internal subversion. In certain Middle Eastern Arab countries the Soviet Union would not have to fire a single shot to reach its aim. Perhaps because of the memory of the recent Suez crisis, there were references in the British press to the assumption that the Eisenhower Doctrine was directed against Britain as much as against the Soviets, for the region which had been Britain's sphere was now being taken over by the United States. Further, the doctrine was the type of diplomatic instrument particularly disliked by countries recently liberated from foreign rule —a unilateral declaration by a strong Western country whose warships were roaming all the seas. It seemed but a new type of "gunboat diplomacy."

How the Eisenhower Doctrine fared will be shown in the narrative of later events.

Toward a United Arab Republic

Egypt was now moving toward unification with Syria in the United Arab Republic. Before that happened, however, a crisis occurred on the Syrian-Turkish border in the autumn of 1957. Egyptian forces were landed in Syria. The two countries were making common cause in the face of what appeared to be a common danger. In a few months the two countries became one— the U.A.R. That was thought to be only a beginning, however. Why should there be a dozen weak Arab states? Why not one powerful Arab nation, perhaps all the way from Casablanca to Aden, across the "northern tier" of Africa, the "Fertile Crescent" countries, the Arab peninsular quadrangle?

In his "philosophy of the revolution" Gamal Abdul Nasser closed his meditations with the words: "And now I go back to that wandering mission in search of a hero to play it. Here is the role. Here are the lines, and here is the stage. We alone, by virtue of our place, can perform the role." *

* Gamal Abdul Nasser, *Egypt's Liberation*. Washington: Public Affairs Press, 1955, p. 114.

The role about which Nasser spoke was that of unification—of the Arabs, of Africa and of Islam. The unification of the Arabs, he wrote, was the primary task, and it was incumbent upon Egypt. But Egypt became embodied in Nasser, her "man of destiny." In the field of foreign relations, the unification of the Arab world acquired top priority.

This problem of Arab unification is a highly important one. What is it? Do the Arabs want it? How strongly do they want it? What are its chances of success?

The difficulties of answering these questions with any degree of assurance are great. How does one get the answers to such questions? Public opinion polls help, but the Middle Eastern Arab countries have not yet got into the habit.* The newspapers are unrepresentative and, in many cases, utterly biased. Personal interviews, especially if they reveal a strong trend, may be significant. But even if they were to manifest an all but unanimous view it is impossible not to question the permanence of their validity. An analogy may prove the point.

In his younger days, the author of this book was a resident of Vienna, where he worked as a newspaper correspondent for several Central and Western European newspapers. Like so many other people, he was greatly interested in the much-discussed problem of *Anschluss*—union of Austria and Germany. He found in the course of his work that the Austrians were unanimous on this issue, even though they rarely agreed on any other political problem. There were two leading parties in Austria, the Christian Socialists and the Social Democrats. They were constantly fighting, but they agreed that there was one solution only of Austria's problem—*Anschluss*. The alternative was national bankruptcy.

Since the Second World War the author of this book has often returned to the scenes of his younger days, and, following up his

* The Bureau of Applied Social Research, Columbia University, undertook field studies in Egypt, Iran, Jordan, Lebanon, Syria and Turkey, as to what changes occurred in a traditional society in transition. The question of Arab unity was not within the researchers' frame of reference. See: Daniel Lerner, *The Passing of Traditional Society*. Glencoe, Ill.: The Free Press, 1958.

earlier interest, he has been asking questions about the desirability of union with Germany. Again there are two great parties in Austria; the former Christian Socialists, who now call themselves *Volkspartei,* People's Party, and the Social Democrats. He has not found one person of either party or anybody without party affiliation that wants anything to do with *Anschluss.* The issue is so completely dead that it has become slightly absurd to ask the question. And this complete reversion of public opinion has taken place in a highly literate and articulate country, where "people know what they want."

Traveling in the Middle East, the author of this book feels transplanted into Austria, at least as far as this one question is concerned—everybody wants a union. Those who do not want to state their preference in public, feel the necessity of paying lip service to it. Arab unity has become an article of faith. Bearing the Austrian precedent in mind, one is bound to ask: why and for how long?

The Middle Eastern Arab air is literally saturated with this idea of union. The radio is the most potent instrument for the creation of public opinion and the air waves of the Arab world are dominated by Cairo. It has succeeded in shifting the loyalty of most of the people from the individual country, be it Egypt or Jordan or another Arab land, to the "Arab nation." To take a continental analogy: there is no more an Arab Saxony, Bavaria or Thuringia—there is only an Arab *Reich,* not as a reality, as yet, but an expectation.

"Folk" or "Nation"?

The unforgettable, traumatic experience of the Middle Eastern Arab world was the 1948 war with Israel. In the wake of that war revolutions occurred in one country after another, and basic changes are incubating in still others. The overwhelming Arab numerical strength succumbed to the Israeli. There appeared to be two main reasons for this disaster: lack of unity and lack of

125

moral *grandeur*. Under the Umayyads and Abbassides, in the early Middle Ages, the Arabs were united and powerful—the rest of the world went to school to them. As they became disunited they lost their greatness; the masters became the servants, first of the Turks and, more recently, of the "Western imperialists." These latter employed the methods of "divide and rule," and thus came into existence a bevy of Arab countries, with their separate governments, petty intrigues, vested interests, "village pump" mentality. The great concept of Arab unity, the foundation of greatness, was lost.

Toward the end of the Second World War an attempt at Arab integration was made by the then independent Arab nations and the result was the Alexandria Protocol, which set forth the aims of the new Arab synthesis. Thus came into existence the League of Arab States, better known in the West as the "Arab League." It was not a full synthesis, not a Greater Arabia but merely a co-operative enterprise for specific and limited purposes. The individual Arab countries remained in possession of national sovereignty. The League was analogous—in the opinion of some Arabs —to the "league of friendship" under the Articles of Confederation of the American states. It was the precursor of the federation adopted later under the Constitution of the United States. "Acting under similar objective and subjective compulsions, many Arabs have persisted, since the founding of the League, in their efforts to evolve the League into a union, or failing that, to erect structures of political unity independently of the League."

The Arab League did not fulfill the expectations attached to it. In political matters its record has been largely a negative one— against Israel or against France. Even in nonpolitical matters its achievements have not been exceptionally impressive.

Of decisive importance was the failure of the Treaty of Joint Defense and Economic Cooperation, which had been approved by the League on April 17, 1950. This Treaty, which had been reluctantly ratified by some of the contracting States, continued to be inert despite the fact that it was finally ratified by all members of the League and that formally it entered into effect in 1952.*

Then there was the other cause of the débâcle, the sins of the *ancien régime,* feudal, corrupt, lacking in patriotism. Today this is admitted in countries where a revolution has occurred, denied in others.

Arab unification, then, is the keynote. The Arab "nations" are what in the United States are called the "states," component parts, not the finished product. Two Arab words throw light on this distinction. Both mean nationalism but in two different senses. One refers to the nationalism of the component parts within the present boundaries, *wataniyah* derived from *watan,* nation, more like *la petite patrie* of the Frenchman—Normandy, Anjou. The other word is more comprehensive, *qawmiyah,* derived from *qawm,* the people, the folk, referring to the spirit of collective nationalism among all the Arabs, irrespective of the present state lines, the Greater Arab Fatherland, *la grande patrie,* France.

Several Arab constitutions have made this distinction. The first one was that of Syria, framed in 1950, which proclaimed that the people of Syria formed part of the "Arab nation." The Egyptian constitution of 1956 was even more specific, announcing that Egypt was an "Arab state" and that the Egyptian people were "part of the Arab nation."

And the Advantages?

Thus the glories of the past would be re-created, one nation, united and indivisible. They would acquire strength through larger numbers and occupying the real "heartland" of the old world—the core, which is recognized as such by non-Arabs, too. They could have a large army. True, they would have fewer votes in the comities of nations but those votes would carry far greater weight

* "Arab Unity," *Information Papers, No. 5.* New York: Arab Information Center, p. 6.

because they would be backed by strength and numbers. Now some of the Arab countries are poor in natural resources while others are rich. In Greater Arabia the resources of the entire Arab nation would be pooled and it would be a rich country. Being rich, it would be respected. It would have a large internal market, a common customs frontier. In this age of integration the future, as thoughtful Arabs see it, belongs to integrated units, the United States and its allies, the Soviet Union and its satellites, the emergent European Common Market.

Nasser would not be consistent with his philosophy if he did not carry this thought further. Egypt is not only a Middle Eastern country but also an African one, at the great intersection of world routes, a hub that has always been important. Either Egypt dominates Africa or she is dominated. Among the "native" countries she is the most advanced, although less populous than Nigeria. Egypt as the hub of Greater Arabia would naturally aspire to leadership in Africa, with its 220 million people. And then there is the third circle about which Nasser wrote in his philosophy, the Islamic one, with a population of about 440 million. A Greater Arabia could possibly collect additional hundreds of millions of people to its flag.

The Gravitational Pull

What are the forces of Arab unity? History—up to a certain point—not the history of the ancestors of the present Arabs, but the image of their history. The Arabs are a synthetic people, as are other people. They are more so, however, because of their origins and their habitats. The whirlwind conquests of the original Arabs swept countless ethnic strains into a common container. The descendants of the original "basic" Arabs of the Quadrangle desertland are a minority, while the descendants of the "derivative" Arabs from Casablanca to Aden are the majority. Basic or derivative, they have been kneaded into one Arab mass of people. The ancestors of the majority of the Arabs in the Levant must

128

have been Christians, but having fallen under the spell of a new ideology that memory is washed out of their minds.* A common history was not the share of the ancestors of the modern Arabs, but it is their share as a historic memory.

What makes an Arab? His language and his way of life. Arabic is a Semitic language, its script derived from the Aramaic, which was the language of Jesus.

Even in Arabia itself the Arabic language exhibits dialectic differences, and such variations are still more marked in countries more remote from the land of its origin. But the written language has almost invariably conformed to that type which has been conveniently denominated as classical Arabic, characterized by an extraordinary richness of vocabulary and the logical, systematic character of its grammatical structure.†

Classical Arabic is that of the Koran, the Muslim Holy Script. Yet, there are numerous Christian Arabs, no less devoted to their "way of life" than their Muslim countrymen. In their case, an inversion of the derivative process has taken place.

And what is the Arab way of life? Is that the life of the nomad in the Syrian desert, the townsman in the Baghdad bazaars, the graduate of the Sorbonne in Beirut, the poor sharecropper in the Litani valley of Syria, or the millionaire factory owner in Cairo? That way of life—in the Arab world as elsewhere—is far less physical than mental, a feeling of community, an emotion linked with ideology, what the French call *mystique*—"togetherness."

This mystique can flourish or perish, depending on the climate of opinion which, in turn, is subject to manipulation. In the history of mankind more people have gone to their deaths in wars and revolutions for ideas generated in other people's minds than for their own interests.

---

* There are numerous contemporary parallels to this situation. The famous German scientist who a few years ago was attempting to devise weapons to wipe out America, today is a much-honored champion of the "American way of life."

† "Arabic Literature," *Encyclopaedia Britannica*, 1947, Vol. 2, p. 192.

The Lesson of History

Have there been other attempts at Arab integration? What about the centuries of Ottoman rule? What about attempts to take advantage of Turkish decay? What about irresistible forces of integration after the downfall of the Ottoman Empire in the First World War?

The answer to these questions has to be tentative. Under the Ottoman Empire the Arabs were subject to a regime which, while not theirs, shared their creed and in those days the people of the Middle East were living within a religious framework, Islam. To organize themselves differently would have meant to generate another religious loyalty and that was inconceivable. The "Arab way of life" during all these centuries was incorporated in the Ottoman way of life, under the guidance of the supreme religious leader, Caliph, who was at the same time the supreme secular head, Sultan.

The Arabs did not participate in plans to subvert or wreck the empire of the Turks. Nearly everybody else did. History knows of few cases in which an empire was on the "critical list" as long as the Ottoman realm. It was a miracle that it survived as long as it did. It was only in recent times that some Arabs—the sophisticated Western-oriented ones—began to think of the Arabs in terms of a nation, and not as adherents of a religion. The "Arab awakening" * was not a popular mass movement but the stirring of an elite. It was a general aspiration, without structure and a clear-cut program. There was to be an Arab country, but nobody knew what shape it would take, what its boundaries would be.

The victorious Allies after the First World War imposed their policies upon the Arab world. Britain created an additional Arab country, Transjordan, because of Arab pressure to prepare a throne for another Arab leader. Constantly the Arab leaders of the Middle Eastern regions, mandates, protectorates, nominally independent

* George Antonius, *The Arab Awakening*. Philadelphia: Lippincott, 1939.

countries, were scrapping among themselves. Some of them sought to establish integrated units for their own aggrandizement, and to overwhelm a rival. There was no real attempt of the Arabs themselves to create a larger unit, submerging the separatist interests of the rulers.

The Arab League itself was suggested by Great Britain in order to help integration in a way beneficial to herself. However, the Arab countries could have taken what they got and could have attempted to reshape it in the interests of greater Arab unity. This they did not do. The "birth certificate" of the Arab League, the 1944 Alexandria Protocol, was specific that the new body was to be formed of "independent Arab states." "Unanimous decision" was required even to take measures to repulse aggression; no decision of the League Council was binding upon any of its members and even the majority decisions were merely expressions of certain members' views. The League had no development from its inception and things just happened to it. "It has responded to outside pressures, but its responses have almost always been conditioned by its inner weakness." *

It was employed as the tool of diplomacy of different Arab countries. It became the instrument of politics of Egypt and Saudi Arabia, at first, and was then directed against the politics of the Hashemite dynasty in Iraq and Transjordan. At other times, Iraq became the strongest instigator of the League. The first Secretary General of the League, Abd al-Rahman Azzam Pasha, was pro-Egyptian and anti-Hashemite. Under the second Secretary General, Abd al-Khalek Hassuna, former Egyptian Foreign Minister, the League became largely a boycott organization against Israel. That was the only issue on which all the Arab countries agreed. "Arab unity does not exist," wrote T. R. Little. "I question whether it has ever existed. The empire of the Arabs was created by Islam, which fused the Arabs into a single purpose but did not give them real unity beyond that purpose."

* T. R. Little, "The Arab League: A Reassessment," *Middle East Journal*, Spring 1956, Vol. 10, No. 2.

In Geographic Unity There Is Strength

What about the geography of the Arab world, its natural frontiers? Looking for a parallel for the natural conditions of unification, one thinks of the United States, Germany and Italy, as illustrations. The two oceans form the two lateral boundaries of the United States. In natural resources it is one of the richest countries, if not the richest one. Germany has no natural boundaries, but she is a compact territory of closely related people, speaking the same language, and with a strong sense of history. Italy is the one country in Europe which has natural boundaries on all sides. She has great dialectal varieties and great differences between north and south; but, at the same time, the conviction that all parts of the country are interdependent and that unity is in the best interest of the nation.

The Arab world is a "world" indeed, an amorphous mass of territory, with no features common to all its parts. There is a natural boundary in North Africa—the Mediterranean—and hardly anything else. Some of the world's greatest deserts are within the boundaries of this "Arab nation." The very opposite of its aridity is the Fertile Crescent, a chain of mountains flanking the eastern Mediterranean shore and the Anatolian high plateau, before trailing off into the headlands of the Persian Gulf. Rivers are characteristic of two Arab countries, Egypt and Iraq—the land of the Nile and the land of the Tigris and Euphrates. Then there is the great Arab Quadrangle, filled by the Saudi Kingdom, and the coastal British protectorates. And finally, there is the "happy Arabia" of mountain-girt and rain-drenched Yemen.

A glance at the map shows that this vast territory has no geographic unity. It is a disconnected area of "islands," settled regions with fertile or semi-arid soil, in the midst of very large oceans. These huge seas are dry—they are deserts, far greater obstacles to travel than the "wet seas." The Mediterranean, for instance, has been a connecting link, weaving the fates of southern

132

Europe and of northern Africa into a common destiny through many centuries. On both sides of this "wet bridge" a white civilization came into existence. On the other hand, the "dry ocean" to the south of Africa's northern tier served as a barrier, so effective that Africa in the north had no link with the Africa to the south for millennia. Situated on the same continent though these two Africas were, the one was white, the other one was black. The former was the setting of the oldest part of our Western history, while the latter formed the backdrop of the youngest events.

The Arab islands, in their desert settings, are scattered all over the landscape: the settled portion of Mesopotamia; the Syrian coast; the toe and heel of the Arabian peninsula, a part of the Red Sea coast; the Nile valley; the Barbary Coast. Within the deserts which separate them are smaller islands of settled population around the oases, with nomads voyaging on "ships of the desert." The Arabs themselves call certain parts of their land masses "islands" even though the seas are far away. There is the "Island of Syria," Gezira—island—lying around and to the east of the inner Euphrates, which flows through the northeastern corner of Syria into Iraq; and then there is the other Gezira, in the Sudan, to the south of the junction of the White and Blue Niles. There are other such "islands," too, surrounded not by sea but by deserts.

"The Arab nation" is not an entity delimited by ethnographical data, nor the fortuitous result of geographic or historical association, but the function of an act of will, according to the noted Arabist, H. A. R. Gibb.

Persians have had far longer and closer relations with the people of Iraq than have, say, the Tunisians; yet Persians and Iraquis believe themselves to belong to quite separate national groups, whereas Tunisians and Iraquis, despite external differences, are conscious of real kinship with each other.*

* Philip W. Ireland, editor, *The Near East, Problems and Prospects.* Chicago: The University of Chicago Press, 1942, p. 70.

Nasser saw Egypt in the role of bringing closer the Arabs, Muslims and Africans. "To me Arab nationalism means many things," he wrote in an American magazine. "Above all it is a spiritual drive, a voluntary solidarity of the Arab peoples everywhere based on a common heritage of language, culture and history. This is a feeling that comes from the heart; it cannot be imposed."

The record, however, seems to tell another story. The Arab countries profess desire for unity but, perhaps, not under the leadership of Nasser. It has become routine for Arab countries to absent themselves from Arab League meetings because they consider it too much under Egypt's thumb. Nasser has kept on delivering slashing attacks on Arab sister nations. "The rulers of Lebanon betrayed us and stabbed us in the back," he said over Radio Cairo upon his return from a visit to Moscow, on May 16, 1958. "The downfall of King Hussein and his reactionary government," wrote the Cairo daily *Al-Shaab,* quoted by Radio Cairo on November 13, 1957, "will help crush the American Zionist plot. . . ." Several times he declared about the sheikhdom of Bahrain: "Egypt will never permit the continued existence of the British residency because the people of Bahrain are Arabs connected with their brothers . . ." and so on.

Geography placed another serious obstacle among the Arabs: oil. The largest known petroleum reserves are situated in the Arab world. As of now, the fabulous deposits are found in the most backward areas: Saudi Arabia, Kuwait, Qatar, while the more progressive regions have no petroleum, as in Lebanon or, not too much, Egypt. Why should the oil-rich territories share their wealth with the poor ones? The sense of national unity stops at the royalty statements. Recommendations that these royalties should help the poorer Arab countries have gone unheeded so far.

Possibly, the creation of Arab unity was within the grasp of the Arabs at one time or another. However, they never seized this opportunity. Assuming that it would have been possible, in spite of the natural handicaps, there were the obstacles of vested interests, political and economic. In the course of years the Arab nations developed institutions best suited to the interests of their ruling minorities. Why disturb them? The forces of inertia were beginning to operate at an accelerated rate.

Again assuming that Arab integration was a historic force, what Arab country should be the "Prussia" or "Piedmont" of this development? "Our land is the land of prophecy," said President Nasser. Why Egypt? Why not Syria or Iraq? Why not Saudi Arabia? Egypt has the largest population among the Arab countries, and some of the most important Arab regional institutions. But Egypt is not one of the most Arab of the Arab countries. Many people of the country make a sharp distinction between Arab and Egyptian. They are Egyptians with a history than which there is no older in the Western world, the cradle of civilization which witnessed the "dawn of conscience" telling man that he did not live by bread alone; that he was part of a wonderful human community. Compared with Egypt's millennial history, the secular story of the Arabs is only from yesterday.

Egypt is not the Prussia of the Arab world. Prussia established her claim to unite the German lands through her superior energy and strength, having vanquished the Austrian and French foe in east and west. On the other hand, Egypt was vanquished by a country a mere fraction of her size not once, but twice, under two different regimes. What was the justification of a defeated country to claim the victor's laurels and undertake a heroic task?

If the task of unification is not undertaken by Egypt, what Arab nation should be the unifier? The Saudi Arabians are the descendants of "real" Arabs and the Arab way of life originated in their towns, Mecca and Medina, in a book conceived by Mohammed, a townsman of Mecca. But Saudi Arabia does not yet belong to the world of modern nationalism. It is partly tribal and partly feudal. Her rulers seem to cherish the security which the country's isolation behind its desert ramparts seems to vouchsafe. It does not look at present as if Saudi Arabia were going to be the Prussia of the Arab world.

What about Iraq? The history of the Arab world since the end of the First World War has been largely the history of conflicts, overt or covert, between Egypt and Iraq. Here are the two great river civilizations, both of them looking back at their golden ages. The zenith of medieval Arab civilization was reached in Baghdad under the Arab Abbasside dynasty. Iraq is situated in the heart of the Arab world. She has oil and great potential riches, and is not entirely dependent upon the bounties of her rivers alone. On the other hand, Iraq has a much smaller population than Egypt and has been far less exposed to influences now stirring the world—especially modern nationalism. Egypt today is far more a global hub than Iraq. Also, many of the other Arabs look down upon the Iraqi as poor relations. Their standing in many Arab eyes is like that of Mississippi in the United States.

Syria and Lebanon are two small countries. One of them has already joined the United Arab Republic. The other one, Lebanon, while Arab, is more Christian than Muslim, according to official statements. Lebanon has the highest living standards in the Arab world, the highest literacy and the lowest sickness rates. But it is not the country to become the Arabs' leader.

Is unification an inevitable trend? In North America there are two countries, speaking the same language, cherishing the same institutions, with a common background. Yet they are two countries. In Latin America there are about a score of countries with identical backgrounds, cherishing similar faiths, all speaking Latin languages, most of them speaking Spanish, and yet there is no thought of integration.

Then, the task of unification needs the work of the unifier. America had George Washington, Italy Count Cavour and Germany Prince Bismarck. Will Nasser be equal to them? The propagation of the idea was done effectively by the various media at his disposal but how was the implementation to be effected?

"In the lives of nations," President Nasser said on February 1, 1958, "there are generations, ordained and solely chosen by destiny to witness decisive turning points in the history of mankind."

136

On that day a formal announcement was made about the merger of Egypt and Syria into the United Arab Republic. This was, indeed, a turning point in history.

Syria Before Unification

Syria passed through an extended period of troubles before it became a component part of the United Arab Republic. Between 1920 and 1941 she was a French mandate and a constant source of trouble to the French. This was due, partly, to the selection of French High Commissioners, such as General Maurice Sarrail, who lacked the tact needed for the performance of diplomatic tasks. His administration in Syria was severely criticized. During a rebellion he bombarded the native quarters of Damascus, causing great loss of lives. The trouble in Syria was partly due also to the fact that the British, who were the mandatories in neighboring Iraq, gave that country far more freedom. The Syrians, more Westernized than the Iraqi, looked down upon that region as more backward. Mainly, however, these difficulties were due to the influence of a sophisticated urban population which resented its being treated as mere "natives." This urban elite was intensely nationalistic.

During the Second World War, General Georges Catroux, an associate of Free French leader General de Gaulle, proclaimed Syria's independence, in order to encourage her co-operation with the Allies. However, it took more than two years before the power exercised by the French was transferred to the Syrians. It took the concerted effort of American and British diplomacy to induce the French to relinquish their hold in Syria.

In mid-May, 1948, Syria joined the other Arab countries in their attacks upon the newly established state of Israel. Like the other Arab states, except for Transjordan, Syria was defeated. This unexpected event produced a reaction which incubated for months. Finally, in March 1949 a *coup d'état* was staged in Syria, the leader of which was Colonel Husni es-Zaim.

137

This adventurous Syrian belonged to the important Kurdish minority (Muslim mountain people speaking a Persian dialect), and was conversant with recent Turkish history, having served as an officer in the late Ottoman army. The record of the founder of the Turkish republic, Mustapha Kemal Atatürk, had made a deep impression on him. He realized that while Syria's march of progress had been impeded by French tutelage, now the road was open to reforms.

It was on the bold pattern of Kemalist reforms that Husni Zaim attempted to introduce his own version of a New Order. He shared his illustrious model's belief that the dead hand of Islam must be removed if the nation was to command the citizens' loyalty. He effected the separation of church and state. He also held that the land which kept its women in bondage was only half a nation and he introduced women's suffrage, an adventurous undertaking among the tradition-bound Arabs. He introduced a modern Civil Code, holding that the solution of the problems of modern life could not be based solely upon the Koran, created for another age. He saw the real cause of the defeat at the hands of the Israeli— the impossibility of scoring victories on the battlefield by soldiers who were afflicted with disease, ignorance and poverty. First among the Arab rulers, he took notice of the majority.

The parliament in Syria was a popular institution only in name. In reality it was a meeting place for the retinues of the "people of influence," a semifeudal assemblage. Unable to find support there for his plans, he treated it in a cavalier fashion, dissolved it, nominated himself Premier, then, in quick succession, Marshal and President. He pledged himself to help the underprivileged against the feudal lords, who ruled over their lands like little kings. But he was swept off his feet by his own power-drunk importance, became arrogant and dictatorial. Seeing himself thwarted at every turn, he decided to join the feudal lords. He was overthrown a few months later and was killed in August 1949.

For the next five years Syria was ruled by military dictators, most important of whom was Adib Shishakli, former chief of police, then security chief, who grabbed power on December 19, 1949. He was disliked by politicians and commoners alike because of his previous posts, but he made no common cause with the feudal families, and this was his drawing card. The program he presented was public-spirited and impressive. However, power overwhelmed him, too, and he developed a mania of grandeur, surrounded himself with a palace guard and began to live like an Oriental potentate—and that he was. Finally, on February 24, 1954, he too was overthrown.

"The Treason of the Clerks"

In reaction to the social indifference of the feudal power elite the "angry young men" of Syria—known as the "young effendis" —rapidly veered toward the extreme left, less out of conviction than as a gesture of protest. An investigation conducted in 1951 by the Bureau of Applied Social Research of Columbia University of New York revealed that it was the frustrated and unhappy middle-class intelligentsia of young lawyers, journalists and writers who were the main supports of the radical wing. Under the prevailing system they despaired of seeing their country turn to reform in an orderly, democratic manner. Several of them were sucked into the apparatus of the Communists operating under such guises as the "Syrian Students' Union," and the "League of Arab Writers," among others. The Communist Party in Syria operated semi-legally until 1956 and then it ventured into the open. Its leader was one of the most colorful Arab Communists, Khalid Bakhdash, an "intellectual," because he was a graduate of a secondary school. He, too, was a Kurd and thus familiar with the restrictions imposed upon minorities. His voice had an amplifier, the Communist daily, *People's Voice,* of which he was the dynamic editor. He endorsed the popular causes, such as opposition to "Western imperialism" and to Zionism.

Even more rabidly anti-Western than the Communist Party was the Arab Socialist Renaissance Party. The army officers, many of

139

whom were recruited from the lower social echelons, also turned toward the left after a series of abortive military coups. Prominent among the left-oriented officers was Colonel Abdul Hamid Saraj, head of the Syrian army intelligence service. By 1957 the group headed by him had most of the army under its control. They were pro-Russians because the Soviets were against the West. The "image" of Russia attracted a large number of people, the Columbia University poll showed. They visualized the Soviet Union as a country where people were treated as equals, where there was no unemployment and the poor were being helped. The Syrians thus polled had never seen Russians and were therefore free to idealize them. On the other hand, they had met Americans. They resented the fact that Americans were so much richer.

In the Shadow of Russia

In the 1954 Syrian elections the majority of the elected deputies tended to a neutralist foreign policy while the representatives of the traditional parties gained no more than 45 of the 142 seats. For the first time in the history of the Arab Middle East the head of the Communist Party obtained a parliamentary seat. A Columbia University Research team observer foresaw that the future of Syrian politics depended on the Communists' ability to broaden the country's social base. Meanwhile, the army's pro-Soviet attitude kept on gaining ground while officers suspected of rightist inclinations were being purged. By the late summer of 1957 pro-Soviet officers were in full control of the army.

Britain's former Minister of State for Foreign Affairs, Anthony Nutting, gave this eye-witness account:

Damascus, when I was there, had the sinister atmosphere of a typical Communist satellite. It was impossible to talk to any one there. The Prime Minister, Sabri el-Assali, gave me an hour of the Soviet gramophone record in its rudest and most violent form, boasting that when I entered the room he had been signing cheques for more Soviet armaments. "The Russians are our friends," he said. "The Eisenhower

140

Doctrine would make us America's prisoners, it would destroy our positive neutrality." *

Moscow was the destination of a group of Syrian army officers headed by the Syrian Defense Minister, Khalid al-Azm, in August 1957. It reached an understanding with the Soviets quickly. They were to provide Syria with military equipment, training assistance, and credit at a low rate of interest, "with no strings attached." Also, two-way trade between the two countries was to be increased and the Soviets were to help Syria carry out several economic projects.

The United States entered the scene as the "villain." The Syrian government named three officials of the American Embassy as participants in a plot to overthrow the regime. Syrian "traitors," including the deposed ex-dictator, Adib Shishakli, were said to be involved in the plot. The United States government rejected the charges as ridiculous and retaliated by declaring the Syrian Ambassador in Washington *persona non grata*. Syrian-American relations reached an all-time low.

Addressing himself to the West, the Syrian Defense Minister, returning from the Moscow trip, declared: "We are at the outer edge of that policy [neutrality]—don't force us beyond that!" The State Department believed, however, that Syria had moved beyond that outer edge. Reports reaching Washington described the Syrian situation as extremely grave, which could have serious effects "on the security of the entire free world." A "trouble-shooting" expedition into the Middle East was undertaken by Loy Wesley Henderson, the American career diplomat: former Minister to Iraq, delegate to the Baghdad Pact Conference, former Director of Near Eastern and African Affairs in the Department of State, former American member of the Suez Commission, Cairo. He visited Turkey and Lebanon, where he collected most of his information, but he did not visit Syria. Both Syria and

* Anthony Nutting, *I Saw for Myself*. New York: Doubleday, 1958, p. 83.

141

Egypt were to charge that this visit was linked to the events that followed.

American arms shipments were rushed to the Arab countries that were not on good terms with Syria: Iraq, Lebanon, Jordan, Saudi Arabia. Fresh arms shipments were not needed in Turkey, which was receiving them regularly under the Truman Doctrine, Eisenhower Doctrine, Baghdad Pact and NATO auspices.

After Henderson's visit an atmosphere of crisis developed quickly. Secretary of State Dulles declared at a White House conference on September 7, 1957: "The President affirmed his intention to carry out the national policy expressed in the Congressional Middle East Resolution which had been adopted, and exercise as needed the authority thereby conferred on the President."

American arms deliveries to selected friendly Middle East countries continued at an accelerated rate. President Eisenhower expressed the hope that the "international Communists would not push Syria into any acts of aggression against her neighbors and that the people of Syria would act to allay the anxiety caused by recent events."

Notable in the President's statement was the reference to the "people of Syria" acting to allay the anxiety caused by recent events. This appeared to be an appeal to the people of a country over the head of its constituted authorities. Or was it an invitation to the people to act against their government? If so, the action would have been in the form of a revolution. Were events in Syria to be interpreted as acts of international communism, as implied by Secretary Dulles? On the other hand, no Middle East country had as yet invoked American aid. Was the Eisenhower Doctrine tacitly amended to mean that the United States could move into the Middle East against international communism even without being asked to do so by a country in the region? Against whom was the doctrine to be employed? The Soviets may have had technicians in Syria, but no armed forces. In the case of a reinterpretation of the Eisenhower Doctrine, what was to be the

142

attitude of the Arab countries in the region? The Arabs were scrapping among themselves up to a point. When that point was reached they usually closed their ranks.

Turkish Army Maneuvers

In September 1957 the Turkish army was holding its fall maneuvers along the northern boundaries of Syria. The government of Syria in Damascus charged that Turkish and American military aircraft was violating the country's air space. Clashes were reported along the Turko-Syrian frontier. The Soviet press, which began to take a deep interest in this matter, reported that Turkey was moving additional armed forces to the Syrian border. The Chairman of the Council of Ministers of the Soviet Union, N. A. Bulganin, warned Premier Adnan Menderes of Turkey on September 11 not to follow "American advice" by attacking Syria. The Soviet Foreign Minister, Andrei A. Gromyko, made the unequivocal charge that Turkey and the United States were plotting to attack Syria. The United States Sixth Fleet in the Mediterranean engaged in landing maneuvers at the port of Alexandretta which was now part of Turkey but which had belonged to Syria. The theme of the Syrian and Egyptian press was "Gunboat Diplomacy—New Style."

Earlier in the year President Eisenhower had declared that the United Nations could not be considered a wholly dependable protector of freedom against the Soviet Union. The General Assembly of the United Nations was in session at this time and Syria appealed to it to investigate the situation which she claimed was a threat to peace.

"Turkey now faces growing military danger from a major buildup of Soviet arms in Syria on its southern border," Secretary of State Dulles declared in the general debate of the Assembly, "a buildup concerted with Soviet military power on Turkey's northern border." Taking the offensive against the Soviets and Syria, he declared that Russia's attitude was in conflict with the

143

1949 General Assembly resolution which called upon all nations to "refrain from any threats or acts, direct or indirect, aimed at impairing the freedom, independence or integrity of any State."

In turn, the Soviet Union made the proposal to renounce interference and force in the internal affairs of the Middle Eastern countries. Soviet Communist Party Chief Nikita S. Khrushchev spoke urgently about the imminence of a Turkish attack on Syria. Behind the scenes, King Saud, considered friendly to America, was working to allay American fears. Khrushchev warned again that in the case of a Turkish attack the Soviets could not remain passive. He told the Turks that once the cannons started to shoot and the rockets to fly it might be too late. In an interview he gave to James Reston, correspondent of *The New York Times,* he leveled serious charges against the Middle East policy of the United States. He charged that Loy Henderson had gone to the Middle East in order to incite Syria's neighbors to attack her; that the Arabs refused to do so and thereupon Henderson made preparations to have Turkey take aggressive action.

Unabated, the crisis continued. The State Department warned the Soviets that it should be under no illusions about American policy. Turkey was a member of NATO and Washington took its obligations under that pact seriously. Also the United States was determined to carry out the national policy expressed in the Joint Congressional Resolution on the Middle East.

The Crisis Increases

Soviet party chief Khrushchev addressed a series of letters to the Socialist parties in Western Europe, telling them that the Middle Eastern situation was getting out of hand and urging them to help save the world from a devastating war. Under the 1955 solidarity pact President Nasser dispatched a battalion of Egyptian troops to Syria. At the United Nations, Foreign Minister Gromyko declared that if peace was violated it would become the duty of all United Nations members to render armed aid to Syria. The Soviet Union was prepared to participate in the suppression of aggression and the imposition of sanctions against the violators of peace.

Secretary of State Dulles spoke on October 16: "The eyes of the world are sufficiently focused on what is going on here, so that it is unlikely that there will be an outbreak of war. I think that it is one of the great advantages of the United Nations . . . the fact that it is in session. . . ."

And the Arab Countries?

What was the attitude of the Arab countries in this Syrian crisis? Syria was very unpopular among the Arab countries, with the exception of Egypt. The oil-producing countries had every reason to be apprehensive about Syria, which wielded great power over them through the pipelines that passed through her territory. Yet, as the United Nations debated the crisis, all the Arab countries spoke up in favor of Syria and against the application of the Eisenhower Doctrine. The Republic of Lebanon, which had hailed the doctrine, now turned against it.

The Syrian-Turkish crisis in October 1957 provided the Soviet Union with an excellent opportunity to strike a pose as the champion of the Arab cause. The crisis abated, but its consequences persisted. In a post mortem on the crisis *The New York Times* wrote that Foreign Minister Gromyko of the Soviets was exploiting the advantage he gained to the full. "This advantage derives from many things: the nature and history of the region, Soviet resourcefulness and American mistakes." *

In the wake of the crisis, Syria concluded an agreement with the Soviet Union for the execution of a twelve-year development program. The U.S.S.R. was to provide Syria with technical aid and credits at an interest rate lower than the one the International Bank for Reconstruction and Development had offered.

* Wallace Carrol, "Brinkmanship Again," *The New York Times,* October 17, 1957.

The Reason for the Merger

The Turko-Syrian crisis may have been one of the reasons why the merger of Egypt and Syria was accomplished and the United Arab Republic established. The Syrians may have become convinced that Egypt could afford better protection than any of the other aspirants for unification. According to another view, the union was rushed through in order to head off a Communist coup which appeared to be imminent in Syria. It was the conservative circles of Syria that were pressing for the merger, according to this view. On conclusion of the union the leader of the Communist Party fled Syria and in forming the government of the U.A.R. and choosing the Syrian members of it, Nasser excluded all Communists and pro-Communist elements. It was this version of the background of the merger President Nasser gave to R. K. Karanjia, editor of the Indian news magazine, *Blitz*. The unification had to be rushed through in the face of an impending Communist plot.

The real reason for the unification, presumably, was the desire of the Arabs to have a United Nations of their own or, even more, a United States of Arabia. Would the other countries want to join? Under what circumstances? How soon? What would be the advantages of the union? But first, what form did this union take? How did the two parts of it adjust themselves to changed circumstances?

As the union was consummated the names of Egypt and Syria disappeared as independent nations. Egypt now became the Egyptian Region of the U.A.R., and Syria's name was changed to the Syrian Region. Egyptian and Syrian embassies disappeared the world over. For the first time since its inception, the number of the members of the United Nations decreased. The Arab League also lost a member.

The capital of the new country was Cairo. The President of the new state was Gamal Abdul Nasser. In February a plebiscite took place in both regions of the republic to confirm the union.

146

The plebiscites resulted in near-100 per cent majorities. Full executive authority was vested in the President, assisted by a cabinet —Council of the Republic—responsible to him. Four Vice-Presidents of the Republic were appointed—two Egyptians and two Syrians. Political parties were dissolved and a National Union —in lieu of the parties—was formed. Members of the legislative council—Common Council—were appointed by the President, and its functions were merely advisory. At least half of its membership was to be drawn from the preceding Egyptian National Assembly and from the Syrian House of Representatives.

Separate executive councils were established in both regions, and their members, too, were appointed by the President of the Republic. The aim of the two councils was to co-ordinate the work of the government in the two regions and to increase executive efficiency. Egyptian and Syrian laws were to remain in force until changed. Only the conduct of foreign affairs and national defense were unified promptly.

The new republic, Nasser said, would adopt the system of "presidential democracy," the executive authority of which was to be vested in the head of the state, assisted by ministers appointed by him and responsible to him. Obviously, this type of "democracy" was to be run by a dictator. President Nasser was thus not only Egypt but also Syria. Nothing could conceal the fact that *l'état c'est lui,* or, as a wag put it: "Progress, it's wonderful. Instead of old Egypt, we now have new *Nassiristan.*"

The former Syrian President called the union "the first step on the path to entire Arab unity." The Secretary General of the Arab League described the formation of the United Arab Republic as the beginning of the "union among all of the Arab states." The permanent observer of the League at the United Nations viewed the union as a "new alliance on the road to complete Arab unity."

The Life of Newlyweds

President Nasser compared the merger to the life of newlyweds, in which certain inevitable adjustments had to be made. What were the assets and liabilities the newlyweds took into their marriage? What were the early indications of the success or failure of the U.A.R.? What were the indications of its serving as a rallying point for further unification? What was the stake of American foreign policy in this union?

Both regions had different backgrounds for long periods of time. Egypt had sprinted ahead of the other Arab regions in the first half of the nineteenth century, establishing an aggressive, semi-autonomous position under the Ottoman Empire. On the other hand, Syria remained directly under the Sultan, except when foreign powers intervened for the protection of Christian lives. Then Egypt fell under British rule, while Syria remained under the Ottoman regime until the end of the First World War. Then she became a French mandate.

The cultural influences in both regions have been more French than English, probably because France was working harder to retain her traditional cultural hold in the Middle East, going back to the Crusades. Even in Egypt the educated classes' *lingua franca* has been French.

Both regions developed social classes of great competence— people of good education. However, much of the education was of the general cultural, liberal-arts type. Recently, there has been an increasing awareness of the importance of technical subjects, particularly engineering. Not a few of the young people of Egypt received their technical education in Britain, the United States, Germany, Switzerland and France. On the other hand, top-echelon Syrians claim more competence in economics and, particularly, in finances. Even today many of them do not think too highly of the financial aptitudes of their fellow countrymen in the Egyptian region.

The economic systems of the two regions have been different, especially in recent times. The "Socialist" system in Egypt tries to foster a mixed economy. Under a government-operated Economic Organization the private and public sectors of the country's economic life have been co-ordinated. Priorities have been established in order to stimulate the growth of those sectors of economic life which the regime considered of great importance for the country. This mixed economy, however, did not want to discourage private initiative.

On the other hand, Syria until the unification was the classical land of *laissez faire* in the Middle East. In some respects it was a typical "robber baron" economy, with the accent on distribution rather than production. More than Cairo, if possible, Damascus was the heaven of the entrepreneur. Products which the entrepreneurs never possessed physically—never even saw—changed hands with miraculous rapidity, leaving a trail of gold along their line of march. "Only stupid people work physically," was the motto. "People who work have no time to make money."

Even greater is the difference in the cultivated areas of the two regions, much more in Syria than in Egypt. In Syria there are nearly three acres of cultivated land for each person, while in Egypt there is only one-quarter of an acre. Still greater is the discrepancy if the Syrian cultivable area is taken into account. In Syria it comprises 17,059,000 feddans (one feddan is 1.038 acre), of which 11,016,000 feddans are actually cultivated. In Egypt, it will be recalled, the cultivated area is only six million acres and the "heroic" project of the Aswan Dam would add two million additional acres. In Syria several development projects are to add more land to the arable surface. Chief among the development projects has been the Ghab drainage program, covering about 90,000 acres of marshland. Irrigation systems planned along the Orontes, Euphrates, Kabir, Khabur and Barada rivers affect a total of 336,520 acres.

There is no immediate real solution for the "Malthusian problem" of the Egyptian Region—as the population increase races far ahead of the food supply. Even the Aswan High Dam project is no more than a palliative. The per capita national income is higher in Syria—$175 according to a 1956 estimate—than in Egypt—$111. These figures should be taken with caution, however; they contain a built-in distortion, because the total annual national income is divided by the number of people, so that the millionaire is credited with as much earning as the pauper.

The unification of Egypt and Syria would make far more sense from the point of view of the Egyptians, who have inadequate land, than from that of the Syrians, who have enough of it. It would be in the interest of Egypt to disperse her population among the potentially land-rich Arab countries. However, this would require a large-scale population transfer for which there are no indications as yet. The Egyptian region has far more industries than the Syrian one, while the latter seems to have far more financial skills than the former. This is so because of the greater sophistication of the Syrians and their apparent greater flexibility. In this case, too, population transfer could help solve the problem.

The First Results of the Union

At first there was a duplication rather than an amalgamation of the ministries. Study committees were formed to address themselves to the problems of organization. A constitution was drafted. Except for a few items intra-U.A.R. import licensing requirements were abolished. The Ministers of Economics and Commerce for the two regions agreed to exempt from customs duties all goods of local origin imported from either region, with some exceptions. Economic agreements with foreign countries were now concluded by the U.A.R. This was not yet a full customs union. The currencies of the two regions were not yet united. The hardships of economic integration were illustrated by a Damascene banker's statement: "We must be careful not to attempt any brusque changes in the economics of our countries. After all, the Egyptians are not very intelligent in these matters.

150

Their economy must be run by the central governments; ours flourishes under private management. If we do not change things too fast, the new Union may work out." *

In Syria the big landlords were smuggling millions of pounds to neighboring Lebanon and from there to Swiss banks, and they resisted land reform. The invasion of Syria by Egyptian products and capital lowered profits for the small merchants and the industrialists. The intellectuals in Syria criticized the absence of political and press freedom. While all political parties were banned, the Ba'ath still maintained its political machinery intact for a time. Thousands of businessmen and politicians were dissatisfied, because favors in government contracts or important positions were distributed only to Ba'ath adherents. Above all, the Syrian was resentful that his country has lost its personality as a nation. "How do you want me to feel?" asked a young Syrian diplomat. "Whenever I say I am a citizen of the U.A.R., the only reaction is, 'Oh, a citizen of Nasser.' Often I am in an embassy dominated by Egyptians, who ignore me or underrate my ability. I have become a second-class citizen." †

Since the Syrian army had made the politics of the country before the union, the question arises: how happy is the army? At the outset, for every Egyptian officer sent to Syria, one Syrian was sent to Egypt. But the Syrian officers were usually kept in subordinate jobs and resented taking orders from Egyptian army officers. Open clashes occurred between Syrian and Egyptian officers, mainly in the city of Aleppo, and these led to "purges" and dismissals in the Syrian army.

The United Arab Republic was not yet two years old when, at the end of 1959, Field Marshal Abdel Hakim Amer, President Nasser's special representative, was given full authority over Syrian affairs, to the exclusion of Syrian Vice-Presidents.

---

* Daniel Lerner, *The Passing of Traditional Society*. Glencoe, Ill.: The Free Press, 1958, p. 302.

† P. H. Crane, "Nasser and Kassem: A Study in Acrimonious Coexistence," *The Reporter*, June 25, 1959. Vol. 20, No. 13, pp. 20-21.

The Shape of Things to Come

The mission of the U.A.R. was described by President Nasser in a major policy declaration reported in the newspaper *Al Ahram* and reproduced in *The New York Times* on July 3, 1959. He called upon the Egyptians and Syrians to make their own "great leap forward." He also called for programs to double the national income of the U.A.R. within ten years, and his statement appeared to be intended to generate enthusiasm for that goal. President Nasser said that the seven years since the Egyptian revolution of 1952 were in reality only a period of preparing for the real revolution, which he characterized as the creation of a "co-operative socialist and democratic society." The national objectives would be to increase the national income, eliminate strife among the social classes and provide equal opportunity for all. "Bread for all should be the inevitable prelude to liberty for all."

On March 8, 1958, the process of unification advanced one step forward. An agreement establishing a federal union was signed in Damascus between the U.A.R. and the Imamate of Yemen. This union was different from the integration of Egypt and Syria, which created one country. This new union was more limited, less integral, and referred only to the unification of the defense and foreign policies of the members. Eventually, their economic policies were to be co-ordinated: "Each state will preserve its international personality and its system of government."

Arab unity, promoted in some ways, was retarded in others as a result of the formation of the U.A.R. On February 14, 1958, the Kings of Jordan and Iraq formed the "Arab Federation," which was described as a "Constitutional Federation, composed initially of the Kingdoms of Jordan and Iraq." It lasted only for a short time and was swept aside by the Iraqi revolution in July 1958. The main purpose of this federation appeared to be to stop Nasser by setting up a rival organization.

Nasser, prospective unifier of the Arab world, was engaged in conflicts with most of the Arab countries. He had a border conflict with Egypt's neighbor to the south, the Sudan; was engaged in a quarrel with Habib Bourguiba, President of Tunisia, who accused him of backing the "subversive" activities of the so-called "Yusufites," followers of Ahmed Satah ben Yusuf, an agitator operating from Cairo on behalf of North African Arab integration. Nasser charged that the ruler of Saudi Arabia, King Saud ibn Abdul Aziz, had been plotting his assassination.

"The New Balance of Power"

The U.A.R. continued to maintain cordial relations with the Soviet Union for a time. The Syrian Region received a Russian loan of $140 million for industrial and agricultural projects. The Egyptian Region, it will be recalled, obtained a Soviet credit of $100 million for the construction of the first stage of the High Dam at Aswan. Besides, the Soviet Union extended a line of credit amounting to $175 million for an industrialization program of Egypt, and East Germany Deutsche Demokratische Republik (D.D.R.), advanced $20 million. Both the Egyptian and the Syrian regions received large quantities of arms from the U.S.S.R. and Czechoslovakia.

This arrangement suited both the U.A.R. and the U.S.S.R. The former had been placed "beyond the pale" in much of the Western world because of Egypt's nationalization of the Suez Canal. President Nasser needed funds for his economic development program. Also, the Soviet Union was ready to supply him with arms. This arrangement enabled the Soviets to gain the "inner track" in the Middle East. All sorts of possibilities were opened up to diplomatic operations in the region. Supplying arms to an underdeveloped country has long been the classical opening to maneuvers to obtain a priority position. The recipient country was dependent upon the supplier for personnel to train the armed men in the use of weapons. Also, the recipient nation became dependent upon the supplier for spare parts.

The Soviet Union combined these operations with diplomatic

153

maneuvers within and outside the United Nations. In possession of the veto on the Security Council the Russians were in a unique position to promote the aims of their Arab friends. Threatening action at crucial times in defense of Arab interests, the Soviet Union ingratiated itself to Arab countries even more. The Arab nations disagreed on many issues but they agreed on a common opposition to Israel, an issue which was charged with emotions to such an extent that eventually it became an obsession. The Russians had no qualms about exploiting this issue to the hilt.

Was Nasser not concerned about letting the Communists into his country? He appeared to be confident that he could handle communism. On several occasions he expressed the view that he would follow the policy of Mustapha Kemal Atatürk in this respect. The founder of the Turkish Republic was an arch-anti-Communist who, however, got along very well with the Soviets. Turkey appears to be the only major country in the Middle East in which there are neither avowed nor crypto-Communists. While Nasser made his deals with the Soviet bloc he jailed Egypt's Communists. He was confident that the Kremlin would be willing to sacrifice Egypt's Communists to the Soviets' national interests. He did not seem to reckon, however, with inter-Arab jealousies and with the possibility of his being trumped by another Arab leader, the revolutionary chief of Iraq—Abdel Karim Kassem. Also he helped devise a method of balancing East and West—a new balance of power.

The old balance of power was operated by powerful nations to prevent the emergence of a preponderantly strong country in the world. It was, for instance, Britain's policy to strengthen the weak and weaken the strong in order to establish such a balance. Under this old system, the small countries were pawns in the great imperial game. The "new balance of power" operated in reverse. There a weak country gave a hand to a strong nation to strengthen itself further at the expense of a rival. In order to do so the small country had to have some assets—such as, for instance, great strategic advantage; and that Nasser's United

Arab Republic had. When one of the great powers became too strong the time was ripe to redress the balance by turning to the other power. This is what Nasser did.

Americans were then engaged on a variety of development projects in Egypt—some eighty experts attached to United States missions inside and outside the Embassy. Up to 1956 the United States had allocated $62 million for aid to Egypt. During the Suez crisis further aid was stopped, except that materials already on order were delivered. For two years relations between the two countries were almost at a standstill. At the expiration of that period America gave the United Arab Republic $25 million worth of wheat and $23 million worth of tobacco, barley and vegetable oils, which came out of the towering stockpile the government had been accumulating. Such transactions had very little of the ideological undertone.

The rivalry between Iraq and the United Arab Republic had basic reasons, as we shall see. However, it was also part of the "cold war," in the conduct of which the United States was fully engaged. As Iraq's General Kassem turned to the Communists, for a time at least, so Nasser turned away from him, and it seemed also that the Communists of the Kremlin were less enthusiastic about him. Here was then a chance for the United States to get on better terms with Nasser and for Nasser to practice the technique of the new balance of power.

Late in June 1959, the United Arab Republic and the United States signed a technical assistance agreement, the first one to be concluded since United States aid to Egypt was broken off during the Suez crisis. The amounts involved were small—$6 million for development funds and $1,700,000 for a program to reclaim Egyptian land and settle farmers on it. But the U.A.R. was reported to be ready to apply for a World Bank loan to help finance its $270 million project for widening and deepening the Suez Canal. The Bank approved a loan of $56 million for these purposes at the end of 1959. Regardless of the cost, the fact that Nasser was again accepting money and advice from the United

States was bound to be politically significant in the Arab world. United States aid had long been criticized by Arab nationalists on the ground that it had too many strings.

Cairo's decision reflected the change in the political climate that had taken place since Nasser began cooling toward the Soviets. He became steadily more friendly toward the West as a counterbalance to the growing Soviet influence in the Arab world. The receipt of American aid involved certain political risks for Nasser. For some time his enemies in Iraq were calling him a "slave of the dollar" for accepting United States gifts of wheat and for seeking a loan from the International Bank for Reconstruction and Development.

However, the "new balance of power" did not mean that Nasser would go all out to side with the United States. It was understood that American aid would be accepted side by side with massive Soviet projects in the Egyptian and Syrian regions of the U.A.R. In addition, the Soviet Union was supplying both regions with arms, while the United States had declined to do so. How successful would this new balance of power policy be and was Nasser a sufficiently skillful operator not to get caught in the Soviet trap?

Meanwhile the U.A.R. keeps on stirring up interest in a United Arabia. The Cairo radio, never addicted to understatement, has been touting the greatness of the new regime. Thousands of Egyptian teachers have gone into other parts of the Arab world, missionaries of a new Arab *mystique*. The University of Cairo has branches as far apart as Rabat in Morocco and Khartoum, in the Sudan, straddling much of Africa. Egyptian schools of higher learning play host to some ten thousand students from the rest of the Arab world.

Yet, the success of further Arab integration will not be decided by the radio, teachers and students. It will be decided by the success or failure of Nasser to give more food to Egyptians and Syrians. The paeans he has received were in anticipation of the "economic miracles" his people believe he will be able to perform.

156

CHAPTER 3

The Rival—Iraq

Between East and West

THE Republic of Iraq—the former Mesopotamia—has for long been the rival of Egypt. Her capital, Baghdad, was the seat of the Arab world empire under the Abbasside dynasty about which Arabs dream today. Iraq faces the east, Egypt faces the west. Iraq is situated in the heartland of the Arab world, Egypt on its peripheries. The majority of the Egyptians belong to the Sunni sect of Islam; the majority of the Iraqi Arabs to the Shiis.* Iraq is rich in oil, the U.A.R. is not. Both Egypt and Iraq have attempted to unite the Arabs under various guises. Iraq fostered various Fertile Crescent schemes. When President Nasser established the United Arab Republic, Iraq promptly countered it by setting up the Arab Federation. Instead of uniting, when the Iraqi revolution of July 1958 wiped out the *ancien régime,* Baghdad went on its own way, resisting Cairo, combating it, bringing about a new polarization.

There is a great difference in the outlook of the people and in

* The Sunnis recognize not only the Koran but also the traditions associated with the Prophet and they recognize all his successors, Caliphs. The Shiis recognize only the Koran and they believe that on Mohammed's death he should have been followed by his son-in-law Ali. While it is assumed that most of the Iraqi Muslims are Shiis it is not quite sure. Together with the Kurdish minority, however, the Sunnis form the majority.

157

the characteristics of the civilization of Egypt and Iraq. The traveler in the past was in Europe when visiting Cairo and Alexandria. In Baghdad he reached the real Orient. Because of her location at the eastern crossroads, Iraq's population is more mixed than that of other Arab countries. She has been exposed to contrary influences, of Persia from the east, Turkey from the north, the desert Arab from the south, the Mediterranean from the west. Iraq is close to the Soviet Union; Egypt is far.

The airplane has brought Iraq closer to the West, but that is a recent development. Under the Ottoman rule—which ended only in the First World War—Turkish officials appointed to Baghdad posts reached their goal by circumnavigating the huge Arab Quadrangle (after the Suez Canal had been opened) and then sailing up the Shatt-el-Arab and the Tigris—a trip that may have consumed weeks. The governors were left to their devices, which were not always public-spirited. If they did not embezzle too much of the state funds it was because the climate was enervating or, less frequently, because they were afraid of higher authorities who also wanted to have their cut. As a rule, the administrators swaggered and the people died like flies in the fall.

Iraq's Minorities

In the history of Iraq minorities play an important role. Most important of them are the Kurds, of whom there may be some four million, partly in Iraq, Iran, Syria, the Soviet Union, but mainly in Turkey where they are not recognized as Kurds but are called "mountain Turks." Although Muslims, these Kurds are not Arabs and unlike the Arabs they do not speak a Semitic language but an Indo-European one—a variant of Persian.

The Kurds are mountaineers, mainly, and they display a strong spirit of independence. In Iraq's history they have played a greater role than their numbers would seem to justify and since the establishment of the republic their part in Iraqi history seems to have enhanced. They are Orthodox Sunnis.

158

Iraq has been a magnet to people from many parts of the Middle East. Armenian communities are encountered frequently and Persian is spoken in parts of the central plains. Turkey at one time claimed the northern oil-bearing districts of Iraq, and there Turkish dialects are spoken. Christian communities in scattered locations have salvaged Syriac languages from oblivion. There was an important though small community of Jews in Iraq, but most of them, some 122,000, had been flown to Israel after the establishment of the new state in "Operation Ali Baba." Several exotic creeds survive in Iraq, such as that of the Yazidis, whose creed is a medley of Muslim, Christian and Magian elements and who are sometimes called "devil worshipers" because they hold that since God is unalterably good there is no sense in praying to him. They pay homage to the Devil.

First Among the Arabs

Iraq was mandated to the British after World War I and she was the first among the Arab countries to achieve a measure of independence. In response to their urgings, the Iraqi obtained several privileges from the British, beginning with 1922, and signed a pact with them in 1936 which paved the way to their being admitted to the League of Nations as an independent country. Still, the Iraqi remained in "special treaty relationship" with the British, which meant English advisers and common defense. In practice this meant that in matters of defense and foreign policy the last word was uttered by London, and not by Baghdad. Helping the British in retaining their hold on the country was Iraq's "perennial Premier," Nuri es-Said Pasha. Whenever he was not heading the government, he was pulling the wires behind the scenes.

Nuri was of partly Kurdish origin, born in the oil-rich northern Kirkuk country, a son of well-to-do Arabs in the Ottoman Empire. He attended the Military College in Constantinople and for six years served in the Ottoman army before the First World War.

During a part of it he helped T. E. Lawrence, a leader of the war-time Arab "revolt in the desert" against the Turks. After the British had chased out the Ottomans, Nuri became a commandant in Damascus, then adviser to King Faisal I of Iraq, the first of his line. Lawrence described Nuri es-Said as a man whose courage, authority and coolness marked him as an ideal military leader.

Nuri became conversant with the British parliamentary system and sought to adopt it in Iraq. However, it was a different type of democracy, in which the semblance was democratic but the substance was autocratic. As long as they served his purpose he put up with political parties but dissolved them when they became cantankerous. He used the legislature as a lightning conductor, conveying the erroneous impression to the people that they had the last word about their fate. To his enemies Nuri was a British "stooge" and they thoroughly despised him. His power over Iraq was so great that his opponents spoke of the country as "Nuristan" —Nuri's Land. No leading Arab was more unpopular than he, because of his service to the "imperialists." Nasser particularly despised him. Some Britishers entertained the most favorable view about him. "Wherever and whenever Britain has found herself in a tight corner during the past forty years or more," wrote Anthony Nutting, a former high official of the British Foreign Office, "she has also found Nuri ready and willing to do battle, to stake all for her cause."

Britain wanted a Middle East defense organization pivoted around Iraq. Britain had there the important Habbaniya and Shaiba bases and, above all, she had Nuri es-Said. The policy of Nuri represented everything that Nasser detested—the hated "imperialism" and the pasha rule. In turn, Nasser was the incarnation of subversion in Nuri's eyes—change in the established order, the unchaining of the mysterious and mercurial forces of the incomprehensible and irresponsible masses. Nuri could handle the docile parliament but what could he do with the people?

Nuri Pasha believed that it was in Iraq's interest to have her security underwritten by a friendly great power. It had to be Great Britain which considered the region its own sphere. The United States was building up a world-wide protective fence around the Communist bloc. The Truman Doctrine placed only Greece and Turkey under American protection and the rest of the Middle East remained a gaping hole. Multilateral treaties, such as the charter of NATO, and bilateral agreements, such as the United States–Japanese pact, looked after mutual interests in the rest of the world.

Secretary of State Dulles took a great interest in filling out the power vacuum. In 1951 Turkey and Pakistan signed a friendship pact and three years later it was reinforced. Under this new treaty the two countries pledged co-operation and the exchange of technical information in the case of an unprovoked attack from outside. The pact was open to accession by any state whose participation the two nations considered useful. The Prime Minister of Iraq declared that his country would consider an invitation to join it in the light of its national interests. The Egyptian Minister of War declared that it was not in the interest of any Arab country to join this alliance before achieving full independence. Should Iraq join—as Cairo saw it—the Western powers would be back in the drivers' seat. As a member of a Western-sponsored alliance, Iraq would receive large supplies of arms, which were denied to Egypt. Eventually, Syria and Lebanon would want to jump on the "bandwagon" and Egypt would be isolated in the Arab world.

The Baghdad Pact

For the same reasons, the Western world, especially the United States, wanted Iraq to join the alliance. This might be the beginning of a stampede among the Arab countries to make common cause with them. They considered Egypt obstreperous and a difficult country to handle. The rivalry between Iraq and Egypt erupted anew. In February 1955, Iraq took the important step. She concluded a pact of mutual co-operation with Turkey on

161

February 24. Article 1 of the treaty said: "Consistent with article 51 of the United Nations Charter, the High Contracting Parties will co-operate for their security and defense. Such measures as they agree to take to give effect to this co-operation may form the subject of special agreements with each other." On April 4 of the same year a special agreement between Great Britain and Iraq was signed. Under a previous arrangement Britain was vested with the right to maintain armed establishment at two Iraqi bases. Many Iraqi considered this a restriction of Baghdad's sovereign rights. Under the Baghdad Pact Britain relinquished the right to maintain the two bases which now were placed at the disposal of the Baghdad Pact countries. Consequently, Britain evacuated the Habbaniya and Shaiba bases she had held under the British–Iraqi pact but promptly returned to them as a Baghdad Pact signatory. Pakistan acceded on September 23 and Iran on November 5, and thus the "northern tier" of Western defense was created.

A United States government statement issued on November 29, 1956, set forth: "The United States has, from the inception of the Baghdad Pact, supported the pact and the principles and objectives of collective security on which it is based." America, however, did not join the alliance directly. Eventually, she did participate in the work of three important committees: military, economic and countersubversion. Also, she agreed to defray a part of the cost of maintaining headquarters and of a military liaison office. Would it not have been better for the United States to become a full member? Possibly it would have been, but there were difficulties in the way. Iraq is one of the most important Middle Eastern oil-producing nations and the pipelines from her fields pass through Syria and Lebanon. America's participation in the Baghdad Pact would have antagonized Syria. Also, Egypt was violently opposed to the pact, which she considered a means of the West to re-enter the Middle East. Further, she did not concede to Iraq the right to take such an important step involving the Arab world. The view is held even today that Nasser's first contacts with the Soviet bloc were in retaliation against Iraq's entry into the Baghdad Pact. Then, there was some ambiguity, at first, about Israel's attitude toward the Arab mutual assistance pact. In Arab eyes Israel was Public Enemy No. 1, and that fact could not be blinked even though the pact was directed against the Soviets. On the one hand, the Baghdad Pact diverted attention from Israel and concentrated it on the potential menace from the north. But on the other hand, it was a potential menace by arming an Arab state without an undertaking not to use those arms against her.

The United States was the most effective motive force behind the Baghdad Pact and yet not a member of the alliance. This ambivalent attitude bedeviled America's friends. Premier Adnan Menderes of Turkey spoke for the other pact members, too, when he expressed his unhappy conviction that the policy of the Washington administration confused and depressed its best friends in the Muslim world. The British statesman, Anthony Nutting, went even further: "Mr. John Foster Dulles had virtually invented this alliance and had at first roundly chastised Britain and other countries for being slow to adopt his brain-child. Then for fear of Israeli counterdemands, Egyptian opposition and Saudi anxieties he had calmly left this inadequately equipped infant upon Iraq's and Turkey's doorsteps."

In the end, Iraq turned out to be a weak reed upon which to pivot the defense of the Middle East. "In the Middle East the conclusion of the Baghdad Pact resulted in strains and tensions which offered new openings for the penetration of Soviet influence." * Because of the military aid provided to Pakistan under the Baghdad Pact, Afghanistan and, far more important, India were alienated from the United States. Syria was fearful of the increase in Iraq's power and Egypt resented Iraq's refusal to follow her leadership. Israel became alarmed over the arms made available to Iraq and over her own exclusion from the American-

* Paul L. Hanna, "America in the Middle East," *Middle Eastern Affairs,* May 1959, Vol. X, No. 5, p. 182.

sponsored defense system. An American diplomat singled out the Baghdad Pact as an illustration of a "paper alliance." ". . . We are placing too much reliance on ineffective, weak, 'paper' alliances of a military nature. I have in mind SEATO and the Baghdad Pact as examples. These are provocative, without adding commensurate military strength." *

Desert and Development

Iraq is one of the Arab countries which can expand the limits of agricultural cultivation. Here, too, the comparison with Egypt is revealing. Egypt with more than three and a half times the population of Iraq has less arable land than the latter's present seven million acres. Iraq actually has "two Niles"—the Tigris and Euphrates, sweeping out of the rain-fed Anatolian mountains and traversing the entire length of the country. Not more than one-fourth of Iraq's tillable soil is cultivated, according to an estimate of the Food and Agriculture Organization of the United Nations.

Then, too, Egypt has some oil, but Iraq has much of it and was starting to get about a quarter of a billion dollars in the form of royalties at the end of the 1950's. As a consequence, Iraq has money for internal development. Even in the near past, whenever the snow on the Turkish mountains began to melt, the chocolate-colored floods of the Tigris and Euphrates swept away sometimes thousands of huts and farms, also villages and even sections of Baghdad. Now the excess water has been drawn into useful service—irrigation. The Iraq Development Board was set up under the Nuri regime and it was endowed with 70 per cent of the country's vast oil revenues. Under the provisions of the 1955–1960 Five Year Plan both the Development Board and the

* Quoted by Max Ascoli, "The Silent Diplomats Speak Out," *The Reporter,* July 23, 1959, Vol. 21, No. 2, p. 15, summarizing the statements of fifty retired American Foreign Service officers queried by the Foreign Relations Committee of the Senate of the United States.

Ministry of Development were authorized to expend Iraqi £500 million (one Iraqi dinar is officially $2.80). Two of the seven permanent members of the Board were nominated by the United States and British governments. Other Americans occupied administrative positions in various agencies of the Iraqi government. The United States Operations Mission in Iraq had a total of 140 American personnel. The operations of the Development Board and of the Americans extended to irrigation and power, public buildings and roads, agriculture and public housing, plus a land-settlement administration. The community development program planned the establishment of a nation-wide system of multipurpose village-level workers who were to seek means for getting the villagers to improve their lot.

A large proportion of the government funds went into flood control and irrigation projects. The gigantic Wadi Thartar project, completed in 1956, diverted flood waters from the Tigris at Samarra into a huge natural depression of 761 square miles. On the Euphrates, the Habbaniya project enabled flood waters to be utilized for irrigation. Other flood-control projects included the Dokan Dam of the Lesser Zab, a Tigris tributary; the Derbeni-Khan Dam on the Diyala; the Duyaila, Latifiyeh, Haveeja and the Greater Musseyeb projects. High priority was also accorded to industrialization; the object was self-sufficiency in many materials required for construction and the production of consumer goods. No other Arab country spent nearly as much on development.

However, some basic reforms could not be introduced because of the nature of Nuri's regime. A few hundred landlords owned fully 94 per cent of the land, and they were the country's "power elite" upon which the Nuri regime depended. Remove this elite and Nuri's regime would have been removed. Nuri Pasha found it impossible to break up even a part of the estates of these local potentates for purposes of land reform. He started a modest—too modest—"reform" with the distribution of government land. The large barrages and irrigation projects helped the thirsty land and

165

added to the arable acreage. However, the main beneficiaries were the rich pashas and the sheikhs. Meanwhile, the horrible shacks along the Tigris and the slum quarters of Baghdad and other large cities served to accentuate the injustice of social and economic polarization. As the American director of the United States Operations Mission to Iraq, Henry Wiens, said:

"... The *ancien régime* [of Nuri] failed to appreciate the intensity and extent of popular support for the new Arab nationalism. It chose not to align itself with this force and even gave the appearance of opposing it. ... The dream of recreating a Garden of Eden from the sun-baked deserts of Mesopotamia so enthralled many Iraqis in high places that they failed to see the urgency of alleviating the sufferings of the general populace." *

The old regime, according to Dr. Wiens, appeared genuinely puzzled and hurt that the people did not appreciate its paternalistic efforts. The late Crown Prince of Iraq was quoted as saying that if only the Iraqi people could be put to sleep for five years, they would wake up with deep gratitude to their government!

Soon the revolution was to strike in Iraq, sweeping away the King, the Crown Prince and Nuri Pasha. However, there was no indication of the impending changes in the press of the Western world. Iraq was the only Arab country whose defense system appeared to be fully integrated with that of the West and, therefore, it was assumed that all was well with the country. To be critical of Iraq was tantamount to disloyalty to the Western cause. Anthony Nutting, the British statesman who covered the Middle Eastern countries shortly before the revolution struck, returned home with the glad tidings: "By far the most exciting and hopeful country that I found in the Middle East was Iraq."

There were occasional exceptions to his optimism. The military correspondent of *The Daily Telegraph* of London, Lt. Gen. H. G. Martin, wrote on a visit he made shortly before the outbreak

* "The United States Operations Mission in Iraq," *The Annals of the American Academy of Political and Social Science,* May 1959, Vol. 323, p. 148.

of the revolution that he was profoundly disturbed by what he had learned from his Arab friends. The cost of living in Iraq had soared and the sharecroppers, industrial workers, students and clerical workers were in great want. The gulf between the rich and the poor was a standing incitement to revolt. The common people hated with a pathological intensity the *pater patriae,* Nuri Pasha, the sheikh landlords and the other nabobs.

Death Strikes at Night

Two Iraqi brigades under the command of General Abdel Karim Kassem and Colonel Abdel Salam Aref were on their way to Jordan, by order of the Baghdad government, during the night of July 13, 1958. Jordan was in trouble again. The two countries, under the rule of two young Kings of the Hashemite dynasty, cousins, were members of the Arab Federation. The two officers violated their orders and instead of proceeding into Jordan stopped in Baghdad. They seem to have been preparing for this night. "The idea of waging revolution," General Kassem said later, "began when we graduated from college. We saw that conditions were worsening." They, too, hated Nuri es-Said Pasha in whom they saw the embodiment of "colonialism." The military had replaced the politicians in the key countries of the Arab world, Egypt and Syria, and were to do likewise in Lebanon and the Sudan. The political parties, corrupt, autocratic, pasha-ridden, had lost face.

The military leaders in Iraq seized the centers of national life during the night: key government buildings, telephone, telegraph, radio centers. Apparently there was no opposition to the coup. The royal regime was unpopular, and no arms were raised for the protection of the pashas and the sheikhs. The young King, Faisal II, and his uncle Prince Abdulillah were killed by a shell in the royal palace, according to one version. They were cut down in front of it while parleying with the military emissaries, according to another one. Nuri es-Said Pasha had successfully escaped

167

from his mansion on the bank of the Tigris and donned a woman's garment, veil and all. However, his nervous gestures in the street aroused suspicion; he was found out and tortured to death. (According to one version, he was impaled on the iron fence of his own palace.) Baghdad went wild with joy, and the rest of the country followed suit.

Who were behind the revolution? The ostensible leader was General Kassem, forty-four years old, born in Baghdad, of a lower-middle-class family. He was a graduate of the Royal Military College. At the senior officers' school at Devizes, in southwestern England, his classmates nicknamed him "snake-charmer," because of his ability of influencing his classmates. Yet he was not a good orator, and appeared to be shy. Colonel Aref, the commander of the other battalion, was a younger man, and appeared to be more dynamic. In the first days of the revolution Kassem was thought to be the Naguib of Iraq and Aref its Nasser. That, however, was a mistaken view.

Kassem said later that he alone planned and directed the revolution and had no partners. According to others, the revolution was backed by political parties, particularly the Communists. Under Nuri Pasha it was a capital offense to be a Communist. Yet, no sooner was the coup over than Communists appeared everywhere. Now that the hated Nuri Pasha was dead, the objects of his special hatred became popular. They were facing the Ba'ath party, representing the Pan-Arab Socialist movement of youth and the intellectuals. They were pro-Nasser and wanted Iraq to join the United Arab Republic. Then there were the National Democrats, a non-Communist left-wing party, and the Kurdish Democrats. Overnight all values in Iraq had changed. What was true yesterday became false today. The term "left wing," an accusation one day, became a badge of honor the following day.

Six months ago there was not one Communist publication for sale in Iraq [wrote the *Christian Science Monitor* on December 30, 1958], just as six months ago no Iraqi newspaper dared print a pro-Communist story. Today by contrast it is literally true that no Iraqi newspaper dares to print a pro-Western story, while virtually every Iraqi paper echoes loudly the Communist line. This does not mean that all Iraqi editors have been hidden Communists who now are able to flaunt their true colors. It means simply that the government tells the people what to print on important subjects and the Communists appear to be in control of the propaganda and censorship fields. . . .

Who were the other new masters of the regime? The "street" may have helped Kassem into power by turning against the royal regime and supporting it with frenzied enthusiasm, but it had to depend on liberal dwellers of the mansions, in the same way that nearly all revolutions in history have done. The first Minister of Finance was a rich businessman from Mosul, the Minister of Justice was a former chief justice of the high court, and other ministries and the Council of the Republic were filled with members of respected and, in many cases, rich families.

A new constitution was framed; the monarchy was abolished and a republic established. It was to be an "association of Arabs and Kurds," the latter the largest minority in Iraq, liberty-loving Muslims, mainly from the highlands, who speak a variant of Persian. Kurds were given important roles in the regime. The emblem of the new republic was a program in itself: the eight-pointed star, symbolizing Arab unity; two crossed swords denoting Arab and Kurdish friendship; an ear of grain, a symbol of economic progress; and the legend "Republic of Iraq," surmounting "July 14th," the day of the revolution.

A new Development Committee was set up, on which there were no Americans and Britishers, and it was to draft new economic plans to raise living standards quickly. On short order the per capita annual national income was to be raised from 42 to 350 dinars (considered utterly unrealistic by foreign experts). A land-reform bill was promulgated under which estates of more than 250 hectares of irrigated and 500 hectares of nonirrigated land were to be expropriated and distributed among the landless and the poor peasants. Families were to get 7.5 to 15 hectares of irrigated and 15 to 30 hectares of unirrigated land. The distribution was to be completed within five years, and compensation to the owners was to be paid over twenty years.* The revolutionary government raised the land tax for the rich. It was decreed that owners must not take more than a half of the sharecroppers' harvest. The estates of leaders of the old regime were confiscated and eight former premiers were among them. Public officials had to report their extra income and property. Feudal titles, such as pasha, were abolished.

Judging by the titles of the new ministries, Iraq was to abandon the regime of *laissez faire* and turn to a measure of government planning or, at least, co-ordination. There were ministries of national planning; housing and public works; irrigation and agriculture; agrarian reform; rural affairs; communications; trade; oil. There was not a word said about the nationalization of Iraq's petroleum. On the contrary, the government expressed the hope that the Iraq Petroleum Company would increase production. There was also set up a ministry for municipal affairs.†

Nasser and Kassem

President Nasser of the United Arab Republic was among the first to salute the "great victory of the people of Iraq under the leadership of their hero Abdel Karim Kassem." Many people of Iraq were under the impression that their country would join the U.A.R. Nasser's pictures were to be seen everywhere in Baghdad and he appeared to be the real victor of the coup. Colonel Aref, one of the principal leaders of the uprising, made no secret of his goal: union with Cairo. An important political leader in Iraq, head of the left-oriented National Democrats, stopped short of union by suggesting that his country and the U.A.R. should be

* The republican government made several startling discoveries about the old regime. Only 125,000 of the population had land. The estate owners paid only one per cent of the government's income in land tax. Sharecroppers surrendered normally about two-thirds of the harvest to the landlords.

† For the first time in the history of Iraq a woman became a cabinet member, Dr. Naziha Duleimi, appointed Minister of Municipal Affairs in July 1959.

federated. The Foreign Minister in the new Iraqi government, Hashim Jawad, however, indicated that the proposed marriage between the two countries was not to take place. "What we are trying to do," he said, "is to utilize the great resources of the country to develop our economy and make Iraq a model in the Arab world, rather than risk the uncertainties of a union with the U.A.R. We are a part of the whole Arab nation but we do not want to be a part of the part."

What had brought about this change?—if a change it was. It may have been the realities of power. Now that he had power, Kassem did not want to become a subordinate of Nasser. The "strong man" on the Nile could huff and puff, could utter dire threats over the radio, could attempt to infiltrate Iraq but could not subdue it with force of arms. The revolutionaries may have had a union in mind but they had to change their minds when they were confronted with the real power situation. Their country was one of the fortunate ones with a veritable treasure trove in its soil. What could they gain by sharing their treasure with Nasser's republic? They had great plans for the rapid advancement of the interests of the Iraqi. In case of a union with the U.A.R. they would give away wealth, and would receive intangibles in return: Arab union, a Greater Arab Fatherland. And if that union were to have a practical meaning, there would have to be an equalization of resources, and eventually a part of the oil royalties would be headed toward Cairo and—who knows?—Egypt's famished masses would be headed toward Baghdad. The new Iraqi leaders did not appear to like either form of this modern exodus.

Then, there may have been more basic reasons to explain this second thought. Conflicts between the land of the Nile and the land of the Tigris and Euphrates have been endemic, an upsurge and an ebb tide. There was much talk of Arab unity but little action. Our Western civilization originated in these river valleys, supplementary sometimes to each other, but mostly in conflict. Alternately, Egypt ruled over Mesopotamia or the Land of the Two Rivers ruled over the Land of One River. This rhythm of "push and pull" continued under the Arabs, too. The Tigris ruled over the Nile, as under Harun al-Rashid in the eighth century, and again it was the Nile that ruled over the Tigris, as under the Fatimites in the eleventh century. The first major attempt at Middle Eastern integration at the expense of the Ottoman Empire was undertaken by Mohammed Ali in the first part of the nineteenth century, and he was the ruler of Egypt. Another major attempt was made about a century later, but this time it was by members of the Hashemite family, from Amman and Baghdad. Then there was the rivalry between Nasser and Nuri.

Another issue may have worked—subconsciously—against the union of Baghdad and Cairo. The majority of the Egyptian Muslims are Sunnis, the majority of the Iraqi Arabs are Shiis. This is not an issue which would cause a vital division but it may have turned out to be a factor in tipping the scales.

A Transition Period

Iraq now faced a problem common to underdeveloped countries in an age of transition. That problem was how to create a new "creative minority," a new "power elite"? Under the old regime a small layer of rich and influential people, the pashas and sheikhs, provided the foundation of the nation. They were gone now and Iraq had no large enough middle class to take their place. The fellahin were too emotional and too little instructed in politics to serve as the new foundation. The "bazaar" was no less emotional and it was apprehensive about abrupt change. There was a vacuum in the political life of the country and various elements attempted to fill it.

There were, first of all, the Communist and crypto-Communist organizations which believed that nothing short of the big house-cleaning could serve the cause of the people. Under the Nuri regime the Iraqi were saturated with hostility toward the Communists and therefore it was the better part of valor for these to appear in camouflage. Front organizations began to proliferate in

172

a large variety of guises: People's Partisans; People's Resistance; Students' League; Peasants' Front; League for the Defense of Women's Rights. A People's Militia was formed, of some 35,000 members. The number of "card-carrying" Communists was not large but their influence was increasing. They knew what they wanted more than the others, and then there was the vacuum to be filled. The country was flooded with Communist literature. *Das Kapital* was juxtaposed with the Koran, both of which advocated justice for the common man. Arms began to flow into Basra from the Soviet bloc. Iraq established diplomatic relations with the Communist countries and entered into cultural and trade agreements with them. By the spring of 1959 Iraq seems to have received close to a quarter of a billion of dollars in Soviet economic credits and military aid.

Efforts continued also to line up Iraq with the U.A.R. Colonel Abdel Salam Mohammed Aref appears to have been a leader of this Middle Eastern *Anschluss* movement. Karem gave him a sinecure as Iraq's Ambassador in Bonn, in the hope that the soothing atmosphere of a West German small town would quench his revolutionary ardor. Instead of going to Bonn, Aref went to Cairo from where he was smuggled back into Iraq three weeks later. He was caught, tried and sentenced to death, which sentence, however, was not carried out. Premier Kassem was now the "sole leader" of the revolution. This was stated authoritatively by Radio Baghdad on May 24, 1959: "The slogan the 'sole leader' corresponds to the facts of the revolution, for he alone planned and directed it. He had no partners. The 'leader' does not covet absolute power. When he sees that the revolution is completed, he will step aside." Political parties, Kassem declared, should suspend their activities during the period of transition.

The foundation of the regime was the military, headed by Kassem. Most of the Communists and crypto-Communists were disgruntled and unemployed intellectuals, the type of people who could not form the base of any rule because they lacked substance and cohesion. This was a stop-gap arrangement until the new regime could find its bearings by gaining more substantial liberal elements to its side, the more articulate part of the urban population. In time the peasants would acquire not merely political awareness but also political skills in the selection of their representatives and in the scrutiny of party programs.

Civil War in Mosul

Meanwhile, however, dissatisfaction flared up along the northern peripheries of the country, away from Baghdad which was still in the grip of a carnival sentiment. Up in the oil country of the north, around Mosul, powerful forces were plotting against the government.

On March 6, 1959, there was a mass gathering of the Communist-controlled peace partisans in Mosul. They were strongly opposed by the commander of the Fifth Brigade, Colonel Abdel Wahab el-Shawwaf, one of the original revolutionary leaders. He turned against the peace partisans, whom he identified with the government. Then he called upon the rest of the army to turn against Kassem. What the colonel's program was, nobody seemed to know, but it was suspected that he considered the new Iraqi regime's policy a betrayal of the Arab cause. He appears to have been pro-Nasser. The call to the army went unheeded. Government air forces quickly descended upon Mosul which they bombed. Colonel Shawwaf himself was wounded in the bombing of his headquarters. Then his own soldiers turned upon him and killed him. This flash revolt, which lasted for a very short time, exacted the lives of some two thousand people.

The post mortem of the revolt showed that its main protagonists represented a motley crew. Some of them were die-hards of the old regime, wealthy merchants, rich sheikhs who were opposed to the land reform decreed by Baghdad, and disgruntled officers. "The wealthy men were behind the plot," according to an eyewitness, a French Roman Catholic priest at a Dominican monastery in the Mosul region, quoted in an Associated Press dispatch on March 17. "They were afraid they would be dispossessed. They were going to lose some of their land because of the agrarian reform law."

The largest single contingent of the revolters, however, was formed by some sixty thousand Shammar tribesmen, ranging over much of northern Iraq, Syria and northwest Saudi Arabia. The paramount chief of the tribe owned hundreds of thousands of acres and the other sheikhs, too, were wealthy owners of land, of warehouses and factory plants.

Taking the side of the government were urban dwellers organized into military units and Kurdish tribesmen from their hill country, who welcomed the chance of chasing away the sheikhs and seizing their land. The Shammar tribesmen faded into the desert but several of them were cut down by pro-Kassem villagers.

The Aftermath of the Revolt

Blame for the revolt was squarely placed on Nasser's shoulders by the Baghdad government. It charged that the adjacent Syrian Region of the U.A.R. had supplied the rebels with agents, money and arms. Angry mobs were roaming Baghdad's streets, shouting pro-Kassem and anti-Nasser slogans. The Iraqi government expelled a dozen members of the U.A.R. diplomatic mission and closed the Egyptian-controlled Middle East News Agency. The Communists led most of the demonstrations. "The Baghdad radio emits a round-the-clock stream of Communist propaganda," reported the last American correspondent out of Baghdad, Larry Collins. A Communist, Loutfi Taher, a former veterinarian, now headed the Iraq government press bureau and seldom did the Baghdad papers print articles not friendly to the Communists. The Communist organ, *Ittihad al Shaab,* of Baghdad, summarized the prevailing attitude:

The only way to preserve Iraq's real independence is through the unity of all those who want to resist the ambitions of the fraudulent champion of Arab nationalism [Nasser], who has resorted to the help

175

of thieves, gangsters and swindlers, plus the agents of the oil companies in Homs, Kirkuk and Mosul.

On the other hand, the Communists extolled Kassem as the "one and only leader," praising his glorious army which had saved the country from the "imperialists and Nasserites."

In return, Nasser turned his torrential eloquence on Kassem. He charged him with sowing dissension among the Arabs and trying to place his land under alien rule. He denounced the Iraqi Communists as the stooges of a foreign power and attributed the Mosul revolt to the reign of Communist terror and persecution.

The war of words now flared up on another front and its implications reached deeply into the international field. Moscow lost no time in reacting to Nasser's attacks on the Iraqi Communists and his innuendos about the Kremlin itself. Prime Minister Khrushchev declared that Nasser conducted his campaign against progressives under the spurious guise of anti-Communism. However, he wanted to leave the door open for reconciliation and added that the "differences in our ideological viewpoints should not impede the friendly relations between our two countries and the joint struggle against imperialism." A few days later again he used a somewhat stronger language: "Nasser is a hotheaded young man . . . using the intemperate language of imperialists."

The Western world was hopeful that Iraq would retain her connection with it under the Baghdad Pact, or "northern tier" defense against the Soviets, uniting Iraq, Iran, Turkey, Pakistan and Great Britain in a mutual assistance arrangement. The United States was a "silent partner," but a very active one. These hopes did not materialize. On March 24, the Baghdad government scrapped the Baghdad Pact. Because of Iraq's withdrawal from the organization the bridgehead of the West to the Arab world was destroyed. "We quit the pact," said Premier Kassem, "in order not to provide members of the organization cause for interference in our domestic affairs." Then he added: "Within three years Iraq will be the most powerful nation in the Middle East."

The West Takes a Hand

The northern tier was breached. Baghdad was no longer in the "Baghdad Pact." In replacement of it the United States signed bilateral pacts with Turkey, Iran and Pakistan. Britain was a full member of the organization. CENTO (Central Treaty Organization) was born in March 1959. The secretariat of the organization moved to Ankara, and a Pakistani career diplomat, M. O. A. Baig, became its new Secretary General. "Iraq's defection," he said, "removed the weakest link in our chain of defense."

Meanwhile, in Washington, contradictory opinions prevailed about conditions in Iraq. The head of the Central Intelligence Agency, Allen W. Dulles, had described the situation in Iraq on April 29, 1958, as the "most dangerous in the world today." President Eisenhower, on the other hand, said a few days later at a press conference in answer to a question about the Nasser-Kassem feud: "We are not trying to promote personal quarrels or personal prestige, as such."

Under the 1954 military assistance agreement between the United States and Iraq, the latter had received a battalion of eight-inch howitzers—the biggest weapons owned by any army in the Middle East; a large amount of motor transport and signal equipment; some World War II United States tanks; some big British Centurion tanks purchased by the United States from Britain; and five Sabre jet fighter planes. The last shipment of United States military aid consisted of four shiploads of transport, ammunition and spare parts which were on order at the time of the Iraqi revolution. An eight-member American military-aid mission had dwindled to one officer, who was also to depart. Still in effect between the United States and Iraq were a technical assistance agreement and a cultural agreement that included American professors teaching at Iraqi colleges. Most of the economic assistance program had withered away since the revolution and the last of the professors were expected to leave. Between one hundred and two hundred Soviet military advisers were believed to be in the country, teaching the Iraqis how to use Soviet equipment.

In the spring of 1959 it became known that the Iraqi government was engaged in negotiations with Great Britain with a view to getting from her substantial supplies of arms, including tanks and jet bombers. It also became known that Britain had canvassed the view of the United States and that Washington gave its approval to this transaction. The situation was puzzling. Iraq had the reputation of moving closer to the Soviet bloc and now, suddenly, she wanted to conclude an arms deal with one of the leading countries in the Western alliance. A few months later, in July, the Iraqi Foreign Ministry sent a note to the American Embassy terminating the military assistance agreement on the ground that it conflicted with the country's policy of positive neutrality.

Why Great Britain, the "archimperialist," and why not all arms from the Soviets? This was a paradoxical situation, indeed, which needed an explanation. As a matter of fact, there were several explanations.

This was the most plausible one: The Soviet Union gave its approval to the arms deal with Britain in order to weaken the United States and to pursue its own balance-of-power policy, pitting one ally against the other. Great Britain wanted to obtain a toehold in Iraq and Washington could not veto this policy.

Then there was another explanation: the *new* balance-of-power policy, practiced by a weak country at the expense of world powers. Kassem may have been shopping for the best bargains, playing the Soviets against the West and vice versa. He could play on the rivalries and jealousies of both sides, and get aid from them both.

There was the other puzzle, too. Was the Soviet Union really friendlier to Kassem than to Nasser? Possibly it could not be friendly to both of them, because of the inter-Arab rivalry. Was not Egypt more important than Iraq, with her incomparably better location, larger population, prestige in the Arab world? It is possible that an Arab Ambassador stationed in Washington was right: "Russia would not have put her eggs in the Iraq basket without having sufficient reason to believe that Nasser, as a popular leader for the Arab masses, is suffering a decline. Moscow always sides with the growing popular forces. . . ." (*The Reporter,* June 25, 1959.)

The Epilogue

On the first anniversary of the Iraqi revolution Premier Kassem promised to restore political life in Iraq and to hold elections within a year. Also he expanded his cabinet in what appeared to be a step away from the nation's Communist organization. The main effect of this change appeared to be the trimming of the powers of Dr. Ibrahim Kubba, who had promoted trade relations with the Soviet bloc in his role of Minister of the Economy. The cabinet did not include any Communists and General Kassem was acting in disregard of the Iraqi party's demand for portfolios as a part of a National Union Front.

There was a lull also in the contest of vituperation between the Cairo and Baghdad radios. In his speech on the first anniversary of the revolution Kassem called for "forgiveness" of Arab countries that had offended Iraq—meaning the U.A.R.—and called for solidarity with non-Arab Muslim countries. Still, the question remained to be answered: what was to be Iraq's place in the Arab world? Would it be possible to establish a *modus vivendi* with Egypt?

Would-be assassins shot and wounded General Hassem on October 7, 1959. After his recovery the adulation of Baghdad crowds seemed to have no bounds, and the streets were filled with joyous shouts: "Long live our leader!"

The dormant political parties were allowed to resume activity early in 1960. However, parties had to be licensed by the Interior Minister and were forbidden to be run on military lines. At the same time it was announced that the Soviet Union would assist in setting up ten large centers for the training of more than four thousand experts in such varied fields as telecommunication, electricity, machinery and oil.

The decade of the fifties ended for Iraq with a quarrel with neighboring Iran about a five kilometer stretch of waterlogged country along the Shatt-al-Arab river before it enters the Persian Gulf. No issue could have been more trivial and yet it is sometimes such trifles that cause perilous international incidents.

CHAPTER 4

Lebanon—The Crescent and the Cross

Churches in the Mountains

LEBANON is different from all other countries in the Middle East. It is Arab, but in a very special way. What makes an Arab? History, literature, a way of life, common heritage, common expectation of a future, a *mystique*. About half of the people of Lebanon—and the more influential half—are Christians, whose history, literature, way of life, heritage, expectation of the future and *mystique* are different from those of the other half and from those of all the other Arabs. The history of the Arabs takes pride in the tremendous campaign of conquests which extended the Muslim rule from the Pyrenees to the Bay of Bengal. Arab literature centers around the Prophet, the caliphates, victory over the Christians and—above all—the Koran. In much of this literature the Christians are the villains, their Muslim antagonists the heroes. The Arab way of life, too, is derived from conditions different from those under which the Lebanese live—from the desert, religious dedication and exclusiveness, a sense of superiority. And the expectation of the future? A sense of unity, more in theory than in reality, a kind of Messianic expectation in a nebulous future. Can the Christian Arabs of the Lebanon really share this expectation when all the sons and daughters of Ishmael are gathered together? And finally the *mystique*—the composite of

181

all this and some more, a quasi-religious feeling of being the recipients of a special dispensation—being a nation by the grace of God. Can the Christian Lebanese share this feeling?

Lebanon is the most mountainous part of the Arab world. One thinks of the latter as a desert, the sun beating down on helpless man, and furnace heat. But Lebanon is verdant mountain slopes, crystal-clear air, attractive farms of bottomland, the snow of the tall peaks and people swimming in the Mediterranean in the shadow of those peaks. Lebanon, in part at least, is also the land of churches—more like southern Tyrol than Arabia.

The mountains explain Lebanon's uniqueness in the heart of the Arab world. They are natural sanctuaries for dissidents and refugees from religious persecution. The dissidents were sectaries from the religious persecution of the zealots of the Byzantine Church, then the Christian enthusiasts escaping the Muslims, then the heretics of Islam, and the surviving Crusaders.

Lebanon is different also for other reasons. In an ocean of illiteracy, she is a literate country, where about two-thirds of the people can read and write. She has the highest per capita income in the Arab world, close to the eastern European standards— about $330 per person a year.* Lebanon is a highly important trading area and her capital, Beirut, is the most active harbor on the coast of the Levant.

The Lebanese Paradox

Lebanon is one of those cases of which the record says one thing and the human heart says something else. Cases like this are the historian's despair. One can quote the record but not the human heart. Yet a literal quotation would produce a total distortion.

The record shows that Lebanon was the part of the Ottoman Empire where the Arabs first awakened to the realization of their

---

* The oil-rich sheikhdoms have, theoretically, a higher per capita income, as for instance Kuwait.

national uniqueness. It was there that their modern sense of nationalism developed, that they first discovered the difference between the atavistic and modern interpretations of the church and state. For centuries Islam was the ideology—both religious and secular—of the Arabs as well as of their masters, the Turks. The religion was the state, and the state was sanctified by the religion. This fusion of creed and secular devotion ended under the impact of modern ideas which established the state as the supreme practical guide to men, and relegated the church to theory.

The Arab concept of the modern state and of the mission of the Arabs evolved in the shadow of some of the great Western schools at the foot of the mountains—the American University of Beirut, and the Université de Saint Joseph. There the modern concept of Arab unity was conceived. The Christians of Lebanon pay lip service to Arab unity and yet they are afraid of it. This fear is locked in their hearts, and is not a matter of record. Yet, ignoring it would be to ignore the most important factor in contemporary Lebanese life. The Christians of Lebanon, too, profess belief in Arab unity, because it is "in the air," the guiding idea, but in their hearts they fear it because their Arabism had developed along lines different from those of their non-Christian co-nationals. Also, because they remember history and the grievous losses their fathers suffered at the hands of their non-Christian neighbors. They are apprehensive that they would be completely submerged in a vast Arab sea which would not tolerate their nonconformity.

Lebanon's "Contemporary" History

Lebanon is the country where "contemporary" history began four thousand years ago. A schoolboy in Lebanon, as Philip K. Hitti pointed out, must be able to identify such names as Thutmose III, Sargon II, Darius, Pompey, Timur, Baldwin Khalin ibn-al-Walid, Abd-al-Hamid II, Napoleon, King Faisal—all of whom have affected his life. He is an Arab who is prouder of his "Phoenician ancestors" than of the Muslim conquerors who gave him his language. "Lebanon is one of those lands that could be described as microscopic in size but macroscopic in influence." *

The name of the country is a Semitic word and Lebanon means "white as milk," referring to the snowy peaks. The Lebanese often refer to themselves as "mountain people."

The recent history of this region was that of the Ottoman Empire, master of these parts for centuries. The Ottomans ruled over a conglomerate of ethnic groups, many of which were not Muslims. Since the secular and religious government formed one indissoluble unit, the treatment of the non-Muslims had to be different. They formed separate units called *millets* and lived under the direct control of their religious heads.†

The Christians of the Lebanon, too, lived under their religio-secular heads. They were, as a rule, better off than their neighbors, the Muslims and followers of the esoteric sect of the Druses, whose creed is a mixture of Islam and other beliefs. This aroused jealousy and greed. In mid-nineteenth century Lebanon was wading in blood. Tens of thousands of Christians were slaughtered, scores of villages and towns were laid in ashes. By now the Ottoman Empire was so decrepit that it lived under Western tutelage. Among the Western Great Powers France claimed precedence on the coast of the Levant because of her dominant role in the Crusades and because French was the *lingua franca* of the elite. A French force of some seven thousand was dispatched to restore order in Lebanon. This strengthened France's claim to the region. Thousands of Lebanese Christians fled their mountains to find sanctuary in less enchanting but safer countries, particularly in the larger cities of the Western Hemisphere.

After the First World War, Syria, which included Lebanon,

* Philip K. Hitti, *Lebanon in History*. London: Macmillan, 1957, pp. 4-5.
† The Ottoman attitude in this respect was well expressed by *millet* which in Turkish means both religion and nation. There was no difference between the two.

184

became a French mandate. Subsequently detached from Syria, Lebanon did not have a happy life under French mandatory rule. On August 29, 1943, Lebanon declared her independence, supported by the United States and Great Britain. At first it was only a nominal independence, still under French control, but three years later it became real. She became one of the founding members of the Arab League in the work of which Beirut took an active part. Lebanon followed the Arab League "line" on most major issues. However, her opposition to Israel has been less violent than that of most of the other Arab states, and Jews not only were not molested but also retained full civic rights. Lebanon sided with Egypt over the Suez Canal issue and with Syria over her quarrel with Turkey. She was the only Arab country to hail the abortive Eisenhower Doctrine but did not follow Iraq in signing the Baghdad Pact of mutual defense, in spite of the fact that Lebanon was more Western-oriented than any other Arab country. Dr. Charles Malik, her foreign minister and UN delegate for long periods of time, was known as a staunch friend of the West.

The "National Covenant"

The Lebanese leaders agreed among themselves that the country had a Christian majority. This has not been confirmed by a census. On the contrary, it is to be assumed that this is no longer the case, as the Muslims in the country have a higher birth rate than the Christians. However, in the interest of communal amity it was decided not to take a census.

It was found convenient to define Lebanon's "personality" in view of her special problem—an Arab country with a presumed Christian majority. This was done in the "National Covenant" of 1943, which may be compared to the "Mayflower Compact." The two signatories of this pact were a Muslim and a Christian. The Muslim signatory was Riyadh es-Solh, who was to play a distinguished role in the history of his country as a premier, and Bechara el-Khuri, a Christian of the Maronite denomination (who

185

are in communion with Rome but employ Syriac liturgy). Bechara el-Khuri served his country as its President. The National Covenant described Lebanon as an Arab country which was never to seek aid from non-Arab nations, to the detriment of her Arab sister states. On the other hand, the Muslims of Lebanon were never to seek the dissolution of their country in a "larger unit." There were many Muslims who would have liked to see Lebanon join Syria, which would have resulted in the Christians' being swamped by Islam. The Covenant was to prevent this.

Communal strife between Christians and Muslims could have assumed a serious aspect if it had not been for the common-sense approach of the Lebanese. They agreed among themselves in a gentlemen's agreement to apportion the main public offices among the delegates of the larger creeds. It was decided that the President of the Republic—who is a real power—should be a Christian of the Maronite creed, the Premier a Sunni (orthodox) Muslim, the speaker of the Chamber of Deputies a Shii (minority sect), the Foreign Minister a Greek Orthodox, and the Minister of Defense a Druse.

Likewise, seats in the Chamber of Deputies were to be apportioned according to the presumed numerical strength of the various creeds: so many Maronites, Sunnis, Shiis, Druses, Armenians, Greek Orthodox, Greek Catholics, and even Protestants and Jews. This apportionment was based upon a constitutional law and not a gentlemen's agreement.

This system worked reasonably well, although communalism was not wholly absent. Christian extremists banded together in the Maronite Falangist Party, which stressed purely Lebanese patriotism and wanted to have no truck with Pan-Arabia. On the other hand, extremist Muslims formed a para-military organization to promote this very Pan-Arabia and which significantly called itself *najjada*—the helping hand.

Different though Lebanon was from the rest of the Arab world, there were also similarities. Real power there, too, was concentrated in the hands of semifeudal dynasties which dominated the political parties. The Arab word for feudal loyalties is *mahsubbiyya*—favoritism, and it indicates a patron-client relationship. Some of the great Christian families dominated the mountainous north—the local dynasties of the Farangieh, Karam, Duweihi, Shehab; while in some of the coastal regions, around Tarabulus (Tripoli) and Sur (Tyre) it was the Muslim families of Al-Khalil, Az Zayn, Usayran, the Al-'Ali and Al-'Uthman who reigned. In other parts of the mountains there were the great Druse semifeudal dynasties, a prominent member of which was Kamal Jumblatt, a Socialist and founder of the Progressive Socialist Party, and Majid Arslan, an anti-Socialist and leader of the Yazbaki Druses. Communal differences did count in these family feuds. "The confessional balance between Lebanese Christians and Muslims, far from being the result of genuine tolerance, was maintained at best by mutual fear." *

The Boiling Cauldron

The emergence of Nasser in Egypt accelerated the pulse of many Lebanese Muslims. To them he was the embodiment of the Arab national ideal, the realization of a collective dream. The Suez crisis encouraged these Lebanese Nasserites to speak with a louder voice, capitalizing on the general upsurge of sympathy for Cairo. The Arab world denounced Britain and France as aggressors but Beirut maintained diplomatic relations with them. After the crisis was over, the Eisenhower Doctrine was adopted—rejected by most Arab lands but unconditionally accepted by the government in Beirut. Arab governments considered this a flagrant violation of the "National Covenant."

Probably under the influence of France, Lebanon had adopted the parliamentary form of government. However, elections were largely formalities at which the retinues of the land barons were

* "The Lebanese Crisis in Perspective," *The World Today,* Sept. 1958, Vol. 14, No. 9.

elected. The President of the country, as we have seen, had to be a Maronite Christian. According to the constitution, he was elected for a single six-year term by the Chamber of Deputies. Such an election took place in 1952 and the choice fell on Camille Chamoun, a former Minister of Interior, ex-lawyer, journalist, rich landowner, a member of the Lebanese oligarchy.

As a result of the propaganda of Nasser and the Suez crisis a strong anti-Western sentiment developed in Lebanon, even among rich landowners. While there was no communal dividing line between the sects, a large proportion of the anti-Westerners was Muslim. Parliamentary elections took place in 1957 and they were rigged, as usual. This time the pro-Westerners had the upper hand under the leadership of President Chamoun. As a result many prominent politicians, some of them representatives of leading interests, lost their seats. The Prime Minister was Sami es-Solh, who, according to the gentlemen's agreement, was a Sunni Muslim. In his younger days he had the reputation of being a rabble-rouser, and he had served in several previous cabinets. The Minister of Foreign Affairs was Charles Malik, former professor of philosophy at the American University of Beirut, previously on the teaching staff of Harvard University, recipient of numerous American doctorates and of the medal of Holy Sepulchre from the Greek Orthodox Patriarch in Alexandria, a crusader for the Western cause and free enterprise, *persona gratissima* in the State Department in Washington, "more American than Arab," according to his opponents.

As the time for a new presidential election approached, rumor spread in Lebanon that the governing party was about to amend the constitution through a coup making it possible for President Chamoun to be elected for a second term. Neither the President nor his entourage denied or contradicted this assumption. There was a great deal of excitement in the bazaars, especially in those of the northern city of Tripoli where the Muslims are preponderant and where they have never made a secret of their desire to belong to the neighboring Syria.

The Powder Box and the Match

It was in the midst of this excitement that a journalist, Nasib Matni, on the staff of the Beirut newspaper *Telegraph,* was murdered in a Beirut street. This happened on May 8, 1958. The newspaper supported the anti-Chamoun opposition. The murderer was never found and the opposition claimed that the government itself was responsible for the crime which it called an *accident d'état.*

The opposition called a nation-wide strike and as tension mounted, firing began in the crowded Basta quarter of Beirut and in the bazaars of Tripoli. The government radio denounced the opposition as slaves of foreign influences, enemies of the nation. It was feared that now that adjacent Syria had become a part of the United Arab Republic, Nasser wanted to round it out by adding Lebanon to it. The opposition retorted that the government was not only in the service of foreign powers but was also utterly corrupt, unrepresentative and unconcerned with the problems of the people.

The strident radio voices of the U.A.R. now took Lebanon under a cross fire, from Cairo, on one side, and Damascus on the other. These voices denounced the Lebanese "ruling clique" as beholden to alien powers, treasonable and pursuing policies contrary to the interests of the common Arab cause. What started out to be a mere domestic squabble degenerated into an international conflict.

The government was supported mainly by influential Christians, but there were numerous exceptions. The highest dignitary of the Maronite Church, Patriarch Paul Meouchi, sided with the opposition, which was mainly Muslim and Druse. On the other hand, the Prime Minister, Sami es-Solh, was a Muslim.

The rebellion broke out in April. In Beirut it was led by a former Prime Minister, Saeb Salam, a wealthy man, whose fortress-like mansion in the capital's Basta quarter was a revolutionary center. The leader of the revolution in Tripoli was another

189

former Premier, Rashid Karameh. Other revolutionary leaders were Abdullah Yaffi, several times Premier and holder of a doctor of philosophy degree, and Charles Helou, former Ambassador to Italy. Most picturesque of the opposition leaders was Kamal Jumblatt, whose name has already been mentioned. His castle of Moukhtara in the midst of his large domain was another revolutionary center. This feudal lord opposed President Chamoun on the ground that the government's "feudalistic capitalism" ignored the needs of the poor.

Basically there were two issues involved in this uprising. One of them was the question of Arabism. Many Muslims in Lebanon saw no justification for the separate identity of their country, which they considered an artifice created by the former French mandatory power for its own administrative convenience and not for the benefit of the people. Then let Lebanon join Syria, they said; and thus join the United Arab Republic which appeared to them the cornerstone of a United Arabia, the goal of their aspirations. The other issue was economic. Lebanon, in the opinion of the opposition, failed to keep step with the times. She continued to pursue an antiquated policy of feudalism and early capitalism. Everywhere else, as they saw it, there were attempts to eliminate the vast span between wealth and poverty, to execute land reforms, introduce higher standards.

The forces of the government were led by the commander of the army, Fuad Shehab, a Maronite Christian. In this strange civil war—*drôle de guerre*—the army left the shooting to the opposing sides, trying to avoid bloodshed. The commander tried to take a sensible stand. The majority of his soldiers were Christian, the majority of the opposition were Muslim. Should the Christian soldiers start to shoot at the Muslim rebels a serious communal problem might arise and this he was determined to avoid. Also, General Shehab qualified as the President of the country. Nearly everywhere else in the Arab world soldiers had the power. Also, he was a Maronite. President Chamoun now ordered General Shehab to take more energetic action. Thereupon the general agreed to contain the insurrection but he was not ready to crush it and stated his reservations openly. It was not the army's task, he said, to take sides in a "political brawl." He intimated, more than stated explicitly, that since his army consisted of Christians and Muslims it might fall apart if ordered into action.

Yet, the ostensible issue in this civil war was not a major one. The opposition wanted the President to resign, but his term of office was to expire in a few months anyway, and according to the constitution, he could not be re-elected. By this time, however, the Lebanese *drôle de guerre* had become an international issue.

"Much Ado About Nothing"

The U.A.R. radio continued its incendiary talk. The Beirut government leveled specific charges against the government in Cairo, charging it with "massive, unprovoked and illegal intervention." It alleged that some three thousand men armed by Nasser had infiltrated into Lebanon to back up the rebels. First Beirut took its case to the Council of the Arab League, which, however, could reach no agreement. Thereupon, it took its case to the Security Council of the UN, which acted quickly. Its first task appeared to be to establish the facts. A team of 139 observers, mostly trained military personnel, was promptly flown into the area. The team could keep watch only on the part of the frontier between the Syrian Region and Lebanon which was open to it. After several days of study the UN body presented its report on July 4. It stated that the large majority of the opposition forces under arms consisted of native Lebanese. "It has not been possible to establish where the arms [of the rebels] were acquired. Nor was it possible to establish if any of the armed men had infiltrated from the outside."

The Lebanese government protested that the report of the team was based on insufficient evidence obtained along a limited sector of the border during an inadequate time period. The team had neither the authority nor the strength to restrain the combatants. The revolt kept on flaring up in urban centers and in the mountainous regions. Many streets in the capital were turned into miniature battlefields but this was a "limited revolution" in which both sides gave evidence of their desire not to hurt the other side too much.

The revolution could no doubt have been liquidated if President Chamoun had resigned, but this he did not do. United States diplomacy entered the fray and the American Ambassador in Beirut issued public statements upholding Chamoun. The perfunctory fighting continued. It was a hot summer and both sides took long siestas.

The Iraqi Intermezzo

At this point, the revolution in Lebanon meshed into events in Iraq, a sister Arab country. It will be recalled that on July 14 flash riots swept the streets of Baghdad, army units seized power, the monarchy was brought down and the republic was established. This was preceded by the usual incendiary radio voices from Cairo and Damascus, attacking Iraq's "perennial Premier," Nuri es-Said Pasha, as the straw man of the "imperialists" and a traitor to the Arabs' cause. It was assumed that the downfall of the Nuri regime in Iraq would be followed by an attempt on the part of Nasserites to seize power in Baghdad, and thereby add the third unit to the United Arab Republic. Nasser's having Iraq, besides Egypt and Syria in his hands, the situation of Lebanon would have been untenable. That thoroughly Western-oriented country would be lost to the West and the entire Middle Eastern heartland would have fallen into the hands of the man who was on the best terms with the Soviets.

The "Eisenhower Doctrine" in Action

The Lebanese government now appealed to the United States for military aid on the ground that the integrity and independence of the country were being threatened by foreign intervention. President Eisenhower transmitted a message to Congress informing it that he had ordered United States marines into Lebanon at the request of President Chamoun. He quoted the Lebanese President's warning that his country would be unable to survive in the face of the rebellion supported by the U.A.R. unless it received American assistance quickly. The American President announced that the marines were being landed on the beaches of Lebanon to "assist the government in the preservation of the country's territorial integrity and independence which have been deemed vital to the United States' national interest and world peace." The President said further that "the Soviet Union and the U.A.R. sought to overthrow the legally constituted government of Lebanon and to install by violence a government which would subordinate the independence of Lebanon to . . . the United Arab Republic."

Meanwhile, however, the revolution in Iraq had been so completely successful that it was over almost as soon as it got started. The King was dead and Nuri Pasha was killed by street mobs. The regime of General Kassem was established. Troops were flown by the British to the neighboring Jordan, where the throne of the young King appeared to be tottering. By that time American troops were in Lebanon and it would have been less costly to dispatch some of their contingents to the Jordan capital, Amman. However, Great Britain considered Jordan to be within her sphere of influence.

The order to carry the American troops to the Lebanese shores was given to the Sixth Fleet of the United States under command of Vice-Admiral C. R. Brown. The first line of attack against the Lebanese shores consisted of two carriers, 42 lesser ships and 130 aircraft.

Eleven hours after orders had been issued the first 1,800 marines stormed ashore in St. George's Bay of Beirut in full battle formation, under the air protection of the Composite Air Strike Force with 150 combat and support planes, with all its maintenance crews and auxiliary equipment. The sudden descent of so large a force created a bottleneck so that the full strength of American armed might could be displayed only several days after the landing in mid-July—a total of 14,000 army and marine troops. More forces kept on crowding into the Beirut beachhead, 80 transoceanic transports of the Tactical Air Command; 50 transoceanic aircraft of the Military Air Transport Service and additional planes of the Civil Reserve Air Fleet, acquired from commercial lines. The combat aircraft used in Lebanon was designed primarily to deliver nuclear weapons ("nukes"). Military commentators of European newspapers pointed out that it would have been difficult to use such weapons in a crowded Oriental city with no definite military targets. Nor were the stringent security precautions of the advancing troops needed. There was no resistance to the troops and the only obstacles they encountered on the beaches were the attractive and pleased young women in bikini suits.

In the meantime, President Chamoun had denied any intention of wishing to run for a second term. Had he made such a declaration earlier there would have been no civil war in Lebanon, no landing of the American troops, and perhaps not even a revolution in Iraq. The revolution in Iraq was not followed by the extension of the sway of Nasser. Indeed, the President of the U.A.R. denied emphatically that he ever contemplated a union with Iraq. This is what Nasser wrote a year after the Iraqi revolution:

. . . I at once sent word to Abdul Karim Kassem, the Iraqi revolutionary leader, that the U.A.R. was not seeking union. I advised him that his first job was to unite his country so that it could face the threats that would come from outside—from the British and Americans then in Jordan and Lebanon. In fact, I do not believe I would have accepted union even if Iraq had sought it. I thought that any such action at that time would invite intervention, especially by the British. Therefore, when an Iraqi delegation came to me four days after the revolution, I suggested that our military agreement, plus economic and cultural agreements, should be the sole basis of solidarity between our countries.*

The tension in Lebanon gradually ceased, not before, however, the Soviet Union had again appeared on the stage as the protector of the Arabs. There appeared to be some danger for a time that the Russians would follow the example of the United States of flowing their troops into the Middle East, to "safeguard peace" at the "invitation" of their Arab friends. This, however, they did not do. Instead, they presented a draft resolution to the Security Council of the UN to call upon the United States and Great Britain to remove their troops from Lebanon and Jordan. Only the Soviets voted for the draft resolution. Diplomatic maneuvers continued.

President Eisenhower broadcast a message to the American troops in Lebanon telling them that they were there as friends to help the Lebanese people remain free and that they would be withdrawn as soon as Lebanon's integrity and independence were assured. At the same time, he commissioned Deputy Under Secretary of State Robert Murphy to visit the Middle East as his special representative. Murphy conferred with both sides in Lebanon, seeking an agreement on a compromise candidate.

The End of the Strife

It was agreed to hold elections without delay. The Chamber of Deputies met on July 31 and elected the President by a vote of 48 to 7—only a minority of the members participating. The majority of the votes were cast for the revolutionary war's "donothing" General Fuad Shehab. In accordance with the gentlemen's agreement, he was a Maronite Christian. Also, he was a descendant of one of the country's large landowning families. The United States welcomed the election as a step toward restor-

---

* Gamal Abdel Nasser, "Where I Stand and Why," *Life,* July 20, 1959, Vol. 47, No. 3, p. 102.

ing stability and making possible the withdrawal of the American troops.

The civil war in Lebanon now had to be liquidated and this time it was the General Assembly of the United Nations which served as the sounding board. One after another the Arab members spoke and all ten of them submitted a draft proposal giving assurance that they would scrupulously observe Article 8 of the Pact of the League of Arab States and agreeing to respect the governmental systems of all other Arab states, and to abstain from any action calculated to change the established system of government. They called upon the Secretary General to make such practical arrangements as the governments concerned would accept and thereby facilitate the early withdrawal of foreign troops.

The question now remained: who would become the Premier of the newly constituted ministry? He had to be a Sunni Muslim, in accordance with the agreement. Finally, on September 24, the choice fell on Rashid Karameh, a former Prime Minister and leader of the revolt in Tripoli during the recent civil strike. This was, then, a victory for the revolutionaries. However, Karameh was far from being an extremist. The liquidation of the recent strife followed quickly. The government of Karameh negotiated the withdrawal of the American Sixth Fleet. The new government also withdrew Lebanon's charge against Nasser for "breach of peace."

The intervention of the American Sixth Fleet and the landing of United States troops in Lebanon had some paradoxical results. Lebanon now joined the other Arab countries in repudiating the Eisenhower Doctrine which she had accepted. She signed agreements tripling her trade with the Soviets. At the same time, she accepted $10 million from the United States "without strings." Lebanon, too, was beginning to operate the "new balance of power," a small nation playing off one Great Power against the other.

At a meeting on the Syrian Lebanese frontier in the spring of

196

1959, Presidents Nasser and Shehab agreed on Lebanon's neutrality. Another paradox developed when former President Chamoun, who had called in the American troops to protect his country against the pro-Communist neighbors, now endorsed the even more pro-Communist Premier Kassem of Iraq. He did so probably not because he liked the Baghdad strong man but because he disliked the Cairo strong man, who was feuding with Kassem.

The People's Livelihood

Inter arma silent musœ, and perhaps nowhere in the contemporary world is it truer than east of Suez that the Muses fall silent in the midst of the clash of arms. The student of contemporary affairs would like to spend far more time on the discussion of what these poor Middle Eastern countries are doing to raise the living standards of their people. Unfortunately, an inordinately large part of the time of these governments is spent on peripheral issues, quarreling among themselves, striking martial attitudes, wasting the country's substance on arms. Because of her high mountains, Lebanon's sector of the Fertile Crescent has adequate precipitation in several spots. In other places more water could be used. Lebanon is the only Arab country most of which is cultivable. Three-fourths of such area was under cultivation. The government established a Planning and Development Ministry which mapped out a Five Year Development project, most important feature of which was the Litani River scheme, to cost $114 million, to develop both power and irrigation. The Litani rises in the Anti-Lebanon range, in the eastern section of the country, flows down the Bekaa valley, between two ranges, and flows into the Mediterranean north of Tyre. For 115 miles the stream is within the boundaries of Lebanon. Even after the maximum possible use of the water of the river for Lebanon's own purposes, a substantial quantity will still flow unused into the Mediterranean. This unneeded portion could easily be diverted to Jordan, Syria, and Israel, each of which needs all the water it

197

can get. For the realization of this and other related water projects the government of the United States had offered $200 million. Up to now, however, nothing has been done to share the Litani's water. Again, as in so many other cases, politics seems to have been given the precedence over economics.

As we look at the contemporary Lebanese scene, the problem of the country seems to be how to safeguard its unique qualities in the contemporary Arab world. Lebanon is a bridge between East and West, with higher standards than her Arab neighbors. It would be a pity to see those standards falling victims to a leveling down process.

CHAPTER 5

Jordan—A River and a Legion

Diplomacy Creates a State

IT was over brandy and cigars that the sovereign nation of Transjordan, today's Hashemite Kingdom of the Jordan, was created.* The West, as H. G. Wells had said, forced Oriental people who had never heard of nationalism, to take it "as they took the cigarettes and the bowler hats of the West." The Emirate of Transjordan had neither a history nor a *raison d'être* when it was created by the British after the First World War. It was created as a convenience, to discharge a social obligation. It has no more *raison d'être* now than it ever had and it is being maintained as a convenience in order not to tilt the balance of power.

During the First World War the British obtained the help of influential Arab circles to fight the Ottoman Empire with which they were at war. Most notable of these Arabs was the Sharif of Mecca, Hussein ibn-Ali who expected to rule over the Middle Eastern Arab world after victory. However, he was not strong enough to resist Ibn Saud, ruler of the Nejd, later of Saudi Arabia, who ousted him. It was for the convenience of one of his sons, Abdullah, that Transjordan was created. Possibly it was created also for diplomatic convenience, as a counterbalance to French influence in adjacent Syria. Or there may have been other

* *The Times*, London, April 27, 1957.

reasons. The will of the people was not one of them. There were some 300,000 of them, and many of them were nomads. "Most of Trans-Jordan is usable only for pasturing the sheep, goats and camels of the Bedouin tribes who in the heat of midsummer migrate to Wadi Sirhan (Saudi Arabia) or to the edge of the cultivated lands, where water is obtainable." * The capital of the little country, Amman, had an estimated population of 25,000.

The ruler of the country thus created had no government, no army, no money, nor any other attribute of the modern state. He was truly a career man, a self-made King, who created a government, an army, a treasury, a nation, with British help.

Even though the British proclaimed Transjordan an independent country in 1923, she remained under their tutelage. A few years later they authorized Emir Abdullah to appoint consuls (but not diplomatic representatives) to other Arab lands. Then, on the eve of the Second World War they agreed to have the Emir appoint a cabinet, responsible to him, filled mainly with Transjordanians who, however, were advised by the British. The country subsisted on very meager income, supplemented by grants-in-aid. Full independence was achieved in 1946 when the Emir was authorized to assume the title of King.

The British created the Arab Legion in the interbellum period. Its first commander was Captain F. G. Peake, leader of the Camel Corps during the First World War desert campaign. He was one of those British expatriates who loved simple people unsullied by competitive greed, and held that people in the desert lands were far more human because they were in the presence of nature's overwhelming might. Among the virtues he found in the desert were frankness and loyalty. While he idealized the character-building faculties of the great open spaces he did elicit those virtues.

The Legion's command was later assumed by a man who became far better known to the outside world, Brigadier John Bagot

* "Trans-Jordan," *Encyclopaedia Britannica*, 1948, Vol. 22, p. 410.

Glubb, known as Glubb Pasha. In the course of years, he became a legend. He was a dedicated soldier, devoted friend of Jordan, admirer of King Abdullah, blunt to the point of rudeness, an excellent organizer. There was nothing spectacular about him. Glubb was matter-of-fact, endowed with that undefinable something which may be called leadership magnetism. People liked him because he liked them; he spoke their language, even Bedouin dialects. And that was different from the attitude of many officers in other Arab armies, speaking a language that, even though Arabic, the common soldiers did not grasp.

The Arab Legion was at first mainly a police force but under the stress of war conditions became a full-fledged army, with armored cars, artillery, all services. In 1942 it had only 47 officers and 1,577 men. Jordan at that time also had a frontier force of 700 men. At its peak it was 23,000 men strong, further reinforced by a National Guard. The Bedouins called the soldiers of the Arab Legion "Glubb's Girls" because of their accouterment: white cotton robe, plaited hair falling to their shoulders, red and white checkered headdress. During the war they turned to short hair and khaki.

Jordan and the Arab Lands

Abdullah was an ambitious, shrewd, realistic politician. T. E. Lawrence, leader in the First World War desert warfare in Arabia, wrote that the Arabs thought Abdullah a far-seeing statesman and an astute politician. "Astute he certainly was but not greatly enough to convince us always of his sincerity." His object was the winning of Arab independence and the building up of Arab nations, but he meant to keep the direction of the new states in the family.

Although he never admitted it in public, Abdullah realized the anomalous position of his unnatural little country and so he envisaged the creation of integrated Arab countries in the Middle Eastern hub. He was the author of Fertile Crescent schemes to include Jordan, Iraq, Syria, possibly Lebanon, too. Naturally, he wanted to be the head of the new state. However, he ran into the jealousy of neighbors to east and west, Saudi Arabia and Egypt particularly, with much larger territories and populations—not artificial little "desert monsters." He was disliked by his Arab neighbors also because he worked with the British, the "arch-imperialists."

Abdullah's country was next-door neighbor to Palestine, which was to be a "Jewish homeland" under the British government's wartime Balfour Declaration. Other Arab countries entertained contemptuous views about the Jews. Not so Abdullah, who followed a policy of moderation. His British advisers may have had a hand in that policy. Naturally, they did not want the Middle East to erupt in flames. Jordan was a member of the Arab League but Abdullah was so distrusted by its more important members that he was not admitted into their inner councils.

This is not the place to tell the story of the war in Palestine and the establishment of the state of Israel. However, we have now the testimony of Glubb Pasha about the role the Arab Legion and King Abdullah played at that time.

When the British decided to wash their hands of Palestine and withdraw from it in May 1948, the question arose: What were the Arab countries going to do about it? The Arabs, with the exception of King Abdullah, according to Glubb Pasha, had been deluded by their own enthusiasm. Fond of studying and retailing in public the story of the great Arab conquests thirteen centuries before, they believed themselves a great military people and regarded the Jews as mere shopkeepers. Out of touch with the situation in Palestine and too inexperienced to find out the facts, the Egyptians, Syrians and Iraqis assumed that it would be easy for them to crush the Jews. The Arabs in Palestine, in turn, were unfamiliar with the Arab governments and they assumed that the Egyptians, Syrians and Iraqis would be strong. "The Arab governments did immense harm to the cause of the Palestinian Arabs

202

because they encouraged them to be defiant, and when it came to violence, they failed." *

In Glubb Pasha's view the Arab governments were largely responsible for the Palestinian Arabs' ruin because they had rendered them intransigent by raising their hopes. The Arabs would have fared far better if they had restrained the Palestinians and used their influence at the United Nations to secure a modification of the plan to divide Palestine into Arab and Jewish sections.

The Arab armies were defeated by the Israeli, except for the Arab Legion, their only effective force in the Palestinian War. It held on to the central section of the front, including the walled-in old city of Jerusalem, until truce was signed in the summer of 1948. King Abdullah realized that after the arbitrament of arms the only possible step was to explore the possibilities of peace. The Arab countries could not afford to live on a war footing and to maintain expensive armed forces. They needed peace in order to be able to raise their people's living standards. The war in Palestine had revealed the weakness and backwardness of the Arab nations.

Anxious to help the people of his country as well as those of the other Arab nations, he wrote to several influential Israelis with the idea of exploring the chances of peace and entrusted the letters to a young confidant, Lt. Col. Abdullah al Tell, whom he had promoted over the heads of senior officers. Tell promptly defected from Jordan, turned up in Cairo with the letters and told the Arab world about them. In the capitals of the Arab countries the King of Jordan was a traitor.

The only Palestinian territory (except the small Gaza Strip) which the Arabs succeeded in keeping out of the hands of Israel's victorious army was a 2,165-square-mile section to the west of Jordan. It was thus that the former Transjordan became the Hashemite Kingdom of the Jordan. The country now consisted of two unequal parts, the old Transjordan known as the East

* Sir John Bagot Glubb, *A Soldier with the Arabs,* New York: Harper, 1957, p. 79.

Bank, and a part of former Palestine, the West Bank. Half a million Arabs lived on the West Bank and many others came from the rest of Palestine. In a few years Jordan had a population of some 1,400,000, and her capital, Amman, grew from a small town to a metropolitan center of a quarter of a million. The former Palestinians became Jordanian citizens. In the other Arab countries the refugees were not assimilated to the others on the ground that admitting them to citizenship would be a recognition of the state of Israel. Abdullah's action in giving the Palestinians the citizenship of Jordan was also chalked up against him by the other Arab rulers as an act of "treason." The existing situation was taken into account in other ways, too. Ministerial posts were now divided on a parity basis between the East and West Banks.

A Royal Tragedy

The defeated Arab governments now began to take stock of their plight. One of their chief advisers was the former Mufti of Jerusalem, Hajj Amin al-Husseini, a bitter enemy of the Jews. During the Second World War he worked with the Axis powers against the Allies. Now he was back in Cairo, speaking for the Arabs of Palestine. He set up a "Palestinian government" in his own home. Its authority was supposed to extend to the Gaza Strip.

Under the guidance of the former Mufti the radio of Cairo, which is heard in the Arab Middle East, drew upon the "rich and almost unbelievable irresponsible vocabulary" of bitter political antagonists—in the words of Glubb Pasha—to denounce the King of Jordan as a friend of the Jews, the enemy of the Arabs, in the pay of imperialist plotters. The hysterical, emotion-charged voice of the radio appealed especially to hysterical, emotion-charged people of whom there is no shortage in a mercurial Middle Eastern world. The object was to generate a bottomless hatred against the Jordan King.

In spite of the frenzied campaign of propaganda against him, King Abdullah was unaware of danger. He noticed only the expressions of loyalty of his subjects, which were explosive, too. Even on the throne he retained the informality of the desert. On Fridays, the Muslim Sabbath, he liked to lead the worship in a mosque and then it was particularly easy for petitioners to approach him. Sometimes he motored to the walled-in city of Jerusalem, to worship in one of the oldest shrines of Islam, the seventh-century Al-Aqsa Mosque, built by the Caliph Abdul Malik. So it happened on July 20, 1951, when the King entered the ancient shrine. A young man who had been aroused to a pitch of frenzy by the hysterical voice of Radio Cairo took aim as Abdullah entered the house of worship and killed him. The King's escort cut the assassin down on the spot. Who were the accomplices and instigators? They were tried in the capital of Jordan and the network of the Arab "Murder, Inc." was traced to Cairo. A kinsman of the former Mufti of Jerusalem was among those who were found guilty. The death of King Abdullah had removed a stabilizing influence in the Arab Middle East.

Abdullah had not been on good terms with his son, Talal, the heir to the throne. For twenty years Talal had been brooding in the paternal house. At the time his father was killed, he was in a Swiss sanatorium for the mentally ill. He was flown home promptly and ascended the throne. Little became known about what he was doing there but eventually he was declared incompetent. The succession went now to his seventeen-year-old son Hussein.

Hussein was a student at Harrow and Sandhurst, in Britain, and had the reputation of being a gay young man with a strong liking for the pleasures of Europe's glamour cities—Paris, Rome, Geneva, Capri—where he liked to take long holidays. During his minority a Regency Council of three carried on the government's business, two of these elder statesmen from the East Bank and the third from the West Bank, formerly a part of Palestine. It was on May 2, 1953, that young Hussein ascended the throne vacated by his father, Talal.

An Age of Chaos

"You Westerners will never understand us until you realize that there is no Jordan nationalism. There is no Jordan nationality. There is a State of Jordan, imposed on us by the Great Powers who cut up our country for their own ends, but we have only one nationalism and one nation—the Arabs." * This is what a prominent Jordanian told an American newspaperman.

There was thus a vacuum within the vacuum—the Kingdom of Jordan in the Middle East. King Abdullah's strong personality had helped to keep the country alive and to convey the impression that it was a well-established nation. Now that he was dead, several contradictory influences converged upon Amman, attempting to fill out the vacuum. These influences were hostile ideologies, aggressive Pan-Arab nationalism, Great Power intrigues. If Jordan did not collapse, it was because she did not even have the strength to do so. Outside forces appeared to keep each other in balance, fearful that a collapse would involve consequences that would be hard to control.

What was the "power elite" of Jordan, her creative minority? The majority of the people consisted of former Palestinians who considered themselves superior to the primitive desert folk. The "Mayflower" class of Jordan consisted mainly of the nomadic Bedouin who roamed freely across boundaries. Were they in Jordan now, in Saudi Arabia, in Syria?—who knew and who cared? A certain loyalty to the throne did develop among some of the Bedouins close to the capital, but how strong was it?

Then there was the bazaar, the querulous traders whose loyalty was attracted to gold. Most of the people were looking hither and yon, unsure what they wanted, even less certain what they could achieve, anxious to acquire a national identity but always

* Arslan Humbaraci, *Middle East Indictment,* London: Robert Hale, 1958, p. 128. (Mr. Humbaraci had been a correspondent of *The New York Times* in Turkey.)

in doubt whether being a good Jordanian was really a patriotic aim.

Strongest influence on this human jetsam was the loudest radio —invariably Cairo. That radio voice exhorted the Jordanians to despise their rulers and their own nationality, the very existence of which was denounced as a betrayal of the Arabs' hallowed cause.

A civil service can occasionally become the bearer of public responsibility and a substitute for national loyalty. There was no such civil service in Jordan. This was true also of other Arab countries. Glubb Pasha, who likes the Arabs among whom he lived the best part of his adult life, summed up his experience in these words: "In the Arab countries there is no tradition of public service. Anybody who enters politics does so with the sole aim of achieving personal gain or advancement."

The Communists played a role among the outside influences. Nobody knew how strong they were because communism, in the words of a German diplomat in the Middle East, was not *hoffähig*—presentable at court. In Jordan, as in most Arab countries, one could not gauge the importance of communism by the number of card-carrying members. They did not carry cards. Also communism was mostly not a specific ideology, as in the Soviet bloc, but a general protest. Its cacophony had its counterpoint in Arab nationalism. The more communism fell under the official ban the more it seemed to appeal to the "angry young men" of the region. The very fact that it was considered so unspeakably dangerous made it immeasurably attractive. It had the added attraction of being clandestine, therefore mysterious and thence endowed with unfathomable qualities of potency. The more confused the situation became the more communism appeared to appeal to young people, frustrated intellectuals in many cases, real idealists, lovers of danger and adventure. Jordan had parliamentary "democracy" which served the aims of autocracy and concealed its bloodshot face. Communism represented the

207

great housecleaning. Occasionally an outspoken Communist emerged to speak with a stentorian voice, as in the instance of a crippled Damascus physician, Abdul Rahman Shgair, whose emotion-charged voice mesmerized many hearers.

British vs. Americans

The British considered Jordan their reservation. They created the country, elevated Abdullah to the throne, established the only effective Arab force, the Legion, subsidized and officered it, kept the country alive. The Royal Air Force had its bases in Jordan. To Britain the Middle East was more than a transit station to somewhere else. It was more than a strategic pivot. A foothold in the Middle East meant that Great Britain was still a force to be reckoned with, a Great Power.

The United States was a newcomer in the region. For years after the First World War America measured the region in tons of oil. However, now that Washington assumed leadership in the West, strategic considerations began to prevail and this area was a strategic pivot. The United States was now geared to a total cold war, and wars, hot or cold, follow their own rules, all of which point in one direction, victory. To any one traveling in the Middle East it became obvious that there must have been few government departments in Washington that did not want to find out one thing or another—preferably everything—in the area. Each of them appeared to follow its own rules, and so they entered into competition not only with other nations, including staunch allies, but also with one another.

During my last few years in Jordan there were more Americans in the country than British [wrote the outspoken Sir John Bagot Glubb], and they were interfering more in the government than were the British. Whereas the British were inclined to work through the Jordan government, the Americans were in the habit of doing everything themselves. . . . In the Arab countries, America is believed to be Britain's worst enemy. I remember well a prominent Arab personality saying to me that he could not understand why Britain was always worrying about Russia.

[And again, the same Glubb Pasha]:

Some people would have us believe that American Big Business is deliberately endeavouring to oust Britain from all Asia and Africa, in order itself to be able to exploit these countries without a competitor. It is striking how often the U.S.A. seems to lead the attack on Britain's position in some eastern country. It is even more remarkable how often the U.S.A. and Russia speak with one voice in attacking Britain.*

A Fifth Column and the Enemy

Cairo, however, kept on concentrating on Britain, when attacking the Amman court cabal. In the early fifties, after the establishment of the Egyptian *junta* the impression prevailed that it was Nasser's policy to have Jordan form the first building stone in the edifice of Pan-Arabia. In his opinion, too, Jordan was not a nation but an "artifice" and its people were looking for an identity. Also, the endemic rivalry between Egypt and Iraq continued unabated. Jordan was adjacent to Iraq. Also, both countries were under the same Hashemite dynasty, claiming descent from Mohammed the Prophet.

In the eyes of Nasser no crime was more hideous than the signing of the Baghdad Pact of mutual defense of the countries of the "northern tier," contiguous with the Soviet Union. Iraq was not the Soviets' neighbor. The Baghdad Pact appeared to Nasser as the "Trojan horse" of the incorrigible West. What he feared most was that Jordan would commit the inexcusable act, "abomination of abominations," and sign the pact, thereby restoring integral Western rule to the Middle East.

The fact that among all the Arab armed forces only the British-officered Arab Legion gave a good account of itself did not endear it to Nasser. It was humiliating to contemplate that no Arab-officered army was equal to the "Jewish shopkeepers."

* Glubb, *op. cit.*, p. 327.

The Cairo radio sought to weaken Jordan by depriving her of the support of the Arab Legion. A saturation propaganda was launched against the country and its King. Young Hussein had provided many a sign of his esteem and admiration for Glubb Pasha, commander of the Arab Legion. However, in this instance, he decided that this was the time to act on the principle *sauve qui peut* and that, therefore, Glubb had to go.

In view of the uncontested fact that Glubb Pasha had deserved well of the Kingdom of Jordan he might have decided on a painful but serene farewell, explaining to the general what circumstances had forced him to take this drastic step and giving him ample time to wind up his affairs. That was, however, not the way the King acted.

On March 1, 1956, the unsuspecting commander of the Arab Legion, Glubb Pasha, received an urgent telephone call from the Prime Minister, conveying a message of His Majesty the King. It was the sovereign's pleasure to dismiss the commander of the Legion and to order him and his family to leave within two hours.

Why this tremendous urgency? Had anything been disclosed to justify the belief that the officer whom Jordan could thank for her continued existence, and who was the father of the only victory Arab arms had known, was a peril to the nation? Nothing of this kind had been disclosed. The unusual haste was explained by the sovereign's desire to demonstrate to the Arab world that he, too, distrusted and hated "imperialism." It was impossible to leave Jordan within two hours and the time limit was extended until the following morning. The dismissal of the "father of the Arab Legion" deprived the King of the strongest support of his regime, Great Britain.

New Forces to the Fore

The new commander of the Arab Legion was a thirty-three-year-old young officer, Lt. Col. Ali Abu Nawar, who had been educated in Britain. Soon he was advanced to the rank of general. He denounced the Eisenhower Doctrine in Cairo's intemperate language. In the autumn of 1956, Egypt, Syria and Saudi Arabia agreed to give Jordan an annual subsidy of $35 million, to replace the subsidy she had received from London. Also, the armed forces of Jordan were placed under the joint command of the four countries, headed by an Egyptian commander in chief.

The violent political oscillations which characterized the history of Jordan in the following months appear to have two explanations. Nobody was at the helm and the country had no compass, exposed to all the vagaries of intemperate weather. Also, behind-the-scene influences were operating under the cloak of secrecy. Jordan had now become a cold-war battlefield.

Under the influence of Cairo, Hussein now veered sharp to the left. In the new cabinet an avowed Communist had a ministerial portfolio. Other parties in the coalition were the Arab Renaissance, *Al Baath al Arabi,* and the National Socialists. The new Prime Minister, Suleyman al-Nabulsi, was a "Great Arabia" man, doubtful of the *raison d'être* of the country whose government he headed. He announced that Jordan would refuse aid from the United States, as being incompatible with the country's independence, and establish diplomatic relations with the Soviet Union and the Republic of China. It was also decided to cut the last links to Britain and abrogate the Anglo-Jordanian treaty. The ideology of the parties forming the government was indicated by the pamphlet that contained their philosophy, entitled *Eisenhower the Colonizer.*

These were the days of the "Moscow-Cairo-Amman" axis. The West Bank—former Palestine—more sophisticated than the East Bank—former Transjordan—gave its support to the new line. However, the forces of conservatives were quickly emerging to the surface on the East Bank, where the tradition-bound Bedouins were less easily taken in by the new "party line" that Mohammed and Marx represented the same creed.

In spite of all these changes, the days of royalty in Jordan appeared to be numbered in the spring of 1957. Revolution was in the air. It was an open secret that young King Hussein was cast for the role of Egypt's Farouk and that young General Nuwar was to be Jordan's Nasser. The establishment of the Republic of Jordan appeared to be only a question of days. The official flag of the republic had already been designed. The Jordan army, thoroughly Eastern-oriented, appeared to be ready to support the uprising. All of this would have been in line with developments in other parts of the Arab world, where thrones were toppling or on the point of doing so, and military "strong men" were emerging.

The Pulling of Wires

Revolutions in the Middle East—and elsewhere—usually start in city streets. The streets of Amman appeared to be hostile to the King and friendly to the "great change." However, in Jordan there was also another force that could be activated—the desert. In a dramatic gesture which seldom misses the mark in an emotional setting the young King appeared among his desert warriors at the army base near Amman. He found the right words and succeeded in eliciting a fanatic and fantastic display of loyalty on the part of the Bedouin. He knew that not only his crown but also his life was at stake. The desert soldiers acted quickly and soon the streets of Amman were patrolled by the warriors of the First Armored Regiment, and they were ready for action—any action.

When these desert people are about to kill they blacken their faces so as not to be recognized by the dead man's kin and called to account. It was soldiers with blackened faces that appeared in Amman's streets; and the import of this act, according to an eyewitness, was not lost on the city mob whose faces turned several shades paler every time they beheld this awesome sight. At the height of the crisis an excited would-be revolutionary was racing down the street shouting republican slogans. "Long live . . ." he screamed as he turned a corner, but the next word got stuck in his mouth when he saw a black-faced Bedouin. "Long live who?"

212

the Bedouin asked, whereupon the terror-stricken near-terrorist stuttered: "It is not sure yet."

Meanwhile units of the United States Sixth Fleet had been dispatched to the eastern Mediterranean and the government in Washington announced that the independence and integrity of Jordan were a vital American interest. Throughout Jordan martial law was proclaimed, military courts were created and all political parties were dissolved. The young commander of the Arab Legion, Abu Nawar, who had been promoted major general, was dismissed by the King, and his successor, Major General Alai Hayari, a pro-Nasser man, did not last long either. Both of them crossed the frontier into Syria where they launched a violent radio campaign against King Hussein on Radio Damascus. The King of Saudi Arabia now rallied to King Hussein's side. Hussein attacked his Prime Minister, Nabulsi, violently and accused the Egyptian radio of spreading untrue propaganda against him. A new Prime Minister was appointed, Hussein Khalidi, but he lasted only nine days. He was followed by Ibrahim Hashem. Within a fortnight, Jordan had had three governments. The plan to assume diplomatic relations with the Soviet Union was abandoned. Jordan turned to the United States for financial aid and received substantial sums.

Blows continued to be exchanged between Jordan and Egypt, both of them representing themselves as champions of the Arab cause. Egypt called Hussein a traitor and kept on calling on his subjects to overthrow him. King Hussein charged that President Nasser was trying to spread communism in Jordan.

A Federation and a Fiasco

The slugging match between the two groups of Arab states continued. On February 1, 1958, Egypt and Syria formed the United Arab Republic. A fortnight later Iraq and Jordan countered this move by announcing the formation of the Arab Federation, a looser organization than that of the U.A.R. King Faisal of Iraq became the head of the federation, and King Hussein of Jordan his deputy. Nuri es-Said, Premier of Iraq, became the head of the central government. The federation did not last long enough to get down to business. On July 14, 1958, the head of the federation, King Faisal, was killed in Baghdad. Another victim of the revolution was Ibrahim Hashem, former Premier of Jordan and deputy head of the federation central government, who happened to be in Baghdad at the time the revolution erupted.

From Iraq the unrest quickly spread to Jordan. Again the country seemed on the point of complete dissolution as disloyalty to the King in the army came to a head. The young King acted again with energy and dispatch. The disgruntled officers were arrested and Hussein made another appeal to the Bedouin, his staunchest supporters. Also he appealed to the United States and Britain for help. British troops were promptly flown to Jordan. Just as promptly the radios of the U.A.R. stepped up their propaganda broadcasts against the King—"traitor" and "imperialist stooge." For a time, King Hussein regarded himself the head of the Arab Federation but soon recognized that the union was dead.

From May 19, 1958, the Prime Minister of Jordan had been Samir el-Rifai, who had been in power on and off since World War II. He was given credit for having helped the young King safely past revolts, palace intrigue, mob rule, threats of assassination and the Middle East crisis of the summer of 1958. The Premier linked Jordan more closely to America. In the spring of 1959 the King and his Prime Minister paid visits to Washington and London and newspapers reported that their country was to receive an annual subsidy of $56 million from the two governments. Jordan was in great need of such funds. Poverty-stricken though she was, Jordan spent about a half of her meager budget on armed forces.

Egypt continued her violent campaign of propaganda against her sister Arab nation and demanded the withdrawal of British forces from Jordan. The case was discussed in the UN where the U.A.R. received the backing of the Soviet Union. The Arab delegates presented a resolution at the UN envisaging the withdrawal of British troops from Jordan. Before the year was over the troops were withdrawn but King Hussein made it clear that they would be asked to return, should their presence be necessary.

Jordan's existence continued to hang on a thread which, however, may turn out to be a sturdy one. The U.A.R. continued to worry about two possibilities. Should Jordan fall apart, who would pick up those parts? True, Iraq was no longer under the Hashemite dynasty—which now ruled only in Jordan—but an expansive government in Baghdad might not like to exchange a weak government in Amman for a strong government in Cairo, should Jordan be absorbed by the U.A.R.

For years now, Israel's Arab antagonists have been charging that she wanted to expand—had to expand in order to accommodate her increasing population. Transjordan had been detached from Palestine, which was to be the site of a "Jewish national home" under the Balfour Declaration of the First World War. There was therefore the fear in Arab circles that Israel would want to validate a claim to Palestine and thus to the Kingdom of Jordan.

What would be a common-sense reaction of Israel to the problem of Jordan? Should the Kingdom really fall apart, as had been predicted many times, Israel could not afford to let it form a part of the United Arab Republic, which would then all but surround the new state. This could not be tolerated especially in view of the ceaseless threats to Israel about the "second round" which would push the Israeli into the sea.

Would it be in Israel's interest to annex Jordan in order to settle a population that had increased more than threefold in a decade? Israel has already started to obtain additional territory for settlement, but it is within the boundaries of the present state—mainly in the Negev, about one half the size of the country, the potentialities of which have not yet been fully exploited. According to all indications, the type of settlement Israel wants is the "vertical" kind, into the soil, and not the horizontal type, into other countries. The acquisition of the territory of a neighboring nation, such as Jordan, would confront Israel with a grave problem. Jordan has a population of a million and a half Arabs. Were this territory to be acquired the new state of Israel would have about as many Arabs as there are Jews. It would be impossible for a new state to assimilate such an alien body, and it would be most difficult even for an old state. In this case the Jordanians would represent a hostile and very explosive element, thoroughly saturated with anti-Israeli sentiment. In view of this fact it is not at all likely that the government in Jerusalem would welcome such an accretion of territory.

At the same time Israel would have every reason to oppose the acquisition of this territory by the U.A.R. as long as it continues to display an implacably hostile attitude toward the new state. Since it does not appear to be in the interest of Israel to annex it or to have it annexed by Cairo, there seems to be only one way out—and that is the *status quo*. Thus, we are faced with a paradoxical situation. Israel, which Jordan considers an enemy, has every reason to wish that the Hashimite Kingdom should continue in existence.

Also, paradoxical as it may be, Jordan's continued territorial integrity exists and continues in part, at least, out of the U.A.R. apprehension of a clash with Israel. In fact, this apprehension underlines the conclusion that Israel, in the various crises which have encompassed the Middle East, has exerted and is likely to exert a stabilizing influence on the region.

A River and Bread

At the request of President Eisenhower, the chairman of the Committee for International Economic Growth, Eric Johnston,* undertook between 1953 and 1955 to negotiate with Jordan, Lebanon, Syria and Israel a comprehensive Jordan Valley Devel-

* The effect of the Johnston mission on Israel will be touched upon in the chapter about that country.

opment Plan that would have provided for the irrigation of some 225,000 acres. Technical experts of these countries agreed upon every important detail of the unified Jordan plan.

Yet, the Arab League rejected it at its October 1955 meeting, not for economic but for political reasons. Syria, particularly, objected to the project because it would benefit Israel, too. Because of this, "every year a billion cubic meters of precious water still roll down the ancient stream, wasted, to the Dead Sea." *

Jordan worked out a limited plan under which a reservoir is to be built near the confluence of the Jordan and Yarmuk rivers. The water stored there would be led in canals along the Jordan River highlands, irrigating some 100,000 acres and producing electricity. The execution of this project would increase Jordan's income by $7 million, a very small improvement even for a small country.

The Kingdom established a Development Board in 1952 to plan the country's economic future. Under this plan small amounts are to be spent on irrigation, terracing of the land, aid to co-operatives, the improvement of basic communication and the development of potash and phosphate production in the Jordanian part of the Dead Sea. Little money has been allocated to economic development because Jordan has a smaller budget than an American small town and because a large percentage is earmarked for the cost of the armed forces. A full-scale implementation of the Jordan River project would be of great help to the people of the Hashemite Kingdom. But in situations such as this the armed forces come first and bread for underfed people follows at a great distance.

* Eric Johnston, "A Key to the Future of the Mideast," *The New York Times Magazine,* October 19, 1958.

CHAPTER 6

On the Margins of the Arab World

NOW we turn to the Arab lands away from the Middle Eastern heartland, on the margins, in Africa and in Asia. In Africa we shall take a look at the Sudan and Libya, two newly independent countries in their period of travail. In Asia we shall cast a glance at Saudi Arabia, a land of the deep desert and extremely secretive; also the land of "Big Oil." We shall take a look, too, at Yemen, which the Romans called *Arabia Felix* and which, today, it would be more correct to call *Arabia Occulta,* because of the secrecy that surrounds it. Finally, we shall look at the regions fringing the great Arab Quadrangle, and the many conflicts that have been erupting there.

1. SUDAN MEANS BLACK

The Sudan is one of the most recently independent Arab countries and she is also a living paradox. Nothing justified the creation of this country in its present form—neither geography nor ethnography, history or traditions. The Sudan belongs to two entirely different worlds, dissimilar as any two parts of our globe can be. One world is that of North Africa, where our Western civilization originated. It is linked to Europe by the Mediterranean Sea. The other world is that of Central Africa, which is separated from

218

North Africa by the desert, the "Dry Ocean," the most forbidding element in nature.

There is a great difference between these two parts of Africa, parts of the same continent. There is not much difference between North Africa and Southern Europe, even though they are parts of two different continents. As North Africa is the oldest of the Old World, so Central Africa is the youngest of the New World, much younger—if periods of exploration are considered—than the Western Hemisphere.

The Sudan is the land which spans these two worlds that meet there and nowhere else, the oldest and the youngest, the black and white, the monotheist and polytheist and, at one time, the slaver and the slave. Indeed, there is no other region in the world where such extremes meet. And this is so because of a natural and an unnatural phenomenon. The former is the Nile, which traverses the entire Sudan before it sweeps into Egypt. The unnatural phenomenon was the British rule, which swept into the Sudan all the territories that for one reason or another could not be accommodated elsewhere. The British did not find the Sudan too difficult a territory to govern, probably because it lent itself admirably to colonial administrators' employing their favorite device of "divide and rule." For the same reason the Sudan may find it difficult to govern herself.

The word "Sudan" means black, but the country is only partly that. The southern part is black, the northern part is white and mixed. Much of the south is fetish-minded, most of the north has a proto-Arabic, monotheistic, Islamic culture. Only 40 per cent of the Sudanese speak Arabic, even though about three-quarters of them are Muslims. Yet we speak of the Sudan as an "Arab" country because the Arabs are the "power elite" and the nation-builders.

The Nationalist Whirlwind

A convention signed in 1899 established the Anglo-Egyptian Condominium in the Sudan, joint government in which all the substance of power was in the hands of the British, who were also masters of Egypt; and the semblance was in the hands of the Egyptians. The Sudan is off the beaten track of political and cultural changes, broiling under a cruel sun, going on its old traditional way. Yet, after the Second World War the Sudan did not remain immune to the nationalist revolution that was sweeping across the face of the colonial world.

The British gave the Sudan their usual honest and efficient administration, but, naturally, they did not encourage the "natives" to become their competitors. High school graduates in the Sudan belonged to the intellectual elite and it was they who launched a nationalist movement which went under the name of "Graduates' General Congress."

Only a handful of people in the Sudan had the skills to read newspapers and even fewer people could follow the intricate convolutions of politics. However, these few were sufficient to launch an independence movement. The direct stimulation came from Egypt, along the Nile.

Two political groups with diametrically opposite aims emerged in the course of time and they rallied around leaders who exercised religious as well as secular authority. The picturesque name of one of these groups was *Ashiqqa*—Blood Brothers—(later merged in the National Union Party) and they favored an autonomous Sudan under the Egyptian crown, in a personal union. Leader of this group was Sayyid Sir Ali el Mirghani, head of the religious sect known as *Khatmia*—Reciters—those who recite the entire Holy Koran. He was an aggressive person, supported by townsmen, particularly the merchants mainly in the north, which is exposed to stronger Egyptian influence.

The other group was the *Umma*—Nation—also known as the Independence Front. As its name indicated, it wanted to have outright independence, but was ready to accept British aid in a transition period. Its leader was Sayyid Sir Abder Rahman el Mahdi, posthumous son of the late "Messiah" (Mahdi) of the Sudan, leader of the religious sect which calls itself *Ansar*—Helpers—

those who extended a helping hand to the Prophet Mohammed. The Umma followers came mainly from the south, cattle and camel breeders, Africans more than Arabs. Their opponents denounced them as "British puppets."

We have seen that in the dying days of the Egyptian monarchy it took a unilateral action in clearing up the country's main outstanding issues, the Suez and the Sudan, which formed a "tandem." On October 8, 1951, the Egyptian royal regime denounced the 1899 Condominium Convention with Britain. However, this was only a paper declaration, since King Farouk lacked the physical strength to implement it.

The following year he was ousted and in came the officers' *junta* which meant business. An agreement was reached between it and Great Britain in February 1953, under which the Sudan was to have complete independence after a transitional period of self-government lasting not more than three years. The head of the *junta* at the time was General Naguib, partly of Sudanese origin, and the officers assumed that their neighbor to the south would want to share their fate. The two countries' interests were linked through the Nile.

The United States, the Soviet Union, Britain and Egypt were busily weaving their diplomatic plans in the Sudan. America was by now deeply engaged in the Middle East. Washington was reported to be pressing upon the British to deal gingerly with the question of the Sudan. In an attempt to build up friendly relations in anticipation of full independence, the State Department established quasi-diplomatic relations in Khartoum, the Sudanese capital.

The Soviet Union appears to have been particularly active in establishing its diplomatic base along the Nile. Indeed, it was in Khartoum and not in Cairo that Soviet diplomacy carried out its great break-through. The Soviet agent was a certain Peter Egorov, former head of the Russian news agency, Tass. His plan of operations was simple. He was far less interested in the Sudan than in Egypt and he was carrying on a whispering campaign in favor of

221

Cairo. Thereby he was hoping to ingratiate himself with the officers' *junta*. The Soviets were willing to invest a large amount of money in this operation. An American newspaperman who had an inside view of Soviet operations in the Middle East wrote: "I know that eight tons of gold were transferred from the *Banque des Pays du Nord,* the Soviet bank in Paris, to Sudan to finance Russian activities there. . . ." * Also, Moscow and Prague opened liaison offices in Khartoum and, subsequently, Soviet and Czech delegations visited the Sudan.

The British were hoping that the decision of the Sudanese would be to maintain some links with them, possibly in the form of commonwealth status. The Egyptians, on the other hand, considered the Sudan virtually part of their country and they were more than eager to form at least a federation. The union of Egypt and the Sudan would have been the logical starting point for the creation of the much-desired United Arabia.

Both the British and the Egyptians leveled charges against each other, each accusing the other side of wanting to influence the voters of the Sudan at the forthcoming elections that were to decide the fate of the country. The British charged that the Egyptians were bribing and subverting the southern tribes in order to propagate their cause. The Egyptians, on the other hand, charged that the British were stirring up the South of the Sudan against the North, playing upon the fears of the descendants of slaves against the descendants of raiders.

The elections took place late in 1953, and resulted in a great majority for the National Union, which was pro-Egyptian. This, then, was a defeat for the British. The leader of the National Unionists was a graduate of the American University of Beirut, Ismail el Azhari. The Sudan's transition period of self-government began, leading to full independence within the three-year period.

The first Prime Minister of the Sudan was el Azhari, who made important policy declarations in the name of his victorious party.

* Arslan Humbaraci, *Middle East Indictment,* London: Hale, 1958, p. 173.

It stood for complete independence and a "link with Egypt" but no interference from Britain, Russia or Egypt. He wanted to replace the old agreement concerning the allocation of the waters of the Nile between Egypt and the Sudan, and which allotted his country only a one-twenty-third share.

It is possible that the Sudan might have wanted to establish some link with Egypt as long as Naguib was in the saddle. In 1954, however, the general was ousted and many Sudanese considered this an affront to their country. The Sudan did not want Nasser. It is possible that Egypt lost the link with the southern neighbor because of the new head of the *junta*.

Egypt subjected the Sudan to ceaseless propaganda, which was deeply resented in Khartoum. The Cairo radio continually attacked the Sudanese Prime Minister. El Azhari and six of his ministers visited Cairo in the summer of 1955. After their return he said: "If we had represented a foreign power the treatment we received would have made us break off relations." Another cabinet minister declared: "A link with Egypt means domination by Egypt."

While Cairo assumed an increasingly anti-Western stand, Khartoum sided with the West. It signed an agreement with the United States which provided for extended technical assistance to the Sudan, taking the form, among other things, of a campaign against malaria under the direction of the World Health Organization and of a program of fundamental education by the UN Educational, Scientific and Cultural Organization (UNESCO).

The Sudan voted at the end of 1955 for complete independence. The British were disappointed because the Sudanese made no application to join the Commonwealth, and the Egyptians were bitter because Khartoum took no steps to establish special links with Cairo. A constitution was adopted and the Governor General, a Britisher, was replaced by a Council of State of five members— the official head of the state. The government was responsible to parliament. Independence was declared on January 1, 1956. A few days later the Sudan became the ninth member of the League

223

of Arab States and before the end of the year was admitted to the United Nations. Russia opened diplomatic relations and Leonid Teplov, former member of the Soviet Embassy in London, became the first Soviet Ambassador in Khartoum. China followed suit quickly. In 1956 the Sudan accepted a Soviet offer of economic and technical assistance and a long-term loan, while East Germany, the D.D.R., a Soviet satellite, dispatched engineers to work on the problem of the Sudan's water supplies.

To Make the Desert Bloom

As in other economically underdeveloped countries, the government of independent Sudan has given priority to increasing the arable land and improving the produce. The Sudan was the original home of the Egyptian cotton, and the cotton now grown is equal to the produce of the Nile Delta. The largest single cotton-producing area is the so-called "Island"—*Gezira*—south of the confluence of the Blue and White Niles. Originally it was a desert land and there the British had introduced one of the most successful examples of irrigation techniques. The bulk of the country's cotton crop is produced there on a million artificially watered acres. In a good year, the Gezira cotton sells for four times more than the country's other crops combined. Through an intricate network of some 3,000 canals, water for the plains of the "island" comes from the gigantic Sennar Dam on the Blue Nile. The government hopes to be able to cultivate all the potentially irrigable land between the White and Blue Niles—a vast total of some five million acres.

Other dams were projected farther up the Blue Nile, especially at Er Roseires, not far from Ethiopia. The Sudan asked for the consent of the Egyptian government to increase her share of the waters of the Nile. Cairo demurred; Khartoum took some water just the same, increasing the cultivation of the Gezira by 25 per cent.

The Sudanese government refused to be treated like poor relations and seized the initiative in the question of the distribution of the waters of the Nile. The Khartoum government took a leaf out of the book of America's Tennessee Valley Authority. Khartoum assumed the stand that the needs of the entire area should be treated as a unit, including Ethiopia, Kenya, Uganda, Tanganyika Territory. The vast marshland of the White Nile in southern Sudan, the Sudd, was to be drained, the Blue Nile shortened, and several smaller dams were to be built. Thus the water available from the Nile would be increased from 52 billion to 80 billion cubic meters, and not only the Sudan but also Egypt and the other areas would profit.

Under a 1929 agreement the Sudan was taking 4,500,000,000 cubic meters of water, while Egypt was getting 48,000,000. There remained 32,000,000,000 cubic meters, flowing into the Mediterranean. Ten billion of this, it was estimated, would be lost by evaporation from the Aswan reservoir. The Sudan had objected to the building of the High Dam on that account, and had proposed a system of smaller dams and reservoirs in the upper reaches of the Nile, where the evaporation losses would be less.

In November 1959 an agreement was reached between the two countries under which Egypt was to receive 55,000,000,000 cubic meters of water and the Sudan 18,500,000,000. Since the Sudan would not need this full amount in the immediate future, the agreement provided that Egypt could "borrow" 1,500,000,000 cubic meters a year and pay it back when the Sudanese got their own irrigation and power projects under way. The United Arab Republic was also to pay the Sudan the equivalent of $43,200,000 in compensation for lands and property to be inundated by the Aswan reservoir and would move to other settlements 50,000 Sudanese affected by the project.

While this agreement represented an improvement in Egyptian-Sudanese relations, conflicts between the two countries arose from time to time. In the Sudan, too, as in other parts of the Arab world, Nasser's tactics aroused scant enthusiasm.

225

As a result of Cairo's policy, small matters which normally would be overlooked became important issues. The boundary between Egypt and the Sudan since 1902 has been the 22nd parallel, except for a small frontier district to the north of it, administered by the Sudan. While Egypt was preparing for new parliamentary elections in March 1958, President Nasser sent an armed guard and a body of officials into the district to conduct a poll in connection with the plebiscite following the establishment of the United Arab Republic. The Sudanese government protested, then appealed to the Arab League, and finally to the UN Security Council, requiring Nasser to withdraw his officials and troops. After some delay this was done. What was the sense of this policy of pin-pricks? People in the Sudan began to ask if this was the way Nasser wanted to make himself popular in the Arab world.

The 1958 elections resulted in the formation of a government composed of the Umma and the People's Democratic Party. One Communist was elected member of parliament. It will be recalled that before independence Umma inclined to close cooperation with the British. Those days were gone by now. The secretary of the Umma, Abdullah Khalil, was re-elected Prime Minister. He outlined his country's foreign policy in an important declaration. The Sudan wanted to keep out of both cold-war blocs, the Premier said, and determined to maintain friendly relations with all countries. To prove this, he signed an agreement with the United States under which the Sudan was to accept economic aid for the development of the country's resources. At the same time, he said that Khartoum would accept Soviet aid, too, if offered without any conditions.

Paradoxically, the one country with which the Sudan could not get along at all was Egypt. Increasingly, the government in Khartoum complained of unceasing interference in its affairs by the government of Nasser. As a result, trade between the two countries came to a standstill, while recriminations continued. In an interview published in *L'Orient,* of Beirut, Abdullah Khalil made serious charges against Egypt without designating it. He charged that "one Middle Eastern power" had been working with some Sudanese army officers for the last three months to engineer a coup to prejudice Sudan's independence. This power also "bought over the Sudanese press and threw the country into chaos through the classical means by which it has applied pressure on other countries." Asked if he meant the United Arab Republic and President Nasser, Mr. Khalil said: "You mention the aggressor in the Mideast and everybody's finger will point to him."

While the Sudan was in the midst of such troubles her stature was growing in the African world. The Foreign Minister of Sudan was recognized as a "dominating figure" at the Accra conference of the African states in April 1958, and there was no willingness on the part of Khartoum to play second fiddle to Cairo. The Sudan was one of the countries, in the view of Sir Harold MacMichael, her former Governor General, that displayed a similarity of outlook with Ghana and Tunisia in advocating not only adherence to the United Nations Charter but also a sort of Monroe Doctrine for Africa.[*]

The Revolt of the Officers

On November 17, 1958, the head of the army, Lieut. Gen. Ibrahim Abboud, seized power in a move which, it was believed, had been prearranged with Premier Khalil. The army declared that the country's situation was deteriorating; party squabbles were ruining it; the army had stepped in to restore stability and honesty; no parties and newspapers were to be permitted for the time being; good relations with the Arab sister countries were to be maintained. "As for our sister country, the United Arab Republic, we shall make every effort to improve relations with her and to solve all outstanding artificially contrived tension between

[*] Sir Harold MacMichael, "Egyptian-Sudanese Relations," *Middle Eastern Affairs,* March 1959, Vol. X, No. 3, p. 108.

the two sister countries." A roundup of leftists followed. Declarations were made, on the one hand, against military pacts, for acceptance of aid without conditions; and on the other hand, aid was accepted from Great Britain and the United States. An officers' *junta* was set up. General Ibrahim Abboud was an elderly man, vacillating, weak. Power was taken by a younger officer on March 2, 1959, Brigadier Abdul Rahman Shenan, who marched his men into Khartoum, surrounded army headquarters and, carrying a tommy-gun, faced the thirteen-man *junta* and demanded their resignation.

Within a short time two more military uprisings took place. Brig. Shenan was arrested, tried and sentenced to life in the fall of 1959. General Ibrahim Abboud's position was strengthened at the head of the Supreme Military Council. Although the political parties were abolished, the Sudanese dictatorship appeared to be comparatively mild, not the iron fist but the kid-gloved type.

What was the meaning of these quick moves? The establishment of a military *junta* followed the usual pattern of the Arab Middle East, the denunciation of civilian authority and the establishment of a military dictatorship. This had happened in Egypt, Syria, Iraq. In Lebanon and Jordan the aid of foreign armies was invoked. In the Sudan, too, as elsewhere, great and perhaps miraculous changes were expected in the wake of independence. As these expectations failed to materialize, the people became restless, the outs made an attempt to get in, revolutions and coups followed in quick succession. In the Sudan, too, the attempts of President Nasser to force the country into his Greater Arabia boomeranged. The coup by the Sudanese officers had a strongly anti-Nasser tinge.

2. LIBYA—EGYPT WITHOUT THE NILE

Among the poor Arab countries Libya is one of the poorest, much like Egypt, but without a Nile. An embittered Libyan friend of mine called his nation "the world's richest country in nothing."

228

As does the Sudan, Libya consists of disparate regions with widely differing backgrounds and traditions. The very existence of the nation is due to historic accident. When the British took over Egypt they also might have taken adjacent Libya (then known under different names) but they considered her a liability. When the French had occupied Tunisia on the western flank of Libya they made no attempt to penetrate eastward, since the aridity of the region between their protectorate and Egypt did not attract them. This large area remained then in Ottoman hands until Italy began to take possession of it in 1911, more for prestige than economic reasons.

The country consists of three distinct zones. Tripolitania in the west and Cyrenaica in the east face the Mediterranean and contain the country's larger cities, while Fezzan is deep in the Sahara, adjacent to former French West Africa and Algeria's desert portions. Tripolitania and Cyrenaica look in different directions; the former toward the west and the latter toward the east. Between them a desert barrier separates the two worlds and the Tripolitanian urban dwellers are cosmopolitan sophisticates in comparison with the Cyrenians. Because of this basic division, Libya has two capitals, Tripoli and Benghazi, some 640 miles apart and the traveler who crosses the boundaries between the two provinces is subjected to customs inspection. The people of the Fezzan, in their oases, Ghadames, Ghat, Socna, Sebha, Brak, are thoroughly insulated from the rest of the world. For the convenience of the king a third capital was being built at Beida over the plains of a tableland the Libyans call Jebel El-Akhdar, Green Mountains.

Libya, a member of the Arab League, has a majority population that is Arab. The large Negro population comprises about 35 per cent of the total. In addition, there are the Berbers (the name is derived from "Barbarian") who call themselves "free people," because freedom, to them, means wandering on the arid steppes. Their Arab neighbors sneeringly call them "Jabali"—

229

mountaineers, hill-billies. At one time there were some 35,000 Jews in Libya but many of them have moved to Israel.

The per capita income of Libya is one of the lowest in the Arab world. About 90 per cent of the country was illiterate as recently as 1957, though new schools have been built since then. In the entire country there were only fourteen college graduates and fewer than five thousand people had had more than five years in school.

The Heritage of Colonialism

The Italian regime was profitable neither for the rulers nor for their subjects. Italy, one of the most overcrowded countries in Europe, had needed overseas sites for settlement, and the Italian Fascist government had spent large amounts on the Libyan region, certain parts of which were to be turned into show places. Yet, at the height of Italy's efforts at colonization there were fewer than 90,000 Italian settlers in the region, a number so small that it had no appreciable effect on the home country's economic condition.

For many years Libya, particularly the Cyrenian zone, offered strong resistance to Italian colonizers. Leading the resistance was a religious Muslim order, named Senussi after its nineteenth-century founder. These religious zealots expected the forthcoming visit of the *Mahdi,* Messiah, whose impeccable piety would inspire his people to lead temperate and virtuous lives. They had their "monastery" at Zawia Baida, the center of religious fanaticism in the mountains of Cyrenaica. When the Italians desecrated their hallowed land, they defended it with all the fanaticism of their sectarian zeal.

Under the Romans Libya had been part of the North African granary, but in recent centuries she had become more a staging area than a population center and during the Second World War she lived up to her reputation. Along the region's coastal road a decisive phase of the war was fought. This was early in the war when the Axis forces were carried onward by a seemingly irresistible *élan* of victory. The German war machine was mowing down all resistance, while from the East the Japanese moved westward with uncanny rapidity. The plan of the western Axis powers was to crash the British defenses protecting the Nile and vault into the Middle Eastern coreland to sever the Allies' jugular vein. Fantastic as the project was, nothing seemed impossible to the German and Japanese warlords. Day after day the names of the Libyan coastal towns were blazoned on the front pages of the press of the world—such names as Tobruk, Tripoli, Derna, Misurata, Benghazi and Sirte. Two of the war's greatest leaders fought the monumental duel, Britain's Field Marshal Sir Bernard Law Montgomery, veteran of the First World War, and Germany's General Erwin Rommel, the "Desert Fox." The German armor's drive carried it into Egypt, within striking distance of the Nile, but the campaign was won by the British at El Alamein in November 1942. Rommel was forced westward into Tunisia, where the strong Mareth Line was cracked. The German Afrika Korps was doomed and the decline of the Axis forces began.

The defeat of the Axis cost Italy Libya, which was occupied by the British. The postwar question was what should be done with Libya? It would have been anomalous to turn it back to Italy. The Soviet Union demanded that it should be turned into a trust territory, to be placed under the Trusteeship Council of the UN, on which the U.S.S.R. had a seat, but this was unacceptable to the Western allies of the "cold war."

The possibility of an independent Libya was mooted. But how could a country be created which had not even a corporal's guard of college graduates? Since the three provinces of the area had so little in common, how were they to be held together? And, in view of the divergent interests of the different sections, who would head the government?

Though the answers to these questions were not easy to find, there was no other solution. It would have been impossible to have one of the major victors of World War II rule Libya. The

Soviet Union had been one of the major victors. Should one of the Western allies assume power, the Soviets would have acquired an effective propaganda weapon. The problem was thrown into the lap of the General Assembly of the UN, which decided late in 1949 that Libya should become an independent sovereign state as soon as feasible but in no event later than January 1, 1952. The Assembly recommended that all three provinces—Tripolitania, Cyrenaica and the Fezzan—should have a hand in framing the constitution. Thus, in 1950, a Libyan National Assembly was created which promulgated a federal constitution in the autumn of the next year. The United Kingdom of Libya—*Al Mamlaka Al Libiyya Al Muttahida*—was born. The question of the head of the state also was solved. He was the head of the same Senussi order which had fought the Italians so long. On December 24, 1951, King Mohammed Idris I el-Mahdi el-Senussi ascended the throne.

Problems of Nation Building

Libya now had to create a government, an army, a navy, and a police force. A legislature of two Chambers was set up. The Senate had twenty-four members equally divided from among the three provinces, half of which were nominated by the King, and the other half by the three regional legislative councils. The House of Representatives was to be a body elected on the basis of one deputy to every 20,000 inhabitants. Pending the population census, Tripolitania was represented by thirty-five, Cyrenaica by fifteen and the Fezzan by five members. The first general election took place in February 1952.

The setting up of a government for Libya required the assistance of the United States and Great Britain. Their direct annual grant of $20 million was more than one-half of the total national budget of $36 million. The United States signed a twenty-year agreement with Libya for the use of Wheelus Field, near Tripoli, one of the largest American overseas bases. In payment, Libya received $4 million annually from Washington. The British trained a small army of 5,000 which the United States supplied with arms. To help meet the next urgent requirements of the country, the "Libyan navy," a small coast-guard service, also was created, and the British organized the Tripolitanian Police in the west and the Cyrenaican Defense Force in the east.

Responsibility for administering economic aid was assumed mainly by the Libyan-American Reconstruction Commission, while the Libyan-American Joint Service was called upon to co-ordinate United States technical assistance. The object of these and other organizations was to raise Libya's living standards. Arid land is the great problem, for, though there is some precipitation in the country, most of it goes to waste on corroded hillsides. The Romans had established a system of small retaining dams in the dry riverbeds and, with modern methods, the Libyan soil could be improved.

The Libyan Finance Corporation made loans available to farmers, industry and trade. British economic aid came to be channeled through the Libyan Public Development and Stabilization Agency, the main function of which was to finance economic and social development. American, British and UN agencies promoted the establishment of light industrial plants, mainly for the processing of local products, such as grains and dates. Those of the population who had the requisite skills were aided in workshops where the accent was on hand labor and the utilization of dormant aptitudes, such as carpet weaving and other handicrafts. Thus, while Libya was independent, it was reliant for its life as a nation on aid from Britain and the United States. She received $40 million from these countries in 1958 in grants, loans and budgetary support.

The Oilman's Map

The dream of all desert countries is to have large quantities of oil and it seems as if Libya, considered the poorest of the poor,

233

may become one of the oil-rich nations. "The Saraha oil discoveries," according to an authoritative petroleum publication, "put Libya, one of the world's poorest countries, on the oilman's map as an area of major interest." The most promising areas were found in one of the globe's most desolate regions, the Syrtic Desert, near the Algerian frontier, and by the late fifties about a dozen major oil companies, mostly American, but also British, French, German and Dutch, were prospecting. In the summer of 1959 the long search for oil in Libya's desert began to pay off. Esso Standard (Libya), an exploration and producing affiliate of the Standard Oil Company (New Jersey), announced that it had attained production of 17,500 barrels a day in northern Libya. The well was at Zelten, in Cyrenaica, about a hundred miles off the Mediterranean coast. Standard announced that the chances of producing oil in commercial quantities elsewhere in Libya, too, were excellent and that it was going to spend $100 million on exploration in Tripolitania and the Fezzan. It was also felt that the discovery opened a new area of Cyrenaica for further exploration and development and the announcement stated that another drilling rig would be brought in to delineate further the extent of the field. An important factor in the Jersey Standard discovery was the relative proximity of the well to the coast and cheap transportation. Until then, major fields discovered in adjacent Algeria had been several hundred miles from the coast, necessitating the construction of long pipelines over rugged desert terrain. The construction of a pipeline from the Libyan field to the coast was a relatively simple task.

However, before Libya's fond hopes of becoming an oil billionaire can materialize, other money-earning possibilities have to be tapped and the country has one "natural resource" in great abundance—sunshine. There, inclement weather never interferes with a tourist's plans, except during the short winter. Therefore, large sections of the coast might be turned into an African Riviera and the remnants of the Italian population of the country (only some 30,000 are still there) could help in building the country as an attractive tourist center "where the sunshine never fails."

Neutralism for Whom?

Libya lives largely on American and British help, as we have seen. Yet, the country considers itself "neutral"—in line with the general Arab attitude these days, which is the result of historic memories. Nevertheless, while it is true that Libya's experience with her Italian Fascist masters was not favorable, Il Duce, Italy's erstwhile dictator, has been dead a long time and the two Anglo-Saxon powers are helpful.

Though the Libyan "man of the bazaar" likes to do business with American guests, he does not like them. Whatever influence Americans and Britishers exercise over his country is indirect and inoffensive, but the Libyan is deeply conscious of the fact that there is an indirect control which limits his country's independence in fact, even if not on paper. Not very helpful is the attitude of the American serviceman on Wheelus Field, who compares all Libyan customs unfavorably with the air-conditioned, sky-scrapered culture he was used to at home. He speaks of the "natives" with contempt, calling them "Mohabs." Rumors are spread at Wheelus Field that Christians are killed in the old city of Tripoli. "Most American servicemen are apathetic to service in Libya and never leave the base. Others, when they do leave, make asses of themselves. Few understand or even attempt to understand the history, the culture, the problems of the United Kingdom of Libya." *

And what about the Soviet attitude? When Libya was created, the Soviets refused to enter into diplomatic relations with the Benghazi-Tripoli government and they referred to it as a "ter-

* Louis Dupree, "The Non-Arab Groups of Libya," *The Middle East Journal,* winter 1958, Vol. 12, No. 1, pp. 33-44. Professor Dupree of the Pennsylvania State University is an American anthropologist.

roristic police regime" imposed upon the country by imperialists. Then, in 1955, the Kremlin produced a "thaw" and proposed the establishment of diplomatic relations. When the Soviet diplomatic mission was opened its head was one of the Russians' leading Orientalists, Nikolai Generalov. The Kremlin was reported several times to have offered technical and economic aid to Libya. The Libyan government, however, claimed that the offer referred to the establishment of a hospital. Whereas Americans are unpopular, the Russians appear to be very popular. The American and British Ambassadors were jeered, the Soviet Ambassador was cheered at a recent Independence Day parade.

Since both Libya and Egypt are Arab countries believing in Arab unity and since they are contiguous, why should they not be united, thereby enlarging the United Arab Republic? Though this would appear to be a logical step for President Nasser, architect of Pan-Arabia, the record shows that he has antagonized one Arab country after another to the point that few of them are on speaking terms with him. Libya has accused him of interfering with her internal affairs and subverting her citizens—this probably in reference to the highly critical tone which Radio Cairo assumed toward the government of King Idris and family problems in the royal house.

Possibly President Nasser did not want to have Libya attached to the U.A.R. for the same reason that the region had not been acquired by any of the major powers before World War I—it is a financial liability. Then too, President Nasser may have learned through experience that the problems of unification are arduous. Long after the presumed union of Egypt and Syria the two regions were far from being fully integrated. More likely, however, the President of the U.A.R. realized that Libya was under the protection of the two Anglo-Saxon powers which would not want to let her fall into his hands. For the same reasons there seemed to be no indication that Libya was about to join the "northern tier" of African countries, Morocco, Tunisia and, sooner or later,

236

Algeria. Unless she has a lot of oil—which she may have—Libya would not add to the strength of the tier. Meanwhile, Libyans hope that their country may be turned into an African Kuwait—the fabulous little sheikhdom at the head of the Persian Gulf.

3. "HAPPY" ARABIA

"No country in the world today—except Tibet until 1951—has succeeded in keeping itself as isolated as Yemen," says a Royal Institute of International Affairs publication. "It has had periods of historical record interspersed with long periods when, for local and usually violent reasons, it was 'off the map.' Few strangers have ever penetrated its fastnesses, and even today, when the new Kingdom is a member of the United Nations and of the Arab League, the outside world knows little about the country."

Egypt has been described as feudal, Saudi Arabia medieval and Yemen Biblical. Few outsiders have ever seen San'a, Yemen's official capital, a walled town with eight gates which look now as they must have looked in the Prophet's time. The famous granaries of Yemen must be much like those that so well served Joseph, the son of Jacob and Rachel, during his stewardship. East by north of San'a is the famous Saba, reputed home of the Queen of Sheba, a distance of but six days of speedy travel by oxcart. *Al Yemen* means "to the right hand," when facing the sanctuary of the Kaaba in Mecca, and in Arab folklore the right hand is lucky, so geographers called the country "happy"—*Arabia Felix*. The only Arab country into which the monsoons sweep, Yemen has enough rain for agriculture. Between the mountain ranges the plains have heavy mist, which is ideal for raising coffee of the Mocha variety, named for Yemen's coastal town of Mocha. Fruits and grains are also raised in abundance.

The Yemeni ruling family belongs to Islam's Zeidi sect, which traces its descent to the great-grandson of the Prophet's son-in-

237

law, Ali, the fourth Caliph. Yemen's ruler for many years was the Imam Yahya,* an absolute monarch, endowed with secular and religious power over the living and the dead. The boundless power of this sovereign once was demonstrated to the English entomologist, Hugh Scott, who was doing research in Yemen. In the Englishman's presence, word was passed to the monarch that one of his bodyguards had just passed away. Whereupon the King signed and sealed a decree giving his royal permission for the deceased warrior to die.

In 1948, however, the aged Imam Yahya was the victim of a palace revolution. His successor, Crown Prince Seif al-Islam al-Badr, appeared to be more active in governmental affairs. News penetrated to the outside world about periodic outbreaks of unrest in the Arabian "Hermit Kingdom," but the motives of these eruptions were all but impossible to ascertain. At times they appeared to be probing operations to find the weakest spots of a regime which appeared to be little concerned with the welfare of the people and was unable to keep abreast of the times. The dissatisfaction of more progressive Yemenis was reflected, during their trips abroad, in their criticism of the condition of their native country. Basic changes had occurred in many other parts of the Arab world, however, and the effect was bound to be felt eventually even in this country of the forbidding mountains.

The few Yemenites who left their country testified that Nasser was the hero of its articulate younger generation which expected a drastic transformation of the country as a result of its being integrated into the Greater Arab Commonwealth. They were not sure how this integration was to be accomplished but having witnessed the "Arab Revolution" in the Westernized parts of the Arab world, they expected these ideas to penetrate into their mountain fastnesses.

On March 8, 1958, Yemen took the first step of what was thought to be the beginning of integration when her Crown Prince

* "Yahya" means "John the Baptist." Islam reveres the great figures of the Bible.

signed a pact with President Nasser of the United Arab Republic and formed the United Arab States.* Basically different from the union of Egypt and Syria, the U.A.S. concerned itself only with foreign affairs and defense, leaving domestic matters to the Imam.

Since Yemen does not publish motivations or explanations of the actions of her government, and her public officials hold no "press conferences" (there is no "press" in the country), the reasons for the union must be putative. Egypt is at one end of the Middle Eastern Arab world, Yemen is at the other end. The distance between the capitals of the two countries is about 1,500 miles. Cairo and San'a belong not only to two different worlds but also to two different eras. Both are Arab cities, to be sure, but their Arabism belongs to different centuries. Did Yemen join the United Arab States in order to strengthen her defense potential? How great was the strength of Egypt and of the United Arab Republic? Not many months before the forming of the United Arab States, Egypt had been decisively defeated by the Israeli in a matter of hours. There must have been some other reason for the creation of the United Arab States.

The Yemeni to whom I spoke had a "sophisticated" explanation of the union. Yemenite autocracy, as they see it, had been firmly entrenched in one of the most inaccessible parts of the world. In recent years, however, their inaccessibility has been breached by the radio. The voice of Cairo penetrates into the country and, though it is not heard by many people, it has strong resonance because of the amplifying effect of the "grapevine," word-of-mouth transmission, which not only transmits but also exaggerates. The royal clique, apprehensive of Nasser's ability to build himself up as the great Arabian liberator at the expense of their established authority, fostered the union in an attempt to disarm Nasser by appealing to his vanity. It was never the intention of the Yemenite court cabal to implement the treaty of unification, and Nasser had not the means to force it upon the country.

* See page 152.

Another explanation of the union concerns the inability of the Yemenite ruling classes to bring the country into the twentieth century. They cannot advance it even into the nineteenth century. However, the *malaise* which has overwhelmed other underdeveloped areas has not made halt at the country's frontiers and the introduction of basic reforms into Yemen could be accomplished only over the dead bodies of the rulers. In order to divert attention from real issues, therefore, the court found it necessary to produce synthetic ones—the type on which everybody must agree, or face the danger of being considered disloyal. Such an issue is the Yemenite claim to the territory of the British protectorate, the Crown Colony of Aden, and its central portion, the Hadramaut. The royal regime of Yemen apparently was deeply impressed by the skill with which Nasser ousted the British from the Suez Canal, and they feel, perhaps, that union with him will strengthen their own position in regard to Aden.

Soviet Technicians and the Oil Rush

Yemen has followed the example of the U.A.R. in practicing the policy of the "new balance of power." It will be recalled that this is a device by which weak countries seek to control stronger ones by playing on their jealousies and pitting one against the other. Relations between the Communist bloc and Yemen have become increasingly cordial. Yemen and the Chinese People's Republic signed a treaty of friendship and commerce early in 1958, and established diplomatic relations. Technical, scientific and cultural co-operation was agreed upon in a subsequent treaty. Yemen was included in the Arab countries receiving arms from the Soviets and their satellites, and the arms shipments were accompanied by technicians and advisers. It was announced that Soviet engineers were to begin the construction of a new commercial port in Yemen, and plans were reported afoot to turn Yemen's Red Sea port, Hodeida, into a submarine and naval base.

Yemen, too, was caught up in the excitement of the great "oil rush," and concessions were granted by the government to several concerns from different parts of the world. The concession of the C. Deilman Bergbau A.G., a West German corporation, extends to the southern areas and the coast, while the Yemen Development Corporation, owned by Americans, has a concession which covers the northeast two-thirds of the country. The offshore islands, administered by the British, are being explored by the D'Arcy Exploration Company, owned by British Petroleum. Soviet oil companies, in spite of their aid, seem to have obtained no concessions from the Yemenites.

"British Occupied Yemen"

The League of Arab States and the government of Yemen do not recognize as such the Aden Protectorate which occupies the 740-mile coastline in the southwest of the Arab Quadrangle. The Arab League has taken the side of the Imamate which claims this territory for itself. Arabs designate it as "British Occupied Yemen." The case of the Aden protectorate has engaged the attention of the United Nations and the Western press, especially since the recent and periodic eruption of skirmishes in the region.

Aden and the protectorates occupy important positions along Britain's "lifeline" facing the Arabian Sea and near the southern entrance of the Red Sea. Aden, the Crown Colony, is only 80 square miles, but it has a first-class natural harbor in the vicinity of the great junction point of east and west trade, near the Strait of Bab-el-Mandeb, dividing Asia from Africa. Back of the Colony is the large Aden Protectorate, the heart of which is the Hadramaut, named after Hazarmaveth of the Bible who was the son of Jokhtan, a descendant of Shem, eldest son of Noah and eponymous ancestor of the Semites. This territory fades into an utterly bleak desert country over which the British maintain a precarious hold, for the local chiefs are the real rulers. When the British wanted to put an end to the endless series of feudal warfares before the Second World War, the truce document they drew up

241

had to be signed by some 1,400 "sovereign" tribal chiefs. Slavery still exists despite British efforts to wipe it out, though some of the sheikhdoms are more progressive. Lahej, for instance, has a fairly well-organized government.

Most of the territory, however, is very primitive and few explorers have ever ventured into the sun-baked regions. One officer in the British colonial administration, Harold Ingrams, who did travel extensively in the area, wrote revealingly about his trips,* and brought back many interesting bits of information. One of these was a primitive anticipation of a "lie detector." The official scribe blessed a piece of dry bread which the accused was ordered to swallow. The local designation for this piece was the "accursed morsel." The accused then turned his eyes heavenward, invoking Allah's intervention to make the bread stick in his throat if he was guilty. After that he began to eat the morsel slowly. If he was innocent, he swallowed it freely; but if he was guilty, he choked on it.

Primitive though the area is, there is at least one momentous piece of news which has penetrated into it. According to British officials making their rounds in the Protectorate's distant regions, Nasser is the hero there, too, and far more heroic than any man can be. Even children shout their blessings on his head. The idea of Arab unification has captivated the fancy of many people in the large centers, such as Mukalla, Saihut and Ash Shihr.

To counteract the Pan-Arab tendencies the British have been pressing for a federation which, they believe, would strengthen their grip on the region. Several emirates recently were induced to form the West Aden Federation which then signed a treaty with Britain under which it bound itself not to enter into agreements with other countries without Britain's consent. The emirs signed this pact in the hope that they would receive higher British subsidies. In their turn, the British want to carry the federalization further.

* *Arabia and the Isles,* London: John Murray, 1943.

Warlike acts broke out between Yemen and the Western Protectorate in the last weeks of 1956, probably in connection with the excitement which the Suez crisis caused in the Arab world. In the charges and countercharges the British accused Yemen of raiding parts of the Protectorate, while Yemen accused the British of unprovoked attacks on Yemenite territory. The British employed planes to push Yemeni tribesmen back from the border areas of the Protectorate and the warriors of the Imam were not equal to the English planes. Finally, the Imam sued for a truce but negotiations failed soon after they had begun because Britain wanted to confine the talks to the final determination of the frontiers whereas Yemen wanted to discuss the entire question of the Protectorate's status.

Border warfare flared up again in the summer of 1959. Yemen charged that British planes had bombed the "Beidha area of Yemen" which is well within the Protectorate, and that British land forces had launched a heavy attack on El Daleh to assassinate a nationalist-minded sheikh there. Controversy broke out also about the Kamaran island in the Red Sea, off the Yemen coast, which is administered by Britain. The British government granted a concession there to a British oil company, whereupon Yemen protested on the ground that the island was Yemenite territory. Britain rejected the protest.

Yemen's Time of Troubles

Late in the spring of 1959 word reached Aden about a mutiny of Yemenite troops in San'a. The mutineers were reported to have burned down a number of houses, including the residence of the Director of Public Security. Shortly thereafter, word reached the outside world that the mutiny had been put down and the leaders were being punished. Army leaders were reported to be pledging their loyalty to the government and condemning "conspirators and traitors." The Crown Prince was carrying out a shake-up, remov-

243

ing the army commander and police chief, and naming an eight-man parliamentary council.

These cryptic reports seemed to indicate that Yemen was following the established Middle Eastern Arab pattern. There, too, the army was trying to seize power from what appeared to be a discredited regime.

CHAPTER 7

Oil Billionaires and Poverty

Petroleum—a New Fertility

ONE of the main reasons for the great importance of the Middle East is its stupendous oil wealth. The discovery of large quantities of petroleum is, however, a recent development and its effects will be felt only later. What will be those effects in the domestic and foreign fields?

This chapter will discuss the importance of oil in the Middle East and the significant problems of the oil-rich countries, and of other regions of the Arab world: Saudi Arabia; the Sheikhdoms of Kuwait, Bahrain and Qatar. The extension of petroleum exploration also has entailed "oil wars" at the Buraimi Oasis; in Muscat and Oman.

It is the "back yard" of the Arab world and Iran, which are fabulously rich in oil, both mainly primitive and backward areas. The only "modern" oil-rich Arab country is Iraq. Recently, Egypt and Syria have also become oil producers on a modest scale. This unequal distribution of the oil wealth has created problems within the Arab world. In view of the Arabs' attempted solidarity, is it right that a small sheikhdom should receive fantastically high annual oil revenues while other Arab countries cannot feed their populations?

All the Middle East oil belongs to the West, and not a drop

to the Soviet Union which is adjacent to this territory. Within the Western world, the share of the United States has been increasing greatly. While the British had the lead in the region at first, today the share of the American producers is estimated at 60 per cent of the total. The protection of these Western interests in the face of the Soviets' outraged attitude is one of the great problems.

When speaking about the oil wealth of the Middle East, a distinction must be made between proven reserves—oil in the "basement" which is known to be available—and actual production, siphoned out of that basement. So far as reserves are concerned, the Middle East is far ahead of the United States and, indeed, of the entire world, East and West. The latest estimate indicates that the reserves of the area are almost five times those of the United States—174 billion barrels against 36.7 billion barrels—and it is believed that the Middle East reserves are even larger because the estimates are based upon inadequate exploration. Many tens of thousands of square miles have never been explored even though their geological formation indicates petroliferous strata. In actual production, too, the Middle East is forging ahead. The United States has a tremendous headstart, of course, with all the facilities of production and distribution which the Middle Eastern area will acquire only in the course of time. Still, oil production in the United States in 1958 was 7.5 billion barrels; in the Middle East 4.3 billion barrels. The Middle East supplied about 80 per cent of the petroleum needs of western Europe—about 1.4 billion barrels in 1958.

The impact of oil upon the Middle East may best be judged by the rapid increase of revenue. Royalty payments to Middle Eastern countries in 1950 amounted to $188 million, and in 1958 to $1,270 million—a fabulous increase.

In recent years there has been a significant development concerning distribution of profits. For several years the host countries and oil-producing companies split the net profits of production fifty-fifty. Increasingly, the Arab oil-producing countries are pressing for a cut on all profits "from the well to the consumer," includ-

246

ing not only production but also refining, transportation and distribution. A new pattern may have been established in the concession which Saudi Arabia and Kuwait granted to the Japanese Petroleum Export Company in the so-called Neutral Zone, which lies between the two countries. Under the agreement with Saudi Arabia on its part of the zone, the government will receive royalties and taxes of at least 56 per cent of net profits from all the activities of the company—sale, refining, marketing and transportation—not merely production.

The discovery, in 1957 and 1958, of oil in offshore areas tended to improve the terms. Both the Italian concession in Iran and the Japanese concession in the Neutral Zone included offshore areas in the Persian Gulf. In Iran, the National Iranian Oil Company, a government corporation, signed a twenty-five-year agreement in 1957 with the Italian firm, Agip Mineraria, providing for the creation of a joint company and for equal sharing of profits from oil production in certain concession areas. In addition, it provided for the sharing of the remaining half of the profits in proportion to the National Iranian Oil Company's participation in the capital of the joint company which, according to the agreement, was 50 per cent.

A New Deal For Billionaires

The first Arab Petroleum Congress, which met in Cairo in April 1959, broached some interesting new ideas which seem to have been incubating in Arab minds for some time. Great interest was aroused by the so-called "Haliq Paper," presented by Omar Kamil Haliq, former delegate of Saudi Arabia to the United Nations. It described the Middle East oil companies as "contented patricians," interested only in a constant succession of record-breaking profits but not at all in the foundations of prosperity both for the companies and the people of the region. The host countries had become vassals, in consequence, of an alliance between "alien business giants and native vested interests." The

247

companies were supporting forces that failed to conform to the interests of basic Arab objectives. Also they fostered relatively little employment.

No less significant was the recommendation of the spokesman of the Republic of Lebanon at the Petroleum Congress. He proposed that five per cent of the oil revenues realized by the Arab countries should be set aside for the financing of an Arab Development Bank which would do for the Arab countries what the UN's Bank for Reconstruction and Development was doing for a larger clientele. The Arab Bank was to operate according to established banking principles. This proposal expressed a long-cherished idea of those Arab countries that produce no oil, or little of it. They like to consider the oil revenue of the petroleum-rich Arab countries as belonging to the entire Arab world. Why should the tremendous income of a little sheikhdom like Kuwait be only at the disposal of its ruler? these Arabs ask. In the interest of Arab solidarity and the general welfare, the oil revenues should benefit the entire Arab world.

Another suggestion made at the Arab Petroleum Congress dealt with a third great issue. The oil-producing countries should get together, it was suggested, and support one another in such a way as to safeguard their general interests. They should see to it that overproduction does not occur and that a steady and regular flow of petroleum is kept on the international market. Such co-ordination would keep production in line with the market demand and help maintain stable prices.

One of the main reasons the Middle East was enclosed within the "defense perimeter" of the United States and the Western world in general, was its great oil wealth. President Harry S. Truman consulted the American oil companies before his administration decided to move into the Middle East early in 1947, at which time the so-called "Truman Doctrine" was announced, under which America extended its armed forces outposts into Turkey. The President was assured that American oil interests would not be jeopardized by such a move; on the contrary, they would feel more secure. Ten years later, early in 1957, Senator Joseph C. O'Mahoney disclosed that Secretary of State Dulles, just before his trip to London in August 1956 to take part in the first conference dealing with the Suez Canal problem, had held a secret meeting with the spokesmen of the American oil companies. "Papers in the possession of the committee show," the Senator disclosed, "that these major oil companies had the inside track in knowing what our government was going to do."

Saudi Arabia Bows Out

Saudi Arabia became an important country under the rule of her founder King Abdul Aziz Ibn Abdul Rahman Ibn Faisal Ibn Saud. A strong ruler who introduced order into the lawless desert, he employed drastic measures which, however, were effective, and he was much admired not only in the Arab countries but also in the world of Islam. As the master of the Muslims' two greatest sanctuaries, Mecca and Medina, he was a conspicuous ruler. Ibn Saud was popular in the West, with which he made common cause during the Second World War.

For several years Saudi Arabia was the most important petroleum-producing country in the Arab world and was surpassed only comparatively recently by the small Sheikhdom of Kuwait. An all-American oil company operates in Saudi Arabia—Aramco, the Arabian American Oil Company, in which Standard Oil (New Jersey), the Standard Oil Company of California and the Texas Company each have a 30 per cent interest; and the Socony Mobil Oil Company 10 per cent. The Saudi Arabian oil-producing center on the Al Hasa coast, at Abqaiq, is linked with the Mediterranean terminal at Sidon, in the Republic of Lebanon, by means of a 1,068-mile pipeline. The Ghawar oil field of Saudi Arabia is said to be the world's longest, 150 miles. Proved reserves in Saudi Arabia were estimated at 37 billion barrels, far more than those of the United States.

It was expected in United States government circles that Saudi

249

Arabia would play an important role in the Middle East. The Arab world, also, felt that Ibn Saud had impressed Washington, and that nothing would have suited the State Department more than to have him assume the leadership in his part of the world. This, however, he failed to do. Did he refrain for causes inherent in the Arab situation or because of his personal reluctance? Before answering this question we must see how Ibn Saud managed his country.

Saudi Arabia is today the only major Middle Eastern country whose law of the land was written some 1,300 years ago, and was deposited in the Koran. All the other major Arab countries have adopted modern laws, patterned on the West. The law in Saudi Arabia is still the *sharia,* a religious code, which is implied rather than expressly stated in every instance in the Holy Script. The King is Imam, the national leader of public worship besides being the secular sovereign. The ruling Muslim sect in the country is the Wahhabi, which is described as a puritanic creed. It is that in some respects. The Wahhabis' mosques are simple edifices, lacking the splendor of the mosques in Islam's great cities. Wahhabi sectarians are extremely strict about indulgence in alcohol and tobacco. On the other hand, the rich among them are addicted to extravagances that are inconceivable in the far more affluent West.

Oil royalties might have enabled the country to invest in productive enterprises and thus raise the living standards. However, only a fraction of these revenues—20 to 35 per cent—has been so employed. A High Economic Council was established to prepare and submit recommendations to the highest circles about constructive development projects. Largest of these was the desert railway linking the "oil coast" at Dammam and Dhahran with Riyadh, the capital, by way of the cluster of oases at Hofuf, and skirting the large Ghawar oil field. A road-building program was launched; electric generators were installed; schools and hospitals were built. Because of the needs of the petroleum industry the demand was very great for building material, especially cement. Two cement factories were being built, one at Jiddah, at the Red

Sea, and the other one at Hofuf, near the Persian Gulf. There was also an increase in the production of some extractive and processing industries—spinning, wool weaving, tanning and silver mining.

However, a juxtaposition of the description of the improvements and of expenditures on them revealed a glaring discrepancy. The Saudi Arabian government's announcements read:

> In the field of welfare the government has been devoting much study and money to the promotion of health facilities. Every weapon in the arsenal of modern medicine is being used to stamp out the diseases peculiar to the subtropical desert climate like Saudi Arabia's. . . . In the larger cities, dispensaries, hospitals and maternity services provide free health service to the populace.

This claim should be compared with the reported expenditure on health, which was only $1.5 million in 1954. (Saudi Arabia's oil revenue in that year amounted to $225 million.) The entire long-range development project, spread over several years, projected an expenditure of 19 million Saudi *riyals* in 1957. (The official rate of the *riyal* was 37.5 cents.) Thus less than one-third of the oil revenue was being employed on public expenditures, according to official figures which, obviously, would not err on the side of understatement. (On the open market the rate of the dollar was 4.75 *riyals* in 1959.)

Jet Power and Camel Power

The combination of a high-pressure American corporation, Aramco, with the medieval civilization of the desert was instructive to observe. The contact of these two cultures was very sudden. What would be the effect of the engine power of the West upon the manpower of the East? Naturally, Aramco was anxious to create a cultural climate that would help its operations by creating a "stockpile" of local human skills. Also, it did not desire to remain a completely alien body in its exotic setting for fear that such a position would redound to its disadvantage. On the other hand, it could not move too fast for fear that by churning up long-established folk mores a state of unbalance would be created that would antagonize the local oligarchy and stimulate an over-accelerated rate of cultural development. The company, therefore, had to move warily.

Aramco launched an Arab Industrial Development Division to promote local light industries and give technical advice to local enterprise. The company's electric power was made available for local purposes and this, in turn, attracted minor industries to backward areas—plaster, tile, cold storage, ice plants and soft drinks, popular in Islamic countries. National productivity was given new stimulus in company workshops for the training of several skills. The oil company also introduced thrift plans in order to head off potential inflation due to the channeling of much outside money into circulation.

The company had 17,170 employees in Saudi Arabia and, of these, 70 per cent were Saudi Arabs. In 1953 only 37 per cent of the Saudi Arab employees were in skilled or semiskilled jobs; five years later 73 per cent of them were in that classification. Company personnel assisted in preventive medicine, especially malaria control, particularly in studies of insecticide resistance among malaria-transmitting mosquitoes.

"Unquestionably," said an observer of this juxtaposition of ultramodern with ultraconservative, "the conduct these people see is not all good. But there are examples that are good as, for instance, the lean tribesman fattening on a steady job, a mother escaping the boredom of seclusion at the free clinic, a school child painting a picture of a fly and what to do with it, and a busload of workers off for a carefree Friday—their Sabbath day. All these things would have had a place only in dreams a few years ago."

The bad part of this desert relationship was the fantastic polarization between the most advanced West and the most backward East. Here the primitive tribesman saw a vision which trumped his boldest dreams about the beauties of the celestial abode he anticipated. Here were the lush grass and the fresh water, the

252

invigorating air of the air-conditioned company compound, the miracles of refrigeration and electronics, the comforts and luxuries that are commonplace in Texas but fantasies on the El Hasa coast of Arabia. And here were also the products of the Hollywood dream factories, Technicolor, Cinerama, that took his breath away. For hours he sat in the cinema, his jaw wide open, in a trance, incredulous and yet believing it all. Will it ever occur to him that he, too, is entitled to the better things in life? And what will he do then?

We have seen that most of the oil revenue did not go into public projects. The influence of the American company was limited, too. The bulk of the gold went into the pockets of the royal family and its countless dependents—the hangers-on, the local sheikhs in the depths of the deserts, whose loyalty had to be secured at so many gold pieces a year. The sheikhs have made a rapid transition from the camel to the Cadillac, according to *The Economist* of London. It is reported on good authority that some 12 per cent of all the Cadillacs sold abroad are purchased in the Middle East. Not long ago one of the sheikhs was called on by a Rolls Royce salesman who wished to find out how his cars were running. The sheikh was not sure whether he had any such cars and so they went to the garage where they found not only several Rolls cars but other limousines as well, under thick layers of desert dust.

The largest portion of the oil revenue is being spent on an inexhaustible succession of royal princes, bound to be unduly numerous in a world where polygamy is the fashion and where the number of concubines of rich people is limited only by the physical aptitude of the virile male. The Nasiriyah palace in Riyadh was started on the foundations of a comparatively new $11 million royal palace, which was demolished to make room for the new $28 million complex of pink cement buildings set in a garden of tamarisks against a bleak desert background. Responsibility for its construction was placed in the hands of the Director General of Public Works, a brilliant arithmetician from the Hadramaut, the Aden Protectorate, who can neither read nor write. The King

253

himself supervised the work in minute detail, traveling from palace to palace, escorted by staff cars, jeeps and motorcycles, all painted red and gleaming bright.

The luxurious homes, furnishings and extravagances of the members of the extensive royal family have become a Middle Eastern legend. For the government, which contains several royal princes, a "simple" dinner service cost $118,000. In spite of the windfall of more than a quarter of a billion dollars in oil revenues the Saudi royal family floundered in financial difficulties and had to contend with endless overdrafts. Finally, on American advice, they set up a modified central bank. The price of the gold bullion was fixed and imports were regulated, eliminating some of the luxury items. The Saudi Arabian Monetary Agency was given an American governor, and a board of directors appointed by the King.

Hand in hand with extravagance went "appalling corruption," in the words of Harry St. John Bridger Philby, noted explorer in Arabia. Although an admirer of the statesmanlike qualities of King Ibn Saud he also noted the disastrous consequences of too much gold raining down upon the thirsty desert too rapidly. "The traditional anarchy of the Badawin tribes now yields pride of place to the selfish irresponsibility of a new bureaucracy whose thin veneer of education has done in a couple of decades more harm to the reputation of a great country than the wild men of the desert did in thousands of years." *

A Pivot of the Free World

Because of Saudi Arabia's oil wealth and location in relation to a weak point of the Soviet Union in Central Asia, the United States sought and obtained the use of her Dhahran oil field, in the heart of the petroleum country. This transfer was effected in 1951 and has been renewed since then. Two years later Saudi Arabia

* H. St. John Philby, *Saudi Arabia*, New York, Frederick A. Praeger, 1955, p. xviii.

accepted a United States military assistance advisory group. A military academy was established to train officers. The Saudi Arabian defense force, consisting of a regular army maintained by levies, entered the process of modernization and expansion. However, Saudi Arabia barred people of the Jewish faith, including Americans, and this prohibition applied to Aramco personnel and to servicemen in Dhahran. The 1951 agreement had specified that there must be no persons objectionable to Saudi Arabia among members of the American mission. The American Jewish Congress objected to this practice and in answer to numerous complaints, Secretary Dulles stated in 1956 that the acquiescence of the United States did not mean approval of the practice. The practice continued even in the absence of acquiescence and, as the complaints continued, the State Department answered that the "record spoke for itself." The American Jewish Congress finally took to the courts its complaint against Aramco's employment practices in connection with Americans of the Jewish faith.

The Windfall and the Slaves

The unexpected bonanza in the form of oil royalties, and expenditures of the United States in connection with the Dhahran airfield for American aircraft, had a profound influence upon slavery in Saudi Arabia. As the authoritative *Statesman's Year Book* (1958) pointed out, the royalties raised the prices paid for slaves and thereby made it more difficult for the slaves to buy their freedom.

A royal decree of 1936 authorized slave trading by traders licensed by the Minister of the Interior. The same decree regulates the conditions and rights of the slaves. The influx of American royalties has greatly increased the demand and price for slaves ($400 for a man, $1,200 for a girl in 1956) and correspondingly diminished their prospect of buying their freedom.*

* *Statesman's Year-Book*, 1958.

Attention was called, by the French Embassy in Jidda, to large-scale slave trade in Arabia, and several prominent Saudi Arabians, including the head of the municipality of Jidda, were named as engaged in slave traffic. A year later the French National Assembly discussed the question of slavery in Arabia as some of the slaves were recruited in France's sub-Saharan dependencies. Arab agents posing as conductors of free pilgrimages to Mecca rounded up gullible Africans, took them to Arabia and sold them. The parliamentary inquiry, conducted by a commission headed by Deputy E. la Grevière, disclosed that over 600 slaves per year were thus obtained. A more detailed study of these practices was prepared by the Antislavery and Aborigines Society for submission to the Economic and Social Council of the United Nations. According to the report of the Society there were about 500,000 slaves on the Arabian peninsula (largest number in Saudi Arabia; next largest in Yemen) and the King of Saudi Arabia was the "foremost patron of slavery."

With the death of King Ibn Saud the "heroic age" of Saudi Arabia seems to have ended. The late King was the "founding father" of the country, the two major parts of which—the Hejaz, with Mecca and Medina, and the Nejd area—he fused into one country. He appeared to be a strong and effective ruler until the decadence set in, due probably to the sudden increase in income. Members of the royal family, apparently, were unable to adjust themselves to the changed conditions.

On November 9, 1953, King Saud succeeded his father, Ibn Saud. The new king appeared to be a stabilizing influence in the feuds between the Arab factions—Egypt on the one side, Iraq on the other side, Jordan mostly in between, Lebanon on the peripheries and Syria subject to particularly violent oscillations. When border disputes embroiled Turkey and Syria in 1957 the Saudi King offered to mediate; Turkey accepted but Syria rejected his offer. When King Hussein of Jordan was endangered by pro-Soviet and pro-Egyptian intrigue, King Saud sent troops to the border, ready to support Hussein. He approved the United Arab Republic

256

but did not join it. He accepted grants-in-aid from the United States, but not from the Soviet Union.

However, news leaked out of Saudi Arabia about disaffection among the army officers from time to time. This followed the usual pattern in the Arab world. In Saudi Arabia, too, Nasser was considered the man of the hour, the Arab Bolivar, creator of a mighty Pan-Arabia. His Voice of the Arabs and the teachers he dispatched created an aura of mystery and strength. With him and through him the Arab cause appeared to be invincible. The King sought to neutralize the unrest of his officers by reviving the religious brotherhood of the *Ikhvan,* which consists mostly of tribesmen. Saud's neighbor, King Hussein of Jordan, had been successful in his appeal to the tribesmen.

Early in 1958 further word reached the outside world about unrest within the vast desert Kingdom where no Western newspapermen were stationed. The *malaise* which had gripped the rest of the Arab world seemed to have penetrated into the towns, oases and deserts of the country. While most of the country's oil wealth went into royal hands, some of it found its way into the bazaars. As a result of such a change, which could not be halted even by the most forbidding desert, the nucleus of a middle class was in the making. This middle class, far more sophisticated than the tribesmen and the people of the oases, was interested in the fact that, the more money the royal treasury got, the worse the economic situation became, since the country was beset by problems of inflation. In the absence of an effective press, the grapevine worked irresponsibly. Corruption in royal and government circles was bad enough but—living up to its reputation—the grapevine made it appear even worse.

Added to this was the influence of the Arab "re-awakening" the expectation of Messianic times, due to the Herculean strength of the new *Mahdi,* messenger of happy tidings, Egypt's Nasser. The bazaar in Saudi Arabia was not sure what it wanted, but it did want a change. Public opinion, never before strong in desert

257

countries where it cannot crystallize easily—as in crowded streets and in cafés—revealed signs of being on the verge of eruption.

On March 24, 1958, Crown Prince Emir Feisal, Prime Minister and Minister of Foreign Affairs, further was entrusted with control of internal and, particularly, of fiscal matters. In the changes that ensued, some formerly influential members of the inner circle at court were dismissed and foreigners were dropped from the Council of Ministers. New ideas began to percolate even in this desert realm. An editorial entitled "The Changes We Desire" in a Mecca weekly dealt mainly with the advantages of modern education. The newspaper devoted a page to sex education. This, indeed, was something new under the scorching Arabian sun.

Prince Feisal's rule was characterized by strict economy. Officials interviewed by a correspondent of *The New York Times* in late November 1959 acknowledged that money had been spent too lavishly before Prince Feisal took over such things as construction of new government buildings and enlargement of mosques in Mecca. They said nothing about expenditures on the royal family which were also restricted. One of the King's many sons explained that twelve of his teen-age brothers had lately been married in groups of four to avoid excessive expense. The children and grandchildren of the King run into the hundreds.

The change was observable in education, polygamy and even slavery. Apart from the spreading network of boy schools, some girls' schools may also be opened under a new decree. Aramco offered weekly television lessons in reading and writing Arabic, which won an enthusiastic following in Eastern Arabia and the Persian Gulf area. The government prepared to establish its own TV station at the capital, Riyadh. While polygamy remained legal, it was practiced less than formerly.*

Prince Feisal made an important policy declaration. Saudi

* "Change Comes to Saudi Arabia, But Monarchy's Hold is Firm," Dana Adams Schmidt, *The New York Times,* November 20, 1959.

258

Arabia will seek amity with the United States but, at the same time, will pursue a policy of positive neutrality. She will resume relations with the other members of the Western alliance if . . . France frees Algeria, and if . . . Great Britain yields to Saudi Arabia in regard to the boundary between her and some British-protected sheikhdoms along the Persian Gulf. The accent was on "positive neutrality" and this indicated that the government of Saudi Arabia was, for the moment at least, also mesmerized by Nasser.

The Case of the Buraimi Oasis

The Buraimi Oasis is a cluster of nine towns on the undemarcated boundaries of Saudi Arabia and several British-protected sheikhdoms along the Persian Gulf. It is situated in southeast Arabia, on the peripheries of shadowy loyalties. One of these is the Trucial coast of six semi-independent sheikhdoms, extending from Sha'am to Khor el Odeid along a 400-mile strip; so called because the British had concluded "truces" with several petty chieftains in the last century in an attempt to stamp out slave trade and piracy. The Buraimi Oasis is also adjacent to the Sultanate of Muscat and Oman, with a 1,000-mile sea frontage in southeast Arabia from El Katar on the Persian Gulf to Ras Sajir on the Arabian Sea.

Protruding into this region is Saudi Arabia, without demarcated boundaries, spilling over into the Empty Quarter, Rub' Al Khali, the "emptiest place in all Arabia." So little was known about the Buraimi Oasis that it is not indicated on the maps of even specialized publications.

Buraimi became important in connection with petroleum. This terrible desert country may be full of the greatest contemporary treasure, oil. Saudi Arabian oil is in American hands—Aramco. Petroleum concessions in the coastal areas, however, are held by the Petroleum Development, Ltd. (Trucial Coast), and the Petroleum Development, Ltd. (Oman), affiliated with the Iraq Petroleum Company in which British and British-Dutch influences are strong.

Buraimi appears to be the last place in the world to cause wars. It is one of the most recently explored parts of Arabia, having been discovered by the British explorer, Colonel S. B. Miles, in 1876. This unexplored tract extends 250 miles west to Qatar, mostly a gravelly steppe interspersed with oases, shelving down to the salt marshes of the Persian Gulf.

For decades Buraimi slept under the torrid sun, practically unknown to the world and, on its part, caring little about it. The oasis part of the area has rich funds of ground water collected near the foot of high mountains which serve as rain catchments and, because of this, it is the hub of desert trails into the interior and to the coast. The center is a vast emptiness, seemingly of no importance to the Western world. But then the same had been said about the El Hasa coast of Saudi Arabia and of the sheikh-dom of Kuwait, the "emptinesses" which have turned out to be fabulous oil-revenue producers.

A conflict did break out for possession of the Buraimi Oasis region, which could be described as the great oil war between Aramco and the Iraq Petroleum Company. On the surface, the desert warfare was fought by the tribal levies of Saudi Arabia on the one side, and Britain on the other, protector of the Trucial sheikhs, particularly the Sheikh of Abu Dhabi. Saudi Arabia made her first claim to the Oasis in 1949. Of the eight villages in the Oasis six were claimed by the Sheikh of Abu Dhabi and two by the Sultan of Muscat and Oman.

The first flare-up occurred in 1952 when Saudi forces occupied one of these villages and remained in occupation for two years. The desert scout forces of Saudi Arabia were equipped with American arms, and the British-led troops of the coastal sheikhs used English weapons. The skirmishes recurred intermittently until the summer of 1954, when Washington and London decided to settle the matter. A truce was concluded between the contending parties and it was agreed that the Saudi Arabians, who had occupied the village, should evacuate it, whereupon the British would withdraw from their encircling positions. The dispute was submitted to a five-member board of arbitration. Two of these were nominees of the British and Saudi governments, the others being neutrals.

The arbitration board met in Geneva in 1955 and the British opened their case with a charge of bribery by the Saudi authorities. Allegedly the Buraimi chieftains had been bribed to transfer their allegiance to King Saud. On September 17, 1955, the British delegate, Sir Reader Bullard, resigned from the board because of what he termed "the total lack of impartiality" of his colleague, Sheikh Yusuf Yasin, Saudi Arabian Foreign Minister and formerly the state officer in charge of Buraimi affairs. Native levies under British command occupied the Oasis, while Saudi Arabia protested.

Muscat and Oman

The oil war flared up now in another region about which the world had heard little, the Sultanate of Muscat and Oman, in the easterly corner of Arabia, with a 1,000-mile sea front extending from near Tibba on the west side of the Musandum peninsula to Ras Darbat Ali.

Muscat and Oman was important early in the nineteenth century, and the first treaty the United States concluded with an Arab ruler was with its Sultan in 1835. Under that treaty American citizens were not to be tried by local judges but by their own consular courts. This privilege of American citizens remained in force until the spring of 1959, when the pact was replaced by a treaty of friendship and commerce, under which the American government relinquished the previously prevailing right of extraterritoriality for its citizens. Since such rights no longer existed anywhere else, their relinquishment in Muscat and Oman ended an era in foreign relations.

261

This primitive Sultanate is famous for its date gardens, which cover more than 150 miles. Batinah dates are noted for their flavor and they ripen ahead of all other dates. However, good though these Muscat and Oman dates may be, they would not be worth going to war over. Yet a conflict broke out in this region, too, not far from the Buraimi Oasis, and not because of anything the Sultanate has at present but because of what it may have—oil.

In this case, the opponents were Britain, protector of this region, and the Imam (ruler) of Oman, backed by the Arab world and represented by the Arab League. Behind the contending parties again one could detect large oil companies, one mainly British and the other American, both of them backed by their governments.

The legal question to be decided in this case was as follows: The Sultan of Muscat and Oman claimed that his unimpaired rule extended to both Muscat and Oman. On the other head, the Imam of Muscat claimed that the Sultan had no authority over him. The antagonists were Sayid ibn-Taimur ibn-Faisal, the Sultan, and Ghalib ibn-Ali, the Imam. The Sultan was an Iraq Petroleum Company man, while the Imam was an Aramco man.

There are two versions about the beginnings of the conflict. The Imam started it, according to the British, in July 1957, when he rose against the Sultan and, starting from his headquarters at Nazwa, swept into the surrounding countryside. The British forces, led by Colonel A. J. Deane-Drummond, went to the aid of the Sultan, in accordance with their treaty of protection. The Arab League, however, charges that Britain was guilty of aggression against the Imamate of Oman, an independent state. It claims that the British "unleashed their jets and rockets in an attempt to intimidate the Omani people and to suppress their national movement." And why did they do it? "In order to establish so-called legal grounds," the Arabs answered, "for concessions and exploitation rights in the hinterland granted by the Sultan of Muscat to

262

a British company. . . . The campaign was financed by the British Iraq Petroleum Company. Its objective was to occupy the Fahud region, believed to possess great deposits of oil."

The Political Committee of the Arab League took the case to the Security Council of the United Nations where the British rebutted by explaining that this was an internal affair of the Sultan, and that they were acting in accordance with their treaty obligations toward the Sultan. The Security Council refused to consider the case.

The Imam of Oman had had the advantage of establishing strong outposts in a difficult mountain country, with sheer walls, which had the reputation of being impregnable. According to the British commander, the Imam's troops were well equipped with American arms. It is to be presumed that these weapons had been given to Saudi Arabia which, in turn, shipped them to Oman. After desultory and occasionally bitter fighting the troops of the Imam were defeated early in 1958.

Here oil showed itself the great magnet of Great Powers. Should Muscat and Oman be proved to have great petroleum wells, the desert war might again flare up and the desert people again be overwhelmed with sorrow.

The Oil-Rich Sheikhdoms

The Sheikhdom of Kuwait, at the head of the Persian Gulf (the Arabs call it the "Arab Gulf"), sits on the deepest oil well in the world. This small country * is a British protectorate and its ruler, Emir Abdullah el-Salem el-Sabbah, is "in treaty relationship with Her Majesty's government." The law in Kuwait is made by the

* There is wide disagreement about the size of the sheikhdom. According to *The Columbia Encyclopedia* it is: "c. 2,000 sq. mi."; *The Statesman's Year-Book:* "Area about 3,650 sq. miles"; *The Middle East* (Royal Institute of International Affairs): "The area of Kuwait is about 6,000 square miles"; *Britannica Book of the Year, 1959:* "Area: 8,000 sq. mi."; *Islam and the Arabs,* by Rom Landau (Macmillan): "Only 20,000 square miles in extent. . . ." and so on. This illustrates the difficulty of obtaining factual information of this kind in the Middle East.

decrees of an eleven-man family council, and against them there is no appeal.

Before the oil rush, Kuwait eked out a poor existence from fishing, pearls, harbor, some trade—almost nothing was produced from her land. Production of crude oil began only in 1946, yet twelve years later the little sheikhdom was the largest Middle Eastern oil producer—1,396,000 barrels a day and production increasing rapidly.

In 1950, the annual oil revenue of the ruler of Kuwait was $12 million; nine years later it was $500 million, having long surpassed that of the former No. 1 producer, Saudi Arabia, not to mention Iraq and Iran.

The ruler of Kuwait had the "advice" of Britain and so he handled his fabulous revenue far more responsibly than his Saudi neighbors. He was said to have divided his royalties into three parts: one for the use of his large family; another one for investment abroad, presumably in London, as well as in New York and Zurich; and the remaining part for the welfare of his subjects. He himself was not too extravagant, but spent much of his time in the invigorating climate of Lebanon, planting cherry trees. This, he explained, was necessary because the revenue from the trees paid for his expenses. While he lived modestly, members of his family, and the large court retinue, did not. Not far from his old palace one could see at night the lights of what looked like a cruise ship rising right out of the desert. It was a cruise ship and it rose out of the Persian Gulf. It was the home of Sheikh Abdullah el-Mubarak el-Sabbah, chief of both the army and the police. The sheikh lived in unabashed splendor, amid crystal chandeliers, marble dining tables for 210 guests, a private movie theater and a fleet of motor cars. He had claimed great stretches of land for himself by erecting concrete blocks around them. For certain of his downtown properties he received prices as high as $20,000 per square yard.*

* *The New York Times*, May 5, 1959.

264

There was money in Kuwait for social welfare, too. Eighty splendid schools were built within a decade, welfare services provided, large sums were spent on public gardens, roads and, above all, water works. Kuwait has no potable water; in the past, water was imported from nearby Iraq. Now, however, two large distillation plants were erected which produce drinkable water out of sea water for the entire population. Electric power stations and building industries were established for the production of lime and brick and a project was launched to replace the horrid hovels.

Yet, in this happy little land, too, there was much discontent, mainly because the inhabitants were listening to the U.A.R. radios and dreaming about a better future under a mighty Greater Arabia. So vociferous was the celebration of the first anniversary of the establishment of the United Arab Republic that two local newspapers were suspended. A Communist cell was said to be operating underground and, according to local estimate, "could take power in a few days." Kuwait was faced with the problem of what to do when one got rich too quick.

Two Seas and a Fish

"Bahrain" means "Two Seas"—those which surround the several islands, the largest of which is called Samak (the fish), which make up the Sheikhdom of Bahrain, off the Saudi Arabian coast of the Persian Gulf. The place is far better known to the outside world than the more important petroleum-producing areas of the region, such as Qatar. This may be so because Bahrain was a pioneer in Middle Eastern oil production. The Bahrain Oil Company is American-owned, but is registered in Canada. The islands' resources appear to be limited so that they have a thinning production zone. Annual royalties are around $6 million. This sheikhdom, too, is a British protectorate, "in treaty relationship with Her Majesty's government." *

* The type of relationship is indicated by the language of the Exclusive Agreement concluded between the United Kingdom and Kuwait on Jan. 23,

The British adviser sees to it that a proportionate part of the oil royalties reaches the public treasury. The ruler and his two hundred accredited relatives receive about a third of the annual royalty payments.

In November 1957 the Iranian government proclaimed Bahrain an "Iranian province," but Iran could seize these islands only if she could take them from the British. Thus Bahrain has been precipitated into the midst of a minor conflict. What are the legal grounds of Iran's claims?

Like the vast mainland behind it, this archipelago belonged to the "Arab universal empire" of the Middle Ages. After the downfall of this empire, turmoil swept the region and the islands changed hands several times. The ubiquitous and enterprising Portuguese held them for a time but they had to let them go, and the Persians, today's Iranians, possessed them for half a century. Before the end of the eighteenth century, however, Bahrain was taken by the ancestors of the present ruler, Sheikh Sir Sulman bin Hamid al Khalifah. The new masters originated in Kuwait. The majority of Bahrain's inhabitants speak Arabic, but many of them understand Persian and they are of mixed stock.

The British contend that Iran has no legal claim on Bahrain. Besides, why should Iran want the islands? Just because Persians once held them for a short time? On this ground, the British could lay claim to parts of France which their ancestors held for longer periods. Do the Iranians need Bahrain's oil? But the petroleum of the islands is now but a trickle, while Iran is one of the region's richest producers. In British opinion, it makes little sense for Iran to dissipate her energies by raising distant claims, instead of buckling down to the task of raising her people's living standards.

One of the "up-and-coming" Arab oil producers is the peninsula of Qatar, which juts into the steaming Persian Gulf. Even in

---

1899: "The Sheikh Mubarak of his own free will and desire does hereby pledge and bind himself, his heirs and successors not to receive the Agent or Representative of any Power or Government . . . within the limits of his territory without the previous sanction of the British government. . . ."

this world of many deserts, there are not many regions as desolate as Qatar. However, her oil royalties in 1958 amounted to $60 million, compared with $1 million eight years before. Little is known about this little sheikhdom under British protection. It would not be surprising to hear that there, too, trouble begins to brew as money begins to flow.

CHAPTER 8

Turkey—The Watch on the Straits

ON March 12, 1947, the President of the United States, Harry S. Truman, addressed the Congress on a matter of great importance.

"Totalitarian regimes," President Truman said, "imposed on free peoples undermine the foundations of international peace and hence the security of the United States." [It was America's obligation, the President continued, to provide military and economic aid to nations striving to maintain their freedom and independence.] "The seeds of totalitarianism are nurtured by misery and want. They spread and grow in the evil soil of poverty and strife. They reach their full growth when the hope of the people for a better life is dead. We must keep that hope alive. The free peoples of the world look to us for support in maintaining their freedoms. If we falter in our leadership, we may endanger the peace of the world—and we shall surely endanger the welfare of the nation."

Thus the President introduced his request to Congress to appropriate funds for the assistance of Greece and Turkey, and to give permission to American military and civil personnel to go to those countries and to work with them on problems of defense. The presidential address extended America's defense perimeter thousands of miles from the American shores and—it made world history.

268

Until this message was made it was Great Britain that had attempted to contain the Soviets in the Balkans and the Middle East. At the time the President's address was delivered both Greece and Turkey were under strong pressure. In the chaotic situation in which the world was plunged after World War II, the time seemed opportune for the Soviets to realize Russia's age-long search for warm-water outlets in the Aegean and the Mediterranean. In Greece there was a so-called "Free Greek" movement, mainly in the mountains of the north, largely Communist-inspired. The northernmost part of the Kingdom of Greece, a part of Macedonia, is inhabited by Slavic-speaking people. Mountaineers, they are fiercely opposed to government authority, unless it is their own. Athens was a long way off and people there spoke another tongue. The revolt which erupted in the Macedonian strongholds spread to other parts of Greece. The forces fighting the Greek government were supported by the Soviets and their satellites in the Balkans—Bulgaria, Albania, and Yugoslavia (which had not yet broken with the Kremlin). A natural sanctuary for the anti-government forces was provided by the rugged mountains of those Soviet satellites adjacent to northern Greece. Should the so-called "Free Greeks" subdue the official government of Greece, the country might fall into Communist hands. A Communist Greece would then have been in a most advantageous strategic position to threaten Western defense lifelines and to spread Bolshevik influence in the Mediterranean regions. This was one danger the West had to ward off.

The other peril was closely related to Turkey. After the war the Soviets, as we have seen, were bent on changing the regime that regulated navigation in the Turkish Straits under the prewar Montreux Agreement. The Soviets wanted to set up their own "defense organization" in the Straits, camouflaged under a joint defense system with the Turks.

It was in response to these dangers that the government of the United States reacted with the presidential message which, unlike the Monroe Doctrine, placed parts of the Eastern Hemisphere out

269

of bounds to outside powers. This Truman Doctrine enlarged America's defense obligations by many millions of square miles. Thus *Pax Britannica* ended and *Pax Americana* began.

The Danger of the Muscovite

The Ottoman Empire and its partial successor the Republic of Turkey have had many foes in the course of centuries. Sometimes the enemy of today became the friend of tomorrow. In one respect the attitude of the Turks has never wavered: the Russian was always the enemy.* Even today, when the Turk speaks about people who have fought his nation, be they Italians, Egyptians or Greeks, he refers to them by the designation of "Muscovite," the Russians' early name.

This enmity appeared to be terminated after the First World War when most of the Ottoman Empire was metamorphosed into republican Turkey. Her founder, Mustapha Kemal, performed the greatest housecleaning in the Middle East. Determined to make a complete break with the past, both in domestic and foreign relations, he made common cause with the Kremlin, although he was an implacable foe of communism. During the First World War his country had been defeated and after the war the victorious powers placed it beyond the pale of law. Soviet Russia was a fellow victim in the war, weakened even more than Turkey and in no condition to expand. A friendly Turkey was to serve the Soviet regime as a buffer and a shield. Because both countries were outlaws in the comity of nations they were thrown into each other's arms. The Soviet Union undertook to help the Turks' military organization and to launch a modest little program of industrialization.

But Mustapha Kemal Atatürk died in 1938 and with him went Soviet-Turkish co-operation. The Kremlin's attitude also had

---

* Just to prove that there are no rules without exception, the Ottoman Empire accepted Russian aid against its own satrap, Khedive Mehemet Ali of Egypt, early in the nineteenth century.

changed in the meantime. The warm waters of the south looked to the Kremlin more enticing than ever. As for the Turks, they remained neutral during the Second World War but, in the Russians' bitter view, this "neutrality" was slanted against them.

A Turkish Landslide

The Kemalist revolution had been the boldest in the modern world—and not only in the Middle East. Its object was to transform an Oriental despotism into a progressive Western republic—at first paternalistic and then fully democratic. Nearly all aspects of life were completely overhauled—the government, law, even religion, the language and folkways.

The advance guard of the Kemalist revolution was the Republican People's Party, whose program contained the dominant ideas of the republic. One of these was nationalism, in lieu of the dynasticism of the Ottoman Empire. The nation was to be the instrument of progress. Another dominant idea was democracy, instead of autocracy. First, however, there was to be a preparation period, with a Grand National Assembly along Western lines—a kind of "academy" for democratic training. The republican concept, laicism (separation of church and state), was to replace the Ottoman Empire's semitheocratic system of government, under which the secular head was also the religious head of the realm—the Sultan was also the Caliph, presumed successor of the Prophet. Still another idea of the new republic was evolutionism, which was explained as "adaptation to circumstances in a dynamic way," to replace the Empire's apathy. Finally, the republic introduced the system of *étatisme* into the economic life of the country. This was the name for a mixed economy in which the state ran many of the economic activities of the country, partly to speed up these processes through central planning and co-ordination; partly to provide the capital investment funds that were not available otherwise.

Opposed to the Republican People's Party of Kemal—upon

271

whom his countrymen had conferred the name of "Atatürk," father of the Turks—was the Democrat Party, which was against what it called the government's rigidities, especially in economics. The Turkish parliament under Atatürk had been dominated by the People's Party—the Grand National Assembly was a one-party body. In 1946, however, a significant change occurred. For the first time in the history of modern Turkey there was now a sizable opposition of 63 Democratic deputies against the People's Party's 465 members of parliament.

Then came the landslide, something that no political commentator had ever anticipated. New national elections took place in 1950 and resulted in a complete change-over. The party of the venerated founder of the republic was all but buried, capturing only 69 seats against the Democrats' 408. The Grand National Assembly elected a new President, Celal Bayar who, in his youth, had participated in the Young Turks' Revolution of 1908, aimed at the reform of the decrepit Ottoman Empire. He became a leading banker of the republic, then Minister of Economy and Prime Minister. A conservative, he believed in the traditional methods of economics. The new Prime Minister was Adnan Menderes, a graduate of the American College at Izmir (formerly Smyrna). For years member of the National Assembly, Menderes was adept in agricultural economics and land reform.

So hallowed was the name of the founder of the republic, Mustapha Kemal Atatürk, that even the opponents of his policy had to profess adherence to it. This the Democrats did, particularly in regard to nationalism, democracy and evolutionism. They took a different stand, however, in regard to *étatisme* and laicism. Their party program stated: "State enterprise will be limited to certain specified public services and such fields as are not taken up by private enterprise, whose sphere of activity will be enlarged. . . ." The Menderes government was to attain four major aims. Budgetary retrenchment was to bring about a balanced budget, so as to combat inflation. The economic system was to be accelerated by drawing upon private capital and initiative. An over-all plan was to be prepared, combining the public and private sectors. Finally, the excesses of bureaucracy which had grown up under the regime of *étatisme* were to be eliminated.

The Turkish government embarked now on a policy of denationalization—an unusual trend in an underdeveloped country where the opposite usually takes place. Domestic and foreign investors were offered attractive inducements. Foreign capitalists were assured of getting their funds back in their own currencies and not in Turkish lire. Profits and the proceeds from the sale of the capital assets of these foreign investors were thus freed from the restrictions of currency transfer. Foreign oil companies were awarded concessions. The liquor and match monopolies were turned over to private enterprise. A semipublic corporation, the Maritime Bank, assumed control over the State Maritime Administration which had operated the country's merchant marine. Private concerns accounted for increasing quotas of the production of machinery, textiles, food products and furniture.

Yet foreign capital, and especially United States funds, failed to fertilize the economic life of the country. Investors were not attracted by the fact that Turkey was now an outpost of democracy. Outposts are usually exposed and "risk capital" does not like to incur risks in exposed regions. Also, American capital, because it could find more profitable employment at home, failed to manifest the spirit of adventure Turkey would have welcomed.

Industrialization was pushed as a by-product of the Truman Doctrine to help stiffen Turkey's muscles. Yet the country was mainly agrarian; 72 to 80 per cent of the inhabitants made their living on the land. Turkey was not overpopulated, as were some of the Arab countries. She had free land, owned by the state and religious foundations, inherited from the Ottoman regime. In Turkey, too, most of the peasants were poor, but not as wretchedly so as the fellahin in the Arab world. The Turkish government estimated in the mid-fifties that some 872,000 peasants had insufficient land to make an adequate living, and there were more than a hundred thousand who had no land at all. Large estates

273

in Turkey were concentrated mainly in the cotton country, between the Taurus range and the Mediterranean. The land reform act of 1945 provided for the redistribution of certain types of land, such as untilled state property and private holdings in excess of about 250 acres. Redistribution began in 1947 and, in the next eight years, more than 1,686,000 acres had been distributed to some 139,000 farm families. Some of the recipients were Turks who had lived in Bulgaria, behind the "Iron Curtain," and who had been expelled from there.

Problems of Quick Growth

United States government money began to pour into Turkey. Beginning with the appropriation of $100 million in the first year of the operation of the Truman Doctrine, American supplies arrived on a large scale—planes, tanks, arms, ammunition, ordnance, motor vehicles. The real value of this aid was far higher than its "paper value" since prices were calculated for surplus material—ten cents on the dollar. The real value of $100 million could thus have been a billion. Turkey was one of the main beneficiaries of United States aid, together with Korea, Vietnam, and Formosa.

The full amount of what Turkey received from the United States includes armed forces matériel and, thus, is not a matter of record. One can draw conclusions, however, from a few available figures. Between 1948 and 1960 Turkey received $1,000,-000,000 in economic aid and more than $2,000,000,000 in military aid from the government of the United States.

In spite of this aid, Turkey's economic situation was constantly deteriorating. Unplanned industrialization, high government expenditures, a reckless import policy which made little distinction between necessities and luxuries, and attempts to play the "Great Power" began to work havoc with Turkey's balance of payments and, within that, with her balance of trade particularly. The budget deficit of the country more than doubled between 1951 and 1957, and inflation set in; the value of the Turkish currency was shrinking. The cost-of-living index which stood at 100 in 1948 was 181 in October 1957. Turkey was found to be a poor risk by the International Bank for Reconstruction and Development. Turkey's leading publicist, Ahmed Emin Yalman, editor of the newspaper *Vatan,* blamed the country's expensive and wasteful investments for giving bad returns in the form of unstable money, for the disappearance of basic foodstuffs, for low returns on production and for general discontent. "The government, which had kept denying the existence of inflation and was boasting of 'magical economic development,' became aware that no relief was obtainable from the West, unless the existing system was radically changed."

American aid had another paradoxical effect. The Turkish economic system had been fairly democratic, especially on the Anatolian plateau, where small farms predominated. A tractor in Turkey before the Second World War was a rare sight. After the enunciation of the Truman Doctrine the situation changed. The United States realized that it was not enough to supply Turkey with arms. She would have to be strengthened economically, too, so that the peasantry should have a stake in the country which, if worst came to worst, they would defend. Agricultural implements, and especially tractors, were imported into Turkey on a sizable scale. This helped increase the acreage as well as the yield which, in 1952, already was 60 per cent higher than the six-year average up to 1950. Within a short period, wheat production doubled, cotton production trebled, and Turkey, which had been an importer of grains, became an exporter. Under the impact of America's massive help the national income increased by 50 per cent during the five-year period to 1953.

This increase in production, however, was too hurried and export standards were not observed. The grain was insufficiently standardized, was mixed with alien crops, and was inferior to products from the world's "open-air grain factories"—Canada and the United States.

275

The large-scale import of tractors caused disturbances also in Turkey's social balance. Tractors could be employed only on large tracts of land. Once a cultivator had a tractor he could produce cheaper than the peasant with more primitive tools. Also, it was in his interest to maximize his profits by acquiring additional land. The small peasant was constrained to sell his land to the *aga,* the village nabob, and a class of *nouveaux riches* was strengthened.

America could not afford to let Turkey, a bastion of democracy, slide into bankruptcy at the very frontiers of the Soviet Union. "The relationship between us and our great ally," said the President of Turkey, "is based upon mutual respect and confidence. This sincere co-operation will continue to be the pivot of our foreign policy." The relationship between the two countries was also based on greatly increased financial help. The policy to help Turkey from the verge of economic bankruptcy may be called the corollary of the Truman Doctrine.

Aid totaling $396 million was extended to Turkey in August 1958 by the United States, the International Monetary Fund and the European Payments Union. Surplus American goods were given Turkey as gifts. The country was also benefiting from the consolidation of Turkish debts amounting to $400 million and the postponement of payments. The Turkish lira was devalued and the Ankara government had to agree to avoid unsound investments. Economic conditions began to improve.

Breaking with a Political Tradition

Under the regime of the Democrat Party of Turkey there were wide-ranging changes not only in the field of economics but also in social relations. One of the great innovations of the Mustapha Kemal regime had been the disestablishment of Islam as the state religion. Atatürk himself was a Muslim, naturally, though not a practicing one, and he was not opposed to religion. What he was opposed to was theocracy. He saw that the modern states were

276

secular and he also saw that the Ottoman system had perpetuated traditional values which had little validity in the modern world.

Under the new regime of President Bayar, however, the Turkish government revised its attitude toward Islam. The leader of the prayers in the villages and towns, the *hodja,* regained new importance. At the universities, faculties of theology were opened. The call to prayer from the minarets, which could be made only in Turkish under the Kemalist system, was now allowed to be made in the traditional Arabic. This changed attitude toward Islam encouraged the emergence of zealots, including the order of the *Tijanis,* who started waging a camouflaged campaign against Atatürkism in a small but symptomatic way.

The Democrat Party described Turkey as a "mature democracy" demonstrated by the fact that now it had a two-party system, as in Britain and America. However, as the 1954 elections approached, the party in power did not want to be overwhelmed by a landslide such as had all but buried its opponent. The government now passed several restrictive laws which seemed to indicate a return to the previous one-party system. The property of the Republican People's Party—the party of Mustapha Kemal Atatürk himself—was confiscated on the specious ground that it had enriched itself at the nation's expense. A vehement protest was entered against this interpretation by the Republicans who declared that this was an insult to the memory of the founder of the republic. Their protest was of no avail and they walked out of the National Assembly.

Even more disturbing was the next action of the Democrats. They passed a law under which journalists became subject to heavy penalties, including imprisonment, if they did nothing more than criticize the government or public officials. The opposition pointed out that this was the denial of the "mature democracy" which President Bayar's regime had claimed to create. Indeed, it turned out that the interpretation of the law was so loose that almost any political analysis became a criminal offense. It was revealed at the May 1959 meeting of the International Press

Institute, representing the press of the free world, that some 800 Turkish journalists had been jailed during the previous four years, including some of the most highly respected men of the press.

Another victim of the oppressive tactics of the government was the Bahai sect, an offshoot of Islam. This sect, which manifests a strong strain of humanism and belief in the innate dignity of man, was now subjected to indignities in Turkey on the ground that its members formed a "secret society" and held illegal meetings without having obtained official approval.

The government's high-handed methods produced the required results at the 1954 elections when, due to strange electoral arithmetic, the Republican People's Party was all but buried, having obtained only 31 seats out of a total of 541. The Republicans polled 3.2 million votes against the Democrats' 4.4 million. At the next election, in 1957, the Democrats obtained a minority of the votes, 47.91 per cent, but a great majority of the seats, 424 out of a total of 610. Former President Inonu charged that the Democrats had stolen the election in many districts. Names of voters had been arbitrarily removed from the electoral lists. The party of the government, the former President said, had endless facilities at its disposal, including the radio, even planes and jeeps, while the opposition was deprived of radio time. The final results were falsified, he said.

Turkey—a Joiner

Turkey is a member of more defense organizations than any other country except the United States. Already in 1949 she joined the Council of Europe. Only about 3 per cent of Turkey is situated in Europe. The aim of the Council, according to its Article 1, was to "achieve a greater unity between its members for the purpose of realizing the ideals and principles which are their common heritage and facilitating their economic and social progress." The Council is mainly a discussion group.

Turkey and her Greek neighbor were admitted to the North

278

Atlantic Treaty Organization in 1952. The Turkish city of Izmir, on the Aegean coast, was selected as headquarters of the southeastern command of NATO. Turkey joined this organization in spite of the fact that the nearest point of the North Atlantic is more than two thousand miles away. In 1953 Turkey joined Greece and Yugoslavia in a Balkan defense group. Only a very small part of Turkey is in the Balkans. In 1954 Turkey concluded a pact with Pakistan, and in 1955 she signed the Baghdad Pact. When Baghdad dropped out she concluded bilateral agreements with the former members.

Turkey dispatched the largest contingent to the Korean front, for a country of her size. The Turkish contribution was 5,000 men. Turkish casualties were the highest proportionately among all the United Nations forces. The number of Turkish prisoners was uncommonly small and Turkish soldiers appeared to be more immune to "brainwashing" by the enemy than the troops of the other nations. The Turkish troops remained on duty throughout the later years. Altogether 45,000 Turks saw duty in Korea until the beginning of 1960.

An Alliance and More Domestic Problems

"The Agreement of Cooperation between the Government of the United States of America and the Government of Turkey" was signed in Ankara on March 5, 1959, in replacement of the Baghdad Pact. Eventually the organization changed its name to Central Treaty Organization. In this agreement the government of Turkey expressed its determination to resist aggression. In case of aggression, the government of the United States "will take such appropriate action, including the use of armed forces, as may be mutually agreed upon and as is envisaged in the Joint Resolution to Promote Peace and Stability in the Middle East, in order to assist the government of Turkey at its request."

The government of the United States reaffirmed that it was

going to continue to furnish Turkey with such military and economic assistance as may be mutually agreed upon between the two governments, in order to assist Turkey in the preservation of her national independence and integrity and in the effective protection of her economic development.

The foreign policy of the Turkish government was endorsed by the opposition in Ankara. However, the opposition took vehement issue with the conduct of the Turkish government in domestic matters. The opposition demanded equal treatment for all citizens irrespective of their party affiliation; full freedom of the press; a judiciary system which was free of arbitrary political influence; and effective guarantees that the next elections would be fair and honest.

The opposition parties made an attempt to fuse their forces. The Republican People's Party and the small Freedom Party decided to merge under the name of People's Party. Two other small parties, the Nation's Party and the Peasant Party, were also to be incorporated into the united opposition.

Within the government party there were signs of an increasing tendency on the part of the dissenting moderate back-benchers to form a group advocating a more liberal policy. This group called itself *Yaylacilar,* the uplanders. Domestic politics became an increasingly important issue, especially in the cities. Younger people began to take their politics seriously. Political violence between the government party and the opposition flared up sporadically. Outstanding in the fight against the autocratic tendencies of the government was former President Ismet Inonu, who could always be found in the midst of the political struggle in spite of his age. He was seventy-seven years old when he suffered a head wound in the spring of 1959 during a political tour. The ex-President spoke for many Turks when he expressed the hope that his countrymen's common sense in political matters would prevail again and that at the next parliamentary elections the people's true will would be given free scope.

Turkey and the Cyprus Dispute

Turkey was involved in one of the most bitter conflicts in the Middle East—the Cyprus issue.

For centuries Cyprus had belonged to Turkey and is situated some 40 miles south of the Turkish coast. It is the largest island in the eastern Mediterranean, 3,572 square miles. It had a population of 548,000 in the late fifties, and of these 79 per cent were ethnic Greeks, 18 per cent considered themselves Turks and the rest were the Levantine *mélange*. This was the island that attracted nearly all conquerors. "The first recorded conqueror, Thutmose III of Egypt (1500 B.C.) was followed by the armies of Greece, Phoenicia, Assyria, Egypt again, Byzantium, the Franks, Venice, Genoa, Turkey and Great Britain. At times, Cyprus has had several masters at once, as in the seventh century, when the island was divided into ten cities, each under a different ruler." *

In spite of all these heterogeneous foreign influences the bulk of the population remained Greek Orthodox, who spoke a Greek *patois*. The Turks took the island in 1571 and ruled there for three hundred years. One would think that this was a long enough period to enable the Turks to turn the island into a Turkish place of settlement. Turkish officials ruled over the island and Turks settled there, too. However, the Turks remained a minority. In line with their policy, they let the minorities live under the leadership of their religious superiors. The Greek Cypriots paid their taxes to the Turkish officials but, otherwise, they remained largely under the administration of the head of the local Orthodox church, who had a large measure of discretion in the management of his flock. Thus the Turkish ruling minority and the Greek majority lived side by side, following their own customs, speaking their languages and worshiping God in their various ways.

As the Ottoman Empire appeared to be collapsing, Great

---

* "Cyprus," *Aramco World*, June 1959.

Britain signed a compact with it in 1878, which gave the administration of the island to the government in London, while the Sultan retained nominal suzerainty. When the Ottoman Empire joined the enemies of Britain in 1914, the British annexed the island. In 1925 it was turned into a crown colony. There were occasional Greek national demonstrations on Cyprus before the Second World War but they were not of great consequence. During the war itself the British and the Greeks fought the same Axis enemies, the Germans and Italians. The Cypriots co-operated loyally with Britain.

It was only after the war that trouble began to brew on the island. In the wake of the war, a tidal wave of nationalism swept the colonial world from one end of the great empires to the other. This wave struck Cyprus, too, full force. But the majority population of Cyprus, the Greeks, did not want to be independent. They were in favor of *enosis,* union with Greece. The organization which assumed leadership in this struggle for the union was the EOKA (Ethniki Organosis Kypriakou Agonos)—National Organization of Cypriot Struggle. The head of this tough, fighting organization was a tough, fighting man, middle-aged Colonel George Grivas, freedom fighter against the Axis during the Second World War. Archbishop Makarios III of Cyprus was the political and religious leader of the Greek Cypriots.

The Age of Terror

At this point, the Turks of Cyprus and of the mainland entered the scene. They wanted to have nothing to do with *enosis.* To combat the Greeks' *enosis,* the Turks set up the TMT, Turk Nudafa Teskilat, Turkish defense organization, a strong army body. The Turkish government and the Turkish Cypriots were in favor of retaining the island's status as a crown colony. Should that be ruled out, however, they would have accepted only another alternative—*taksim,* the division of the island into Greek and Turkish

regions. Under no circumstances would they have accepted union
with Greece.

Why did the Turks oppose *enosis?* It is true that the two
countries had been foes for centuries but that era seemed to be
over. Now they were Allies in NATO and the Balkan Pact. They
faced a common danger in being overwhelmed by the Soviets
and their satellites. Greece and Turkey were adjacent to the Iron
Curtain. After the age of enmity, the era of good neighborly relations appeared to have arrived.

After the end of the Second World War the Greeks had
acquired an important group of islands from Italy—the Dodec-
anese—which at one time belonged to Turkey. Wherever the
Turks looked they saw Greek islands. The Turkish government
recalled that a few years before, Greece had been on the verge
of being overwhelmed by the Communist forces, moving down
from their Macedonian mountains in the northern part of Greece.
The Greek Kingdom was saved then by the timely help of the
United States and the Truman Doctrine. It was not at all inconceivable that the Soviets would make another effort. Also in
Greece, the Turks said, there were still crypto-Communists camouflaged by the respectable names of conservative political
parties. What would happen if due to strong pressure Greece
should go Communist? Another neighbor of Turkey—Syria—was
also in the hands of "left-wingers," as the Turks saw it. With the
acquisition of Cyprus, Communist regimes might eventually surround the strongly anti-Communist Republic of Turkey.

As to the Turkish Cypriots, they professed to face an immediate and possibly fatal danger in case of *enosis.* The leader of the
Turkish Cypriots, Dr. Fazil Kutchuk, depicted this peril to the
author of this book. According to Dr. Kutchuk the enmity between Greek and Turk was close to the surface and could erupt
on short notice. Such an eruption would occur if the Greek
Cypriots were exposed to the tender mercies of the Greeks. Hatred
between the communities was "in their blood." Under British

283

rule, too, the Greeks, according to Dr. Kutchuk, dealt ruthlessly with the Turks and this in spite of the fact that the British sought to keep the scales even between the two groups. Island Turks at one time, according to their leader, had occupied important professional posts but they had been pushed out by the Greeks.

Realizing that some measure of reform must be introduced, the British government offered limited home rule, which, however, was far short of the regime of self-determination the Greeks wanted. The EOKA went into action and soon terrorism swept the island from one end to the other and continued in 1955-56. The British charged that not only had Archbishop Makarios not used his high office to stem the terrorism but that he was actually in league with EOKA and that he took an uncompromising stand in favor of *enosis*. Terror was now taking a heavy toll in lives. The British now took a determined stand. They arrested the Archbishop on March 5, 1956, when he was about to enplane for Athens. The charge against him was "co-operation with the terrorists." He was deported to the Seychelles in the Indian Ocean. A three-cornered fight was now raging among Greek, Turk and the British.

The relations between Turkey and Greece deteriorated further. In September of the previous year Istanbul and Izmir (Smyrna) witnessed violent anti-Greek riots, in the course of which churches were desecrated and destroyed, hundreds of Greek-owned houses were looted and wrecked. Only after the damage had been done did the police appear. Greek reaction to these outrages had been violent. The Athens government withdrew Greek servicemen from the Izmir southeast headquarters of NATO. Also, Greek forces were withdrawn from the maneuvers of the Treaty Organization.

Terrorism continued unabated, interspersed with occasional periods of truce. Greeks and Turks slaughtered one another, guerrilla Greeks killed those of their own nationality who did not go along with the EOKA, and in the midst of all this turmoil were the British servicemen—unhappiest creatures in creation. The

284

Greeks now charged that the British had created an artificial issue about the fate of the Turkish islanders—a Machiavellian plot of divide and rule. Cypriot Greeks began a boycott against British goods. Life on the island became all but unbearable, terrorism flaring up now in this part, now in another. Additional British troops were dispatched to Cyprus and it was contemplated that their number should be increased to thirty thousand. The death penalty was imposed for "terrorism" and sometimes it was no more than the bearing of a gun. A strict curfew was enforced.

The relations between the two communities became so intolerable that an interior migration began on the island. Turks began to move out of Greek neighborhoods and tried to settle in Turkish villages and towns. The Greeks began a similar migration to Greek sectors. Greek lawyers refused to attend court sessions that were held in the Turkish quarter of Nikosia, the capital. The situation looked absolutely hopeless and even the cleverest statesmen were baffled.

Five times the Cyprus problem was submitted to the General Assembly of the United Nations but no solution was produced. The UN body considered the problem and then produced an innocuous formula such as, for instance, the one in February 1957, when it "expressed its earnest desire for a peaceful, democratic and just solution of the Cyprus problem." In the spring of 1957, the British government found it convenient to release Archbishop Makarios from the Seychelles islands. He was forbidden to return to Cyrus and he went to Athens.

A new governor was sent to the island, Sir Hugh Foote, a liberal-minded and imaginative public official, who tried several solutions. These, however, were rejected by one or the other party—sometimes by both. Prime Minister Harold Macmillan now tried his hand on the solution of the Cyprus problem. There was to be a Governor's Council, including four Greeks, two Turks and a commissioner each, representing the Greeks and the Turks. Then there were to be two assemblies, one Greek, one Turk, to deal with communal problems. Finally, a tribunal was to be set up to which the commissioners could refer legislation which they considered discriminatory. Eventually, all Cypriots would have the right to opt for Greek, Turkish or British citizenship. This regime would be in effect for seven years. At the expiration of this transition period consideration would be given to the establishment of a Tripartite Condominium of Greece, Turkey and the United Kingdom. This plan, too, was rejected.

Enter M. Spaak

Since Greece and Turkey were members of the North Atlantic Treaty Organization the question of Cyprus was of concern to the entire Western alliance. It appeared to be intolerable that one of the most vulnerable parts of the Western world should be eroded by this fratricidal war. At this point, M. Paul Henri Spaak, former Prime Minister and Minister of Foreign Affairs of Belgium, entered the scene. Currently, he was Secretary General of the North Atlantic Treaty Organization. He arranged a quadripartite conference between Britain, Greece, Turkey and the spokesmen of Cyprus. He was accepted as a mediator by all sides. The government of the United States was using its influence to settle this embarrassing problem, and the facilities of the United Nations, too, were fully mobilized. British public opinion had turned to thoughts of maximum concessions to the islanders, as long as they were compatible with the strategic interests of the Western world.

By this time the islanders were also yearning for peace, exhausted by the protracted civil war. As a preliminary step another cease-fire was arranged. This was the proper time to count the casualties. The paradoxical situation was noted that more Greeks had been killed by other Greeks than by their British and Turkish antagonists. When all the casualties had been counted it was found that six hundred persons had been killed in the carnage.

286

The energetic M. Spaak arranged that the spokesmen of Greece and Turkey should meet in Switzerland and there consider a new proposal. On February 11, 1959, they did agree on what became known as the "Zurich Agreement." It was then submitted to the representatives of the island Greeks and Turks, who found it acceptable. The British government considered the plan and accepted it.

The Zurich Agreement provided that Cyprus was to become an independent republic within a year, and its independence was guaranteed by the United Kingdom, Turkey and Greece. The new nation was to have a Greek president and a Turkish vice-president. The Republic of Cyprus was not to have a union with any other country and was not to be partitioned. The British were to retain two Cyprus bases to which they were to have free access at all times. Under the authority of joint military headquarters, Greece and Turkey were to station armed contingents on the island. This agreement was, indeed, different from anything that had been proposed before.

Archbishop Makarios was now free to return to his island and there he was given a hero's welcome. Colonel Grivas, a mysterious figure to the end, who was thought to have been the commander of the EOKA, emerged from hiding, and left Cyprus for Greece where he, too, was given an impressive welcome. The Prime Ministers of Greece and Turkey now took pains to patch up their differences. Greek Premier Konstantine Karamanlis paid an official visit to Ankara where he was welcomed as a friend. Premier Adnan Menderes of Turkey summed up the situation at a state dinner in honor of his Greek guest: "It would be hard to maintain that history has not recorded difficult times between Greece and Turkey. But the failure of the past should only serve to make us more vigilant in the future." *

* Subsequently conflicts arose between the Archbishop and Grivas, as well as between the Greek and Turkish leaders on the island. At the time this book went to press it was expected that they would be settled.

287

The spokesman of the Turkish Cypriots, who had told me a few weeks before the agreement that the hatred between Greek and Turk was so intense on the island that they could never again live together, now told reporters that there was every reason to assume that Greeks and Turks will live as good brothers on Cyprus.

CHAPTER 9

Iran—Nine-tenths Submerged

Variety and a Paradox

IRAN is an iceberg, only one-tenth visible and nine-tenths submerged, wrote *The Times* of London.* Visible to the tourist is the one-tenth of the country, the magnificence of some of the great cities, such as Isfahan and Shiraz, the northern portion of the capital, Tehran, with its massive houses, impressive avenues, inhabited by well-to-do people. Particularly visible is the northern suburb of Shemran, on the wooded slopes of the Elburz mountains, with its quiet aristocratic residences, hotels and embassies. Submerged is the factory district of Tehran, in the southern sections of the capital, inhabited by undernourished workers. Partly submerged, too, is detailed knowledge about the country, largest by far in the Middle East, about 636,000 square miles.†

Built into Iran's present is her past, which is a living reality in this tradition-bound country. A glance at the past may explain Iran's diversity in unity and her unique reactions to outside pressures.

The language of the majority of the people of Iran—called

---

* April 6, 1959.

† The total population was estimated at 19,000,000 in 1958, but the authoritative reference publication *The Statesman's Year-Book* believes that this is an overstatement.

Persia until 1935—is an Indo-European tongue, Persian. However, Arabic—a Semitic language—is spoken by many on the southern peripheries and elsewhere. The language of large enclaves of people in the northwest is Turkic, a Ural-Altaic tongue. Sizable groups of Armenians are also found in Iran—Indo-Europeans, too. Then there are the Kurds, dwellers of mountains all around, and they speak a Persian dialect. Finally, many people in the east speak Pushtu, another variety of Persian.

These and other languages are sediments left behind by wave upon wave of conquering races, attracted to this region because it lies along a historic transversal highway between East and West; by its natural wealth and topography, its mountain sanctuaries, sought out by the oppressed.

Looking at the tattered Iranian peasants and the factory workers, at their sallow emaciated cheeks, the weak bodies of many of their women and children, one would never know what a strong race of people they are. It is almost a miracle that there is an Iran in a continuous line of history from the Medes and Persians of Cyprus and Darius the Great. There is no such continuity in Egypt.* Iran is like Egypt, however, in that she too has always been a magnet to would-be conquerors.

Iran, too, was overrun by the Muslim Arabs and their satellites in the early Middle Ages. But while these conquerors imposed not only their religion but also the Semitic language and ways of life upon the Land of the Nile, the resistance of the Persians was much stronger. There the Muslim conquerors imposed neither their language nor their way of life upon the local population—merely their religion, and even that in a special form. The Iranians belong to the Shii minority of Islam—not the Sunnite majority. They accept the Koran, not the bulk of the traditions; revere the Caliph Ali as half-divine, his predecessors as usurpers. In a way this is a variant of the Persians' ancient Zoroastrianism, with

* In 1960 Iran is celebrating the 2,500th anniversary of her existence. A good argument could be made in favor of the theory that the ancestors of the Persians came into possession of their land nearly three thousand years ago.

its belief in a God of Light and God of Darkness. Even today the Iranians look at the Arabs not as their religious teachers but as an inferior breed. Throughout their long history the Iranians have resisted outside influences—detribalization and also denationalization.

The Sick Spot of Asia

Yet, Iran is the sick spot of Asia, as, at one time, Turkey was the sick spot of Europe. Her affliction was too much history and the debilitating influence of traditions. She was also weakened by the unrelenting pressures against her frontiers. In a way, the weakness of Persia has assured her survival because it forces her powerful neighbors to create a balance.

From the north the pressure was applied by Russia, first the Czarist empire, and, later, the Soviet Union, both explosively expansive, thirsting for the warm waters which history had denied to the monstrously bloated realm. In the south, the counterpressure was applied by the British, whose most precious colonial possession was India. They have now been succeeded by the United States. The following was the line-up between the two power blocs:

The Russians started to push the Persians around at the turn of the nineteenth century, and as St. Petersburg's power of pressure increased, Tehran's power of resistance decreased. Persian claims in the entire Caucasian area were challenged by the Russians in a long struggle which ended with the Treaty of Turkomanchai in 1828. In the second half of the nineteenth century the Czarist regime was moving ponderously into the backward Islamic world of Central Asia, between the Caspian Sea and western China, filling out that "power vacuum" with its monumental presence. The area thus occupied by the Czars was also adjacent to Persia. That country was now placed between the two tongues of the Russians' global pincers. What kept the Russians from cracking her and smashing their way to the Persian Gulf, to the Arabian Sea, the coveted warm waters? Had they been able to sweep into Persia and beyond it the era of their pathetic frustration might have ended and they might have solved their perennial problem of occupying a vast mansion of a myriad of windows but without a single gate—the absence of warm-water outlets, the great Russian tragedy.

The Russians could not smash their way into Persia because at the southern end was crouching the British lion, ready to pounce upon the Russian bear. Great Britain was watching jealously over India, that most precious of all diadems in the British imperial crown. All the world was convinced then that India was the sheet-anchor of British might and that without her the United Kingdom would be reduced to the status of one of the Scandinavian countries. The Russians did not slash into Persia because of Britain. Thus the British and the Russians held each other in check. Occasionally they were on the point of coming to blows but their differences were always composed. Persia owed her existence to the fact that these two world powers balanced each other. Iran was allowed to live as a nominally independent nation even after 1907, when Britain and Russia reached an agreement over her in the face of a common danger looming ominously in the West—the threat of a dynamic German realm.

The Czarist empire vanished and was replaced by the Soviet Union. India no longer forms part of the British Empire and *Pax Britannica* is merely a chapter in history. *Pax Americana* has replaced the British peace, with this difference, however. Britain could lean upon India, a vast local reservoir of power and a strategic location. The United States is not the master of India but hopes to be able to depend upon Pakistan, one of the two successor states on the subcontinent. How dependable is Pakistan as an ally?

As this is being written, the balance of power between East and West is no longer as it existed for decades before the end of the Second World War. United States military establishments are now in Iran, while the Soviets, whose frontiers with Iran are long —about 1,500 miles—are gnashing their teeth. Yet there are indications that not all of Iran wants to be included in America's global defense perimeter. Tehran may turn back to the new balance of power, maintained by weak countries, exploiting the cold-war jealousies of stronger nations.

Then the Puppet

It was the Soviet Union that first succeeded in upsetting the balance in Iran and penetrating into the interior. In the global plans of Allied logistics, Iran played one of the most important roles during the Second World War. Through her Trans-Iranian Railway the Western Allies were in a position to extend a helping hand to the Soviets, engaged in a life-and-death struggle against the Axis. The ruler of the country, Reza Shah Pahlevi, was pro-Axis and too shrewd for his own good. He was convinced that Germany was to smash the British and he wanted to be on the winning side. This time the British and the Russians saw eye to eye on Iran, deposed the King, replaced him by his son, Shahanshah Mohammed Reza Pahlevi, and divided the country into two spheres of influence for the duration of the war. The Tehran Declaration of 1943, signed by Britain, America and the Soviet Union, guaranteed the territorial integrity and independence of Iran. That country became one of the original members of the United Nations. March 2, 1946, was set as the final date for the withdrawal of all foreign soldiers. However, in November 1945 a revolt flared up in the northwest of Iran, adjacent to the Soviet Union, and all the world seemed to know—except Moscow—that it was Russian-inspired. The people in that region speak a Turkic language, Azerbaijani, like their kinsmen across the frontier, in the Soviet Union. The revolt set up an "Azerbaijan Autonomous Republic," headed by Jafar Pishevari, who had been living in the Soviet Union. He promptly launched a massive program of reforms with the idea, no doubt, of making an impression on the rest of Iran as well. A land reform was quickly undertaken and a large number of social security measures was introduced.

The cold war among the Allies, however, began as soon as the

293

hot war with the Axis was over. The Western powers took Iran's case to the Security Council of the United Nations. World-wide public opinion was alerted and the Soviet troops were finally withdrawn, and with their going Pishevari's puppet republic collapsed. However, while the Soviets were occupying their Iranian sphere they were exerting pressure on the Tehran government to help them solve one of their problems.

Iran is one of the world's largest oil-producing countries, but her active petroleum operations are in the west and southwest. Northern Iran's geological formation is such that it, too, could harbor commercial quantities of oil. That region is adjacent to the Soviet Union and Iran did not wish to provide the Kremlin with this key to her front gate. On the other hand, she could not afford to taunt Russia by awarding a major concession to the West.

The Soviet Union has more than enough petroleum but one can never have too much of it. Also, since the West owned Iranian oil in the south, the Soviets felt they should have it in the north—thus establishing a petroleum balance. Also, the Kremlin was apprehensive that Tehran might award a northern oil concession to a Western country. With these thoughts in mind, the Soviets exerted pressure on Tehran to grant them an oil concession in the north. The troops of the U.S.S.R. were then still in Iran. The Iranian government answered that it was agreeable to the plan but that it could not negotiate a petroleum treaty while foreign troops were on its soil. Also, the ratification of any treaty by the national legislature, *majlis,* was needed. The troops left, the treaty was signed, and the legislature said "no." Everybody knew, of course, that the *majlis* was a rubber stamp. The Russians were angry but by that time the United States was watching Iran's northern ramparts.

The Age of Mossadegh

One of the most important lubricants of post-World War II history was oil. Iran owns some of the largest oil fields in the petroleum-rich Middle East and for years it was worked by the Anglo-Iranian Oil Company (AIOC), the country's largest single industry, connected with what was described as the world's largest refinery at Abadan. Hundreds of thousands of Iranians, the workers and their families, were dependent upon the bounties of oil.

With the coming of the American oil companies into the Middle East a managerial revolution occurred there. The Anglo-Iranian believed in giving as little as possible to the government in the form of oil royalties, its share of the revenues. These revenues in the Middle East are very large, as we have seen, because production costs are low, due to the abundance of oil. Aramco, the most aggressive American oil company, believed in making everybody happy and it reached an agreement with the government of Saudi Arabia, under which it was to receive 50 per cent of the net oil revenues derived from the production of oil, in the form of royalties. The Anglo-Iranian, a much more conservative company, considered this a bad precedent but it, too, was compelled to enter into negotiations with Iran about increasing royalties. Indeed, these royalties were to be doubled, according to a supplementary agreement, but even so they would have been much lower than the fifty-fifty agreement, which by that time had become the standard in the Middle East.

Articulate Iranian public opinion, which observed the oil situation with close attention, was upset by this situation. Some of the Iranians wanted merely a larger cut of the revenue, while others wanted also a larger share of the management. Still others preferred a more drastic step and wanted to nationalize the industry. The program of nationalization was writ large in the work of the "National Front," which demanded immediate action. Leader of this movement was an eccentric physician-politician, Dr. Mohammed Mossadegh. Iran's economic troubles, he held, could be removed if the nation took over the oil wells.

The Prime Minister at the time was Ali Azmara. Iran had drawn up an ambitious Seven-Year Plan which was to turn a poverty-stricken and economically backward country into a more

295

prosperous, progressive nation. However, Iran could not afford to carry out this plan as an "Operation Bootstrap," producing much, consuming little, because the country consumed so little that less consumption would have meant starvation. Foreign funds were needed and the Prime Minister knew that outside investors were scared of the very word "nationalization" and that they were suspicious of Middle Eastern countries, anyway. Nationalizing the Iranian oil industry, therefore, would have jeopardized the success of the plan.

This may have sounded good sense to many people but common sense is not always the most appealing campaign issue. Mossadegh had the advantage over the Prime Minister in that he had a very uncomplicated, easily understandable solution for Iran's numerous woes—a panacea. Public opinion in Iran, as in many other countries of the region, is created in the bazaars where people congregate in large numbers and where there is plenty of time for discussions. These people are not always very well informed, but what they lack in documentation they make up in intensity. The bazaar was impressed by the plan of oil nationalization and soon the extremists got the upper hand and they created a climate of hysteria where only emotions counted, not the facts. Those who opposed nationalization were denounced not only as bad Iranians but also as bad Muslims. In March 1951, nationalist-religious fanatics assassinated Prime Minister Ali Azmara.

On April 28, the *majlis* voted unanimously for the nationalization of the petroleum industry "in the interest of the happiness and prosperity of the Iranian nation and for the purpose of securing world peace." The champion of nationalization and hero of the bazaar, Dr. Mossadegh, became Iran's new Prime Minister two days later. He told the nation that there was so much oil in Iran's subterranean caverns that all her people could live "not only in ease but in affluence."

The British protested and denounced the nationalization as an act of piracy. Britain felt justified in seizing oil from the fields

296

of the Anglo-Iranian on its way to foreign markets. But there was very little oil available, because there was not enough know-how in Iran to operate the industry. The Soviets across the frontier must have been observing these developments with great interest but their engineers did not help out Mossadegh, either because they were not wanted or because the Soviet Union concluded that the risk was not worth the game.

The British submitted their case to the Security Council of the United Nations, which could not be of help, and then to the World Court at The Hague, which, however, declared itself not competent to deal with this case. This was a victory for the Iranian Premier but a hollow one. Instead of the Golden Age, Iran was overwhelmed by a new Iron Age. The government treasury was all but empty, business was at a standstill, and the country was worse off than before.

Still, the Prime Minister held on to the helm because no politician dared to defy the extremists. At least they listened to him. Finally, the ruler of the country, Mohammed Reza Pahlevi, who had been consigned to limbo, made an attempt to seize power. The extreme nationalist forces behind Mossadegh, reinforced by religious fanatics, resisted the Shah, who, feeling his life endangered, slipped out of the country and turned up in Italy. Mossadegh dispatched army troops to occupy the royal residences and parliament building.

He, too, however, encountered opposition. The flight of the monarch aroused new interest in him. Foreign influences may have been working in the background, too. Pitched battles were fought in Tehran's streets between the antagonists and protagonists of the Shah. Many officers and men of the armed forces went over to the cause of the Shah. The Premier was arrested by forces friendly to the Shah and he wasted no time in returning to his capital. Mossadegh, now an ex-Premier, was made to stand trial on charges of illegally dissolving parliament, attempting to oust the royal regime and defying the Shah. He was sentenced to three years in prison. He still had many followers, evidently. After

297

having served his sentence he returned into a world which had passed him by. Yet his great gesture while in power, of defying the world, was not forgotten.

The new Premier, Fazollah Zahedi, saw that it was imperative that the oil revenues should be restored in order to forestall budgetary bankruptcy and to continue with the country's major projects. The law of nationalization was to be retained while, at the same time, an agreement was to be reached with the oil company.

A Problem Is Solved

Seeking a solution acceptable to both sides, the United States now entered the scene, as Herbert C. Hoover, Jr., special adviser to Secretary of State Dulles, began to lay the groundwork for a new petroleum pact. Several other oil companies were drawn into this work. Eventually, in 1954, a general agreement was reached between the Iranian government and a group of oil companies, designated as the "consortium." It was agreed that the consortium was to act as the operating body, and that it was to pay the Iranian government about one-half of the net profits and other ancillary benefits. The government, in turn, agreed to compensate the former Anglo-Iranian, renamed British Petroleum Company, with the payment of $70 million over a ten-year period.

Shipment of Iranian oil into the world markets resumed on October 31, and Iran's oil revenues shot up spectacularly. In the last full fiscal year before nationalization Iran received $45 million in petroleum revenues. She obtained no oil royalties at all in the years 1952-1953, and in 1954 she started with a mere $9 million. However, by 1958 Iran was making $246 million.

New oil fields were found southwest of Tehran, at Qum. Plans were made to link Iran with the Turkish Mediterranean ports of Mersin and Iskenderun by means of a 1,000-mile pipeline. Thus Iran was to obviate the necessity of being dependent upon the caprices of the in-between Arab states. Also, Turkey and Iran formed parts of the Western defense system, headed by the United

States. The pipeline was to have a capacity of 30 million tons a year and was to cost about half a billion dollars. However, there was no indication as to where this large sum of money was to be obtained. All the eyes were focused on America and on the international finance institutions with headquarters in Washington.

Iran was better off economically than she had been before, but the country continued to be beset by a large number of political and social problems. The standard of living of the common people was still very low, in spite of all the projects, partly in the form of blueprints and partly in the process of implementation. Even in Iran it seemed as if the times were past when hungry people resigned themselves to a fate of being always hungry.

Social Forces in Iran

Iran, too, consists of two nations, the rich and the poor. "Iran is definitely a very backward nation," wrote President F. D. Roosevelt's special representative in the Middle East during the Second World War, Major General Patrick Jay Hurley, a former Secretary of War (reproduced in *The Memoirs of Cordell Hull*). "It contains really a series of tribes, and 99 per cent of the population is, in effect, in bondage to the other one per cent. The 99 per cent do not own the land. . . ."

Estimates vary as to the proportion of how much land is owned by whom. It is more realistic to say that about 55 per cent of the land is controlled by a few owners, Iran's "200 families," who live in the sumptuous Tehran suburb of Shemran, with all its super-exclusive clubs, and who live a part of the year in the United States, Switzerland and France, and whose money does not work for their country, because it is remitted abroad where it is placed in gilt-edged securities. Some of these feudal aristocrats own up to a hundred villages that many of them have never seen. They are absentee owners and many of them are uninterested in modernization. Iran today is a hungry land and yet only about one-fourth of the arable surface is cultivated.

299

The present King inherited some three thousand villages and about 3,750,000 acres of land from his father as the family's private property. The Shah realized that communism, just across the frontier from his country, could easily take advantage of this situation and in 1950 he decided to introduce a land reform on his own estates. He could not get very far, however. He was constituting a bad precedent, in the eyes of the two hundred ruling families.

He could distribute only 56,500 hectares (one hectare is 2.5 acres) to 8,251 families in 1951 and the following years. By the autumn of 1955 this phase of the royal land reform was completed, and then there was a lull. In October 1958 the Shah further distributed land in thirty-four of his villages. Taken all together fewer than a hundred villages were affected out of a total of three thousand. "The areas involved, however, have so far represented less than 1 per cent of the cultivated area of the country." *

More recently the Shah has been trying to break the rule of the great tribal dynasties of the Bakhtiari, Qashqai and the Lurs, among others. He has ordered the confiscation of the land of the rebel chiefs and its distribution among members of the tribes. It will be instructive to see whether he will be able to carry out this plan. The powerful tribes have their armed forces and in the past they were able to conduct their own foreign policies. Some of the important tribes went again on the warpath against the sovereign, it was reported in 1959, and their delegates were reported to have held a top-level policy meeting in Munich with the idea of setting up a national front against the King.

The condition of the peasants in Iran continues to be very sad indeed. It is believed that some 60 per cent of them own no land, and an additional 23 per cent do not own enough land to make a decent living. They pay 50 to 75 per cent of the crop they harvest to the absentee landlord for rent and water. A good part

---

* *Economic Developments in the Middle East, 1957-1958,* New York: United Nations Department of Economic and Social Affairs, 1959, p. 9.

of the rent is spent on seed, to pay off debts and the traditional levies of the usual parasites—usurers, the officials and the gendarmes who suck the peasants' blood. The peasant has not enough food to keep him until the next harvest and so he must borrow grain from his landlord's steward, thus sinking still deeper into bondage. Within a radius of not more than 100 miles from Tehran, on the road to Shahrud, the visitor still sees tracts of good land of loess which is allowed to lie waste. About a million farm families still lived in virtual serfdom as the seventh decade of the twentieth century dawned. It was then, too, that a bill was put before the parliament in Tehran to reduce the absentee landlords' holdings and to sell them to the peasants. How such a law can be implemented remains to be seen.

Also, the peasants have to pay heavy taxes. It is they and the urban workers who pay most of the taxes—mainly in indirect levies. Only 10 per cent of the government's revenue is derived from income imposts. Avoiding paying taxes by the rich has been developed into a fine art. On the other hand, interest rates range between 20 and 40 per cent.

Industrial Feudalism

Iran is one of the few Middle Eastern countries with sizable industries, many of which came into existence under the stimulation of the present King's father. A center of industrial growth is Isfahan with several cotton and wool spinning and weaving plants; silk mills in the north draw upon domestic supplies. Scattered about the country are beet-sugar refineries. There are also cement and glass plants, also rice mills. Until recently, the sheet-metal and ammunition factories were government-owned.

New enterprises are being launched constantly—four hundred of them in 1958 alone, an investment of $600 million from private sources. The needs of the country in textiles can now be covered, and the production of cement quintupled in five years. Business has never been better but not for the industrial worker. "Here

301

there are practically no limits on profits," an Iranian businessman told a French investigator. "I realize a net profit of 300 per cent a year but could do better with improved management." *

The average daily wage of the industrial worker in the autumn of 1959 was 80 cents, and 90 per cent of this went for housing and food. Rents had risen 20 per cent within a year. Food prices had increased twelvefold in the twenty years until 1956, clothing ninefold, and rent twentyfold, while wages barely doubled.

There is an embryonic middle class in Iran, the people called *fokoli* (from the French *faux col,* collar), who may be called the white-collar class. Members of this class are educated but have no jobs, in many cases, and therefore they are bitter, emotional, ready-made targets for agitators. Then there is the bazaar, highly emotional; the influential *mullahs,* religious leaders; and the generals of the army, who are mostly fighting among themselves, bring up the rear. Some of the army officers appear to have leftish tendencies. Hundreds of them were discharged and several of them were executed recently because of alleged participation in illegal organizations. The university students in Iran, too, have the reputation of inclining to the left.

Plans and Realizations

Iran, too, felt the need of launching a long-range program of economic improvement. As far back as 1949 an ambitious Seven-Year Plan was formulated to raise the nation's living standards. This task was entrusted to an American association of prominent engineering firms, the Overseas Consultants. The aim of the completed project was to encompass the entire wide range of economic and social development in one integrated whole. Through irrigation and soil improvement, farming was to be developed; also a large number of industries, especially for processing domestic raw materials into finished products was to be established; the coun-

* *Le Monde,* September 8, 1959, as reported by Eric Rouleau.

try's water supply was to be increased. Health conditions and education were to be improved and housing developments on a large scale were to be undertaken.

Funds for this large project were to be derived from several sources. A large proportion was to be obtained from Iran's oil royalties. Other sources to be tapped were Iran's banks, the International Bank for Reconstruction and Development, private investment and foreign aid.

The Fourth Point of President Harry S. Truman's Inaugural Address in 1952, envisaging the extension of aid to economically backward countries, had made a deep impression on Iran. She was an economically backward nation, if there has ever been one. Also, she was the next-door neighbor of the Soviet Union. What was more natural than that America should take a deep interest in Iran's project? The Shah himself paid a visit to Washington as his country's traveling salesman. It was there that he learned that Point Four meant technical advice only, and not funds. Shortly thereafter Iran entered a period of doldrums as the result of the nationalization of oil. The Seven-Year Plan appeared to have become a casualty.

It was revived again in 1956, and a Plan Organization was established under the leadership of a former head of the National Bank, Abol-Hasan Ebtehaj. He held to the view that his organization could best perform its task by taking an over-all view of the country's available resources and cutting across the lines of the government departments in making up plans for national integration. This the politicians did not like. He was replaced as Managing Director by Premier Manouchehr Eghbal.

American experts took a close look at the Iranian situation and they did not like many of the things they saw. They did find, though, that the country had vast potential resources, but time and money were needed to activate them and place them under efficient management. The budgetary specialist, Philip Taylor, learned about the weaknesses of Iran's budgetary system—inade-

303

quate taxes, very unreliable, too, because they bore down heavily on the poor and were light on the rich. He, too, found that indirect taxes represented the bulk of the government's revenue, hardest on the poor who had to spend all their income on everyday needs. Taylor learned about the reasons why the people who could best afford to pay taxes were practically immune to them—because they were powerful and could cause trouble to the government. (Also because they entertained no scruples about stirring up the excitable bazaar against the authorities.)

The experts found, too, that the post-nationalization plans were not well balanced. An inordinately large proportion of the funds was to be spent on Tehran, which was already a showplace (in parts) and what was the sense of erecting ornate and monumental fountains in the capital? Why not spend more money in relieving the distress of the poorer portion of the population?

Some projects, however, were found to be highly constructive. Best known of these was the Iranian Tennessee Valley Authority, as it became popularly known in the United States. It was designed to develop the agricultural potential of a large area drained by five rivers in the Khuzistan region, adjacent to Iraq, in the southwest of Iran. It was expected that the whole series of dams will produce 6 million kilowatts, and irrigate 2,500,000 acres of the better land in the region.

In order to help with the implementation of the plan the Industrial Development Bank of Iran was sponsored by the Chase International Investment Corporation and Lazard Frères. It was established in the summer of 1959 with the object of making long-term and medium-term investments in mining and other private enterprises dedicated to the development of Iranian economy. Geared into the plan were ancillary projects to stimulate native "risk capital" to take more risks. Fiscal exemption was granted to new concerns for five years and they were to pay low import duties. A 1955 law was voted, assuring privileged treatment to foreign private capital. Foreign investments and profits could be taken out of the country in the original currency.

Social improvements are also part of the Seven-Year Plan. Today some two million Iranian children are able to go to school, instead of 800,000 in 1955, and 13,000 Iranians pursue their studies abroad. On the other hand, Iran is still very short of hospitals, polyclinics and physicians.

It may be because American advisers believe in the greater suitability of private enterprise that Seven-Year Plan funds have recently been reduced in favor of the private sector. The Plan Organization was supposed to receive 80 per cent of the oil revenues, according to a 1957 program. Two years later only one-half of the oil revenues was assigned to the Plan. Large projects of public use have been sacrificed and the new orientation is toward short-term plans. Also when state enterprises reach the point of showing profits they are turned over to private people, who realize very high returns, while the general public suffers. As high-pressure businessmen were getting hold of the Plan, the country's economy sank into a state of near-anarchy.

The Shah to the Fore

The Shah of Iran has extensive powers, according to the country's constitution. He rules by the "grace of God." The executive power is in his hands and he is vested with the right of delaying legislation passed by parliament. In effect, Reza Shah, founder of the ruling dynasty, was an absolute ruler in the interbellum period. His son ascended the throne in the early days of World War II when effective power was in the hands of the occupying powers, Great Britain and the Soviet Union. His power was further abridged by the establishment of the Soviet-sponsored puppet republic in Azerbaijan after the war. He was young and inexperienced. Many of the Iranian politicians were old and experienced. Power thus came to rest in the hands of the political parties which, in turn, were the extended shadows of powerful individuals and groups, the usual "200 families," working with other established

305

forces, the bazaar, the army, the bureaucracy, playing one against the other.

Clown as he was, Premier Mossadegh also was a perceptive politician. He was aware of the strength of the "revolt of the masses" in the world and was bent on riding to triumph on its crest. He made a crude attempt to turn the common man into a "king." He announced the forthcoming introduction of social reforms. The nationalization of the Anglo-Iranian was extremely popular among the masses. Thus Iran's man in the street was to assert his superiority even against mighty Britain.

The collapse of Mossadegh in 1953 meant also the collapse of the party system. His followers were discredited; the opposition groups were hesitant. The hero of the hour was the Shah, the "young lion," the "country's conscience." Here was his opportunity and he took it—not, however, without prompting from the sidelines. He displayed some of the audacity of his late father, the empire-builder. In politics he revealed a cautious hand. He knew how to play one group against the other and thus maintain a balance. In the wake of the Mossadegh experiment the political parties were prohibited.

In 1957, however, Iran saw the emergence of two political parties. The *Melliyun* (nation) party was founded by Dr. Manuchehr Eghbal (also spelled Ikbal or Ikhbal), who became the Prime Minister. It adopted a conservative program "with a social conscience." The other party, *Mardom* (people) was more to the left. It attempted to reach the workers and to fill the void left by the elimination of radical ideologies. Still, the pivot of Iran's political life continued to be the Shah. The government spoke in the name of the ruler: "This is the will of His Majesty," and then the last word had been said. Certain dangers were entailed by this procedure, in a good many people's view. Should something go awry, the Shah's reputation would suffer.

Before the post-Mossadegh elimination of the political parties the Tudeh movement played a role in Iranian politics. The word means "masses" and the program of the movement called for most of the reforms the region needed, such as, for instance, land reform, a democratic constitution, schools, hospitals, social security. However, the Tudeh acquired the reputation of being Communist or at least a front. Maybe it was. It attracted intellectuals, university people, articulate trade-union members. Many of these were probably not Communists, not even sympathizers. But there was no progressive movement of a less vivid hue. Many intellectuals felt that not only social justice but the national interests of Iran required that she should not fall behind the modernization that was sweeping across the underdeveloped part of the world.

The Tudeh discredited itself by adopting the cause of the Azerbaijan puppet regime. From time to time it was outlawed, but it managed to re-emerge under several pseudonyms, such as the Association to Combat Imperialism. It took a strong stand in favor of Iran's nationalization of oil and just as strong a stand against Great Britain. Thus it was operating on a common front with the jingoistic bodies it fought and which combated it, in turn.

After the Mossadegh experience the Tudeh appears to have been crushed—perhaps not completely. It has fallen a victim of Iran's powerful and ubiquitous secret police, S.A.V.E.K. Today the movement has no coherent organization. Known Tudeh supporters have been jailed, except for those who have been executed. In prison they are exposed to government orientation. The "repentant sinners" are forgiven, but first they have to go through "the procedure." They must sign a statement in which they renounce their past association and the Tudeh ideology. If they are sufficiently prominent, the statement is published in the press, together with their photographs. Then they are released. However, the Tudeh still publishes an illegal sheet, *Sobh Omid* (Dawn of Hope). It is said to be printed somewhere in Europe but it is not unlikely that its place of publication is European Russia or perhaps Asian Russia. In Iran the prevailing tendency is to be suspicious in political matters. It is suspected by some people, for instance, that it was the "200 families" that infiltrated the Tudeh with known Communists in order to discredit it. There can be no doubt of the fact, however, that the Soviets were using the movement for the furtherance of their policies in Iran. The secret Iranian radio, Sedaye Melli Iran (National Voice of Iran) which claims to emanate from within the country but probably originates in Russia, propagates the Tudeh policy.

The Russians in Iran

The northern part of Iran (then Persia) was officially designated as within the Russian sphere of influence in the major diplomatic realignment between Britain and the Czarist empire in 1907. This terminated the "cold war" (or as it was known in those days, the "dry war") between those powers. The father of the present Shah started his career as one of the senior officers of the Cossack Division in Iran, the top command of which was in Russian hands.

After the First World War the Soviet Union and Iran concluded a new treaty. The year was 1921, and it was a time of troubles both for the Russians and the Iranians. Both countries feared attacks by third powers. The pact provided that if a third party should attempt to carry out a "policy of usurpation" through armed intervention in Iran, or if such power should want to use Iranian territory as an operational base against the Soviets, or if a foreign power threatened the Soviet frontiers or if Iran were unable to stop such a menace, the Soviets had the right to advance their troops into Iran for defensive operations. However, as soon as such a danger was removed, Russia undertook to withdraw her troops from Iran.

As Iran joined the defense system headed by the United States, the Russians protested, invoking the 1921 pact which vested them with the right to move into their neighbor's country. Moscow kept on charging that Tehran was privy to American plans to convert the country into a strategic base against the Soviets. Finally, Iran announced the nullification of the two articles of the 1921 pact under which the Soviets might have felt entitled to move their troops across the border. This was in 1959.

The Russians did not move into Iran to punish a recalcitrant neighbor. Instead of that they launched a massive campaign of vilification against the Shah on the radio. They kept on describing him as a profligate lecher leading his decadent entourage in endless bouts of orgies. The reaction of Tehran society was amused indifference. "If the King amuses himself, so much the better for him." But nobody knew what the common people were thinking about these broadcasts.

American Influence in Iran

The cold war began in Iran, with the establishment of the Russian-sponsored Azerbaijani puppet regime immediately after the Second World War. America was Iran's most energetic sponsor before the Security Council of the United Nations. The United States was now putting up fences around the Soviet Union for the protection of the countries that lacked the strength to defend themselves. The government had already offered assistance to Iran in 1947, the year in which the Washington administration announced the so-called Truman Doctrine for the defense of part of the Middle East, Turkey, Iran's next-door neighbor. In the same year the United States signed a pact with Tehran under which a military mission was to increase the efficiency of her army. The pact contained the significant clause that Iranian army matters might not be entrusted to other powers' experts, without American consent.

Subsequently, America moved massively into Iran in both civilian and military matters. An American military mission under General Robert Grow, Second World War commander of the 6th Armored Division, was invited to reorganize the Iranian army. General H. Norman Schwarzkopf headed the American mission to reorganize the Imperial Iranian Gendarmerie. American aid to

Iran was extended over a broad front—through the Mutual Defense Assistance program; through Point Four, the Export-Import Bank, and the Near East Foundation. Indirectly, too, America helped, through United Nations institutions such as the International Bank for Reconstruction and Development. In six and a half years alone, up to June 30, 1957, American aid to Iran was $394 million—and more, since the accounting system in such matters does not reveal all the relevant facts.

Americans were at work in Iran in private capacities, too, side by side with British, French, West German and other teams. A large number of Iranian projects were entrusted to Americans—housing, roads, the Khuzistan Development project and many other phases of the Seven-Year Plan.

Iran was a member of the "northern tier" countries along the southern border of the Soviet Union; these countries formed the Baghdad Pact organization in 1955. The other northern-tier countries were Turkey and Pakistan. Other members were Iraq and the United Kingdom, while the United States remained a partner in the background. In 1958, Baghdad turned against the Baghdad Pact in a revolution which sought to make a clean sweep of the past. The United States was ready to conclude bilateral agreements with the remaining Asian members of the former organization, and one of them was Iran. What should America's commitment contain? Washington was interested in the fence against the Russians, while the Shah was also interested in a fence against a domestic revolution. He had been deeply shaken by the regicides in nearby countries—in Iraq and, before that, in Jordan. America was to underwrite his regime. A revolution at home was likely to be Communist-inspired. Even if it was not, the Soviets were likely to draw benefits from it, as they were doing in Iraq. Also, defense arrangements required a regime undisturbed by domestic convulsions. The Shah wanted the United States to underwrite his regime by protecting it against both foreign and domestic "aggressions." This the administration at Washington was unwilling to do, at first.

The Shah thereupon decided to play out one world power against the other. He approached Moscow with the plan of a mutual nonaggression pact. He went so far as to present the official text he was ready to sign. The Kremlin was interested—very much interested, indeed, and dispatched Deputy Foreign Minister Semionov to Tehran posthaste. At the same time the Shah saw to it that his *démarche* in Moscow should also be noted in Washington.

When Washington learned about Iran's proposed step it dispatched the former Chairman of the Joint Chiefs of Staff of the United States, Admiral Arthur William Radford, to Tehran with the mandate to offer the Shah a more elastic document. Under this pact military assistance was to be extended to Iran not only in the case of outside aggression but in the event of "any aggression," and that is a very elastic concept, indeed, which may include also a revolution at home. The Soviet diplomat had to withdraw; the sovereign signed the pact and the *majlis,* legislature, ratified it on March 8, 1959.

Now that there was no longer a Baghdad in the Western camp, the headquarters of the organization was moved to the Turkish capital, Ankara, evidently felt to be a safer place than either Tehran or Karachi. The name of the organization was changed, too. It was now CENTO, Central Treaty Organization. The United States also signed bilateral agreements with the other Asian members, Turkey and Pakistan, both of which wanted to have American protection against "indirect aggression," "internal revolution" and got treaty protection against "any aggression."

Now that CENTO had replaced the Baghdad Pact the transportation system of at least two of its countries had to be improved, so as to free it from the revolutionary tendencies of certain Middle Eastern regions, particularly Iraq. The decision was taken to build a new railway from eastern Turkey to western Iran, starting at the Turkish town of Mus, and proceeding through Van to Qutur and Khoi, where it would join the Iranian trunk system. On the basis of survey estimates Iran and Turkey applied for help to the

United States Development Loan Fund, a subsidiary of the Export-Import Bank. Iran asked for $38 million and Turkey for $48 million, later reduced to $36 million. There the matter rested—for a time at least.*

* The history of the Iranian maneuvers to have the United States protect her against "indirect aggression" was told in the March 11, 1959, issue of *Der Spiegel,* the West German weekly, which is known to be well informed in such matters. Its account of these events has never been denied by any official source.

CHAPTER 10

Israel—Problems of Growth

East in the West

IN cultural orientation and social attitudes Israel is a Western country, not a Middle Eastern one. Though the preponderant part of her population has come from Eastern Europe and the Middle East, and her political leadership originated in pre-First World War Russia and pre-Second World War Poland, Israel, geographically situated in the coreland of the Middle East, operates within the framework of the Western world.

In this respect a similarity between Israel and the United States is manifest, but it is qualified by a notable dissimilarity. The cultural pattern of America is that of the farthest West, basically Anglo-Saxon, and yet the majority of Americans are not of that origin. In technology, particularly, North America is more Western than most of Europe. On the other hand, leadership in the United States and Canada was drawn from a dominant Anglo-Saxon social strain and from strata which had assimilated its ways. In Israel, however, the leadership merely absorbed the Western ideology but was not predominantly Occidental itself.

"Western culture, as exemplified by the cultural developments of the last two centuries in Western Europe and the United States of America, is focused on the two main and interconnected themes

313

of technical development and mass benefits." * The development of the modern factory system with its mass production, soil chemistry, storage and distribution of food, banking and insurance were made possible by the common denominator of technical development. Mass education, universal suffrage, hygiene, newspapers, books, movies, radio and television, sports and athletics, became available to the masses of the population, and not merely to the privileged few. Also mass-oriented were the characteristic social, ethical and economic doctrines of the West, while the democratic philosophy, religious doctrine and ethics as well as group interests were to render service to every man. This is also true of Israel's Western-oriented culture.

The triumph of Western values is the most significant development of the contemporary world. Israel, the youngest country in the Middle East, launched her national life within this Occidental framework and that makes hers a unique experiment in the region. Her Arab neighbors, on the other hand, began their national lives within a basically Oriental mold. Exposed to the all-pervading contemporary influence of Western values and due to the traumatic experience caused by the emergence of Israel in their midst, they are Occidentalizing. But the road to the goal is arduous and long, and though her neighbors are being Westernized, Israel is Western and thus still is an alien body in their midst. This is the basic factor in their hostile attitude toward her.†

Israel's difficulties with her neighbors revealed a trend of be-

* Raphael Patai, *Israel Between East and West,* Philadelphia: The Jewish Publication Society of America, 1953, p. 29.

† The social, political and economic development of most of the Arab countries in the Middle East was delayed due to the interplay of historic forces and group interests. They remained feudal, semifeudal, and even tribal in the age of the atomic bomb. Large parts of the area remained immune to the influence of capitalism as well as the Soviet type of collectivism. The "great awakener" of the Arab Middle East was the emergence of Israel. One after another the more important Arab countries began to shake off their feudal and tribal yokes. Revolutionary upheavals swept the Arab world from Aden to Casablanca. Israel has turned out to be the great modernizer of the area. The Arabs' boundless hatred of Israel may reach deep down into the darknesses of the human psyche—the hatred of the hand that disturbs a deep slumber.

coming institutionalized. Not one of the Arab countries established diplomatic relations with her and their hostility to her stiffened into a dogma. . . . The motivation of their enmity fed rationalizations that served as synthetic substitutes for constructive programs. Though the Arab League had been established ostensibly to strengthen its members with the positive achievements of integrated and co-ordinated policies, it served its major functions merely as the instrument for boycotting Israel . . . for she provided the most telling illustration of an intrusion, a dynamic way of life. The contrast with the ways of the neighboring countries created the setting for a unique Western experiment in the East. Supremacy was manifest in all phases of social activities: health and social services, education, science and culture; government and administration; defense forces; national institutions and the national economy. Israel ranked with the Western countries in nearly all these fields—in spite of all the difficulties of nation-building in an uncompromisingly hostile environment, Israel's living standards, per capita national income, calories, food consumption, were on the European level.*

The significant factor in Israel's orientation is the modern ideology which interprets freedom not merely as a negative factor —freedom from coercion by the government and powerful individuals—but as a positive force expressed in a conscious endeavor on the part of the collective body to free the individual for a fuller unfolding of his native capacities by shielding him against hazards inherent in society, especially in modern times, and to lend him a hand in overcoming the impact of forces over which he has no control, such as unemployment and the usual human disabilities.

Israel's Power Elite

In a democratic society the leaders are presumed to have reached their positions through their own efforts and to exert their

* For the background information of Israel's problems of nation-building the reader is referred to the author's book, *World Without End: The Middle East* (John Day, 1953), Chapter 9, pp. 277-316.

315

strength in conformity with the will of the majority of the people, with due regard to the legitimate needs of the minority. "The power elite is composed of men whose positions enable them to transcend the ordinary environments of ordinary men and women; they are in positions to make decisions having major consequences." *

The group that sets the tone, Israel's creative minority, is dynamic. It believes in the socially formative power of creative education, in the feasibility of favorable social conditions providing the proper framework for the fuller development of the individual's potentialities, and in the importance of the best attainable social forces being integrated into outstanding national achievement. It is recognized today that the state of Israel has produced statesmanlike qualities which have raised the level of the country's cabinets and diplomatic corps among the highest in the world. In a country where the quality of education is so high and where intellectual gifts abound, the leaders' ability to retain their places in public life can be due only to the recognition of requisite aptitudes.

Ordinarily no hero-worshipers, the Israeli could not help making an exception with their Prime Minister, David Ben-Gurion, who piloted Israel through the hardest part of the fateful fifties. Many saw in him a providential statesman—as distinguished from a successful politician—who possessed the qualities the occasions demanded: to assay situations with energy and dispatch; to "feel" the requirements of the hour; to delegate authority to the most competent deputies; to possess a historical view; to act boldly and, where needed, to compromise with the inevitable.

A native of the Polish town of Plonsk, near Warsaw, David Gruen, age twenty, left the pogrom-ridden Russian Empire and entered Palestine, under Ottoman Turkish rule. The year was 1906. Working there as a farm laborer and watchman, he changed his name to Ben-Gurion, meaning "young lion," and also the name

* C. Wright Mills, *The Power Elite*, New York: Oxford University Press, 1956, pp. 3-4.

of a Jewish hero who fought the Romans shortly after the death of Christ.

He helped establish the Palestine Labor Party, became the editor of its journal, studied law in Constantinople. This labor-union leader was also a scholar and linguist who spoke not only Russian, Yiddish and, of course, Hebrew, but also mastered English, French and classical Greek. During the First World War he took Britain's side against the Turk, and was exiled from the empire in 1915. He went to the United States and helped organize pioneers for settlement in Palestine. He also helped organize British, American and Palestinian volunteers in a Jewish Legion to serve in the war; served as a private with the 40th Royal Fusiliers in General Allenby's operations against the Turks.

After the First World War he became a member of the General Council of the Zionist Organization; the general secretary of the Federation of Labor; member of the executive board and, later, chairman of the board of the Jewish Agency for Palestine, and was thus in the thick of the battle for the establishment of a Jewish nation. It was Ben-Gurion who on May 14, 1948, proclaimed the independence of Israel. He became the Prime Minister of Israel and Minister of Defense. Then came the Arab invasion. What chance did the small strip of land have of defending itself in the midst of the vast Arab world? It seemed that nothing short of a miracle could save the country from being crushed by the Arab neighbors' ponderous weight. These were days that tested strength and Ben-Gurion stood the test. The miracle happened. The invading forces were repelled, and the task of nation-building began.

This, too, was largely directed by Ben-Gurion. He convinced his countrymen that, small as their newly won land was, it must be large enough to receive all those who wanted to enter and, in a decade, Israel admitted a million immigrants "from a hundred and two countries all over the globe" * and the population of the

* Ben-Gurion's radio address on May 12, 1959.

state increased threefold. "Neither in the annals of the First or Second Commonwealth," Ben-Gurion continued, "nor in the history of any other people, has there ever been such a rapid increase in so short a time."

In 1953 Ben-Gurion startled his nation by declaring his intention of retiring from office. Complaining of "spiritual fatigue" he retired into the semi-arid Negev, to the collective farm of Sde Boker, south of Beersheba, to study and to meditate. He felt refreshed being close to nature and the doughty young people upon whom Israel's fate depended—the pioneers in a frontier land, the tillers of the soil. In July 1955 he resumed his double task of Prime Minister and Minister of Defense. Again the times were critical. Israel's Arab neighbors, testing the young country's strength anew, increased guerrilla activities. Ben-Gurion felt that force must be answered with force, since it was the only language the neighbors understood. So the Sinai campaign was launched and it was understood. The guerrilla inroads ceased.

Ben-Gurion also found time to write books—a historical, economic and research survey of Palestine; a volume on the working class and the nation; *The Struggle,* in five volumes; *Vision and Implementation,* also in five volumes; and others. He had some critics who thought the language of his actions was too forceful. But he had more admirers. Some people called him a "Master of Persuasion"; others spoke of the "Happy Warrior of Israel." Seldom has the leader of so small a country acquired a reputation so vast.

Others, Too

Among those who made a strong impression on his country was Moshe Sharett. He studied at the London School of Economics, became an editor of the Tel-Aviv Hebrew daily newspaper *Davar,* headed the Jewish Agency's political section, initiated formation of the Jewish Brigade during the Second World War, and became the country's Minister of Foreign Affairs for eight crucial years, until 1956. He was Prime Minister during the two years of Ben-

318

Gurion's absence from the helm. Probably there have been few foreign ministers with his aptitude for languages—he speaks nine of them well.

Israel's first President was Dr. Chaim Weizmann, a chemist with an international reputation. Active all his adult life on behalf of the Jewish cause, he was president of the World Zionist Organization and of the Jewish Agency for Palestine. In 1917 he helped obtain the Balfour Declaration from Britain in favor of a national home in Palestine. He was also president of the Hebrew University in Jerusalem and director of the Daniel Sieff Research Institute in Rehovoth. He died in 1952 and was followed by Izhak Ben-Zwi, who began his studies before the First World War at the University of Kiev and continued them at the Imperial Ottoman University in Constantinople. He was co-founder and member of the faculty of the Jerusalem Hebrew Secondary School and helped organize the Jewish self-defense group "Hashomer" under the Ottoman rule. The Turks exiled him in 1915 and he went to the United States. After the war he became a member and later chairman of the Jewish National Council. At the time of the establishment of the state of Israel he became member of the Provisional State Council. In 1952 he was elected President of Israel. He wrote many books on many subjects, such as on the lost and regained tribes of Israel; on Arabs and Muslims; Book of the Samaritans; the Modern World and the Arab World; and Research and Articles, in five volumes.

The English-speaking peoples are particularly familiar with Israel's former Ambassador to the United States and permanent representative to the United Nations—Abba Eban. At the age of twenty-three—in 1938—he was a member of the faculty at Cambridge University for research in Arabic and Persian literature (after having received triple 1st honors in Arabic, Hebrew and Persian literature). He prepared the first English translation of an Arabic novel by the Egyptian author Tewfil al Hakim. On the staff of the Jewish Agency he specialized in the study of Arab-Jewish problems. And then his distinguished service as a diplomat

319

began and he was still no more than thirty-five. The late Professor Harold J. Laski used to say that Eban's rhetoric is as sonorous as Winston Churchill's. However, he can do it in seven languages.

One of the picturesque political leaders of the country is Mrs. Golda Meir. She had been a teacher in Chicago, Milwaukee and New York. She speaks English with a Midwestern accent. Shortly after World War I she began her career in Palestine by raising chickens. Later she filled several important government and important ambassadorial posts. She is the only Minister of Foreign Affairs of her sex.

There cannot be too many countries in which officials in the highest positions are so outstanding in the field of learning. The "people of the book," the Israeli, are led by highly learned leaders.

The Arabs and Israel

From the beginning of the establishment of the state of Israel, the Arab countries imposed a boycott on her. The Arab League, which had been established to co-ordinate the member countries' political, economic and social activities—with diplomacy in the van—concentrated its attention on one task only, as the Boycott Committee of the League was advanced to the most important body of that organization. "At the moment," wrote the former Egyptian President, Mohammed Naguib, "the Arab League is devoting most of its energies to enforcing a blockade that is slowly but effectively strangling Israel's economy." *

All forms of co-operation between the Arab states and Israel were prohibited—trade, shipping, travel and cultural relations. To keep Arab goods from reaching Israel and Israeli goods from reaching the Arab countries through middlemen—since direct shipping was impossible—the Arab League set up a unified system of export-import control. Within four years, up to 1959, Israeli exports to Middle Eastern countries declined from 15 per cent of the total to 3 per cent, most of which was consigned to Turkey.

* Mohammed Naguib, *Egypt's Destiny*, Doubleday, 1955, p. 232.

By the end of the decade Israel received only 1 per cent of her imports from the Middle East—again from Turkey—and nothing from the Arab countries. A certain amount of smuggling between Israel and the Arab world went on, of course, but such illicit traffic is not susceptible to statistical measurement.

The goods that Israel was not able to obtain from Arab sources nearby she was compelled to buy in more remote countries, sometimes at a higher cost, because of higher prices and transportation charges. A large percentage of these goods originated in the United States, Great Britain and continental Western Europe. The Israeli developed great ingenuity in exploring new markets, especially in "Black Africa" and in parts of the Far East, as we shall see later.

Particularly hard hit was Israel by being cut off from most of the Middle Eastern oil supplies. Part of the region in which she is situated contains the largest oil reserves of the world—about three-fourths of the total. And yet Israel was compelled to import petroleum from distant overseas places. During the years of the mandate, the oil refinery at Haifa, Palestine, had been linked via pipeline with the Iraq Petroleum Company fields at Kirkuk. The normal annual producing capacity of the refinery was four million tons a year. During the 1948 Palestine campaign the Arabs put the Haifa branch of the pipeline out of commission, and the refinery thenceforth could be operated at only about 15 per cent of its capacity.

The Arab League boycott committee concerned itself not only with Israel but with Jews elsewhere. Questionnaires circulated by it among foreign concerns inquired about Jewish employees as well as financial interests and, because of this, some concerns in the international trade completely suspended or reduced their relations with Israel. Arab airports refused to service aircraft which had called at Israel. The Arab League attempted to blacklist foreign firms under contract to furnish Israel with services and goods.

The Suez Canal continued to be closed to Israel even after the events of late 1956, in spite of United Nations resolutions. After the Suez campaign, further restrictions were imposed on Israeli shipping. No Israeli vessels of any kind were allowed to pass; cargoes consigned to Israel on vessels of foreign flag were refused transit if they appeared on a "contraband list"; foreign vessels carrying cargoes to Israel were blacklisted. In 1959 these restrictions were extended to cargoes from Israel proceeding southward to ports in Asia and Africa. By then more than 330 ships belonging to twenty-one countries were blacklisted. Halted by Egyptian authorities, three ships, *Capetan Manolis, Lealott* and *Inge Toft,* involved interests in ten countries, namely, Ceylon, Denmark, Germany, Hong Kong, Japan, Liberia, Malaya, the Philippines, Switzerland and the United States.*

"Israel desires to make it clear," Israel's Foreign Minister declared, "that she is not prepared to accept and should not be expected to accept a situation in which she is singled out for illegal discrimination. Moreover, we believe that the United Nations itself cannot accept this situation."

Attacks on Israel continued daily and in many languages over Radio Cairo. Typical of this was the statement on July 27, 1959, by President Nasser himself: "Every Arab is looking forward to the next round in which the decisive battle will take place in order to get rid of Israel."

And the Consequences?

The Arab boycott and enmity hurt Israel not merely because she was separated from natural trade contacts but also because of the heavy load of armament costs. However, the Arab challenge stimulated the government in Jerusalem to find the proper responses. Israel was seeking to become self-sufficient in producing the types of food for which her soil was adequate. Actually, she became self-sufficient in vegetables and fruits. Having been cut

* Foreign Minister Golda Meir in a policy statement before the General Assembly of the United Nations on September 24, 1959.

off from Suez, she was strengthening her hand at Eilat. As we have seen, the Israeli think of vertical, not horizontal expansion, the further extension of agriculture by cultivating wastelands, accelerating the rhythm of irrigation, producing more per acre. Through an increased rate of industrial development they can produce many finished products which, in turn, they can exchange for imported food.

And what is the effect of the boycott on the Arab countries themselves? Some of them seem to be hit as hard as Israel, if not more so. There is the case of Jordan, for instance. When Palestine was a mandate, most of her foreign trade was by way of Haifa, the closest first-class port. Israel has made it clear that Haifa could be easily turned into a free port for the use of Jordan, in case of an Arab settlement. In the absence of it, however, the Hashemite Kingdom of Jordan has become all but landlocked. Her exit door through Aqaba is extremely narrow and it also lacks the facilities to deal with normal trade.

No less unfavorable is the situation of the United Arab Republic as a result of its failure to maintain normal relations with Israel. The two parts of the Republic, the Egyptian and Syrian Regions, need the Israeli region as their natural transit line. As long, however, as they fail to recognize the existence of Israel they deprive themselves of the substance of the advantages of their union. As matters stand now, the U.A.R. is not an organic unit; its two parts are separated by a no man's land. Should Israel resume the natural function of this region, becoming a transit territory, the task of integration of the two component parts of the United Arab Republic could be carried out.

Other Arab victims of the Arabs' policy of boycott of Israel are those very people whom the Arab League professes to want to help. These are the Arabs of the state of Israel, constituting about 10 per cent of the total population. Whatever hurts Israel, hurts them, too, and the boycott is designed to hurt the country with which their fates are linked.

Several Arab countries are engaged in the execution of development projects and they need a variety of goods and services which they lack. On the other hand, Israel has certain types of machinery, for example, and chemicals, appliances, rubber products, vehicles and some consumer goods. Israel also possesses an increasing number of exportable services, the skills which many of her citizens' background, and her excellent schools of higher learning provide—a large pool of know-how which would serve Israel's Arab neighbors in good stead. These neighbors could ameliorate the economic condition of their people by exporting their surplus products to Israel.

The Arab nations, nearly all underdeveloped countries, are spending an inordinately large part of their budgets on their armed forces. It is assumed that some of them spend as much as about a half of their budgeted incomes on arms. Expenditures of this nature may be temporarily stimulating in the economies of very rich countries which have to utilize their industrial equipment to keep on producing even when their markets have reached the saturation point. That is not the situation in the Arab countries. There, whatever is spent on arms is deducted from the national income available for the satisfaction of life necessities. In these countries the cost of arms eats into the capital of the nation. Excessive armament expenditures for such nations may become fatal.

Why the Boycott?

In history it is a frequent occurrence that a state of "cold war" prevails. Nations engaged in such a type of "warfare" keep on setting off their propaganda barrages, keep enmity alive, partly to force the other side to submit to its will in the diplomatic field and, possibly, in preparation for a hot war. The Arabs claim, however, that it is not a cold war in which they are engaged with Israel but actual warfare, with a temporary truce. The language of some of the statements emanating from Cairo and Damascus— sometimes also from Amman and Baghdad—sounds occasionally as if war were only a matter of short time. These statements, however, should not be taken literally. Arabic is one of the most flowery languages, and its speakers are not afraid of overstatements. Arab statesmen have not got used to the idea that what they say may be translated into a Western tongue, which is subject to closer control. When, therefore, a flamboyant orator in one of the Arab capitals says: "We are going to exterminate every single man, woman and child in country X," his statement translated into British English would sound something like this: "We are not very fond of country X."

Yet, because of the lack of nuances one is never quite sure. The statesman may mean what he says or, if he does not, his audience may mean it. Public pressures may develop which can easily force the government's hands. The "enormity" of the creation of Israel is constantly stressed by Arab leaders. They will never, never recognize it. Yet they have already done so, not once but several times. They recognized Israel when they launched a war against her. One does not wage war against a nonexistent country. Also they recognized Israel when they failed to walk out of the United Nations after that body had accepted the new country as a member. They have kept on recognizing Israel by participating in the work of the United Nations in which Israel, too, has a hand. They recognize Israel when they keep insisting that the Arab refugees should be readmitted there. A nonexistent country cannot accept refugees.

More directly, they have recognized Israel by insisting that normal diplomatic relations between her and themselves could be restored if she accepted the United Nations' 1947 partition plan. At the time they rejected the plan, whereas the spokesmen of the Jews in Palestine accepted it. The difference in the size of the Jewish part of Palestine under the plan and the present size of Israel is 2,000 square miles. That seems to make all the difference in the world—between existence and nonexistence. In the face of such an absurdity one must look more closely for the reasons.

Arab leaders also assert that "Western imperialists" had established Israel as their Middle Eastern bridgehead and that the

United States, particularly, was employing her as a pipeline into the Middle East. Nasser was complaining to several visitors that the United States was helping Israel by government grants and private donations so as to force Egypt into submitting to her imperialist designs. The United States saved President Nasser at the time of the Suez crisis.

Other "explanations" of the Arabs' fear and hatred of Israel are concerned with the belief the new country wants to expand beyond its present limits, "from the Nile to the Euphrates." Israel could do this only by subjugating and absorbing many millions of Arabs. Her present population is a little over two million. Israel would cease to be a mainly Jewish country if she were to expand. Also, she is surrounded by either congested areas or by wasteland. Expansion would confront Israel with an insoluble problem. The Arab leaders cannot help being aware of these simple facts.

The real reasons of the enmity appear to be of a different nature. Since the establishment of Israel there appear to have been two principal reasons for the enmity.

At the time Israel was established the feudal and tribal-feudal nature of the Arab Middle East was pronounced. It was a somnolent civilization, with a strong accent on the maintenance of the status quo. Great transformations were taking place over much of the rest of Asia, but not in the Arab Middle East. There social and economic conditions had not changed for generations. In the regions directly under Western control, English and French, the political institutions of these countries emerged, with their basic functions entirely perverted. The parliaments were there, proclaiming the triumph of democracy. But this was only on the surface. Within these parliaments the feudal and feudal-tribal systems prevailed. The political parties were no more than the retinues of the pashas and sheikhs.

Israel disturbed the somnolence of the region. Here was a country deeply steeped in Western traditions, bent on letting Occidental ideas prevail. Social justice was to replace social injustice in the very heart of the Middle East. There man was to be

326

the measure, while elsewhere wealth and social status were the determining forces. Obviously, the ruling cliques could not resign themselves to the emergence of a "revolutionary" new factor. The enemy was Israel.

The enmity did not help. Israel did serve as a catalytic agent. Revolution swept off the Farouk regime in Egypt, that of the feudal lords in Syria and, more recently, that of Nuri Pasha in Iraq. The heads of the new regimes should have offered votes of thanks to Israel. Instead, the campaign of vituperation against Israel increased. The golden age in the wake of the great house-cleaning failed to materialize. The basic economic conditions in some of the countries could not be improved with the dramatic speed people expected. The problem of Egypt could have been solved only by producing half a dozen other rivers—additional Niles. Sky-storming ambitions were not supplemented by the requisite skills. Old-established habits could not be changed quickly or, perhaps, at all. People who considered land and gold as wealth could not be induced to exchange their money for pieces of printed paper—securities. There was no capital to invest. There was one solution—the union of all Arab countries. The Arab sun shone brightest when the *Pax Arabica* prevailed. Everybody wanted it and immediately was not quick enough. But when the time came to carry the project into effect people discovered that they individually would lose through unification.

The revolutionary changes effected in the wake of the war in Palestine failed to produce utopia. An explanation was needed and it was right at hand—Israel. It was because of her that there was not enough rain and that the age of miracles was delayed. In the meantime Israel had succeeded in making much of the desert bloom. In the midst of all the failures, she was a success. Not that she had reached the goal, but was on the way. It was explained in the Arab countries that Israel was kept alive by American gold. But it was not explained what happened to the oil royalties of some of the Arab countries and why, if all Arabs were one nation, this great wealth was not distributed among them. If American

327

Jews could help Israeli Jews, why could Saudi Arabs not help Egyptian Arabs?

Again Infiltration

The Sinai campaign by Israel in the late fall of 1956 was set off by the infiltration of commandos from Egypt.* There have been infiltrations also from other directions, particularly from the direction of Jordan. The topography of the region and the way the armistice lines were drawn helped the work of the infiltrators. The boundaries with Jordan are in a mountain region—those of Judaea and Samaria—uphill, downhill, without any natural dividing line, except perhaps an occasional wadi, waterless "river," filled with pebbles and boulders. Israel's land borders extend to nearly 600 miles, while her sea frontier from Rosh Hanikra in the north to Ashkelon in the south is only 117 miles. The country's frontier with the Kingdom of Jordan alone is 329 miles. The frontiers appear to have been drawn in haste, not in their actual setting but on maps. Villages were separated from their fields and waterholes. Along the old road from Jerusalem to Tel-Aviv, at the so-called Latrun Gap, there is a no man's land, a narrow stretch of fertile field, covered with thistles. The shepherd grazing his sheep and the unwary traveler who strays across the invisible line is in danger of being shot. The wire representing the armistice line at Beit Safafa runs down the middle of the road, cutting the town in two. "Here the Jordanian talking to his father in the house across the way in Israel," writes Glubb Pasha, "is guilty of communicating with the enemy." A good sanatorium in the valley below is useless because the armistice line runs right across the middle of the buildings.

Thefts, smuggling, nocturnal harvests, the rounding up of farm animals, were common. The radios in Cairo and Damascus created an atmosphere of hysteria. Israel was denounced as the implacable enemy and it was a virtue to inflict damage on her. And

* For an account of their activities the reader is referred to Chapter II.

328

then politics entered the scene in a complicated series of plots and counterplots. There was the former Grand Mufti of Jerusalem, the one who taught Hitler how to kill Jews. Hajj Amin al-Hussaini, the former Grand Mufti, is their implacable foe. Then there was the Saudi government which hated the ruling house of Jordan—fellow Arabs—no less than the Jews. And this was the plot.

Hajj Amin al-Hussaini had a nest of terrorists in Damascus. These were hired by the Saudi Arabian government to infiltrate into Israel and commit acts of sabotage there. They were to do this by way of Jordan. Why not directly from Damascus across the Syrian border into Israel? Because the Saudis hated the Hashemite dynasty of Jordan and wanted to stir up trouble between it and Israel. The case was investigated by Brigadier Glubb. His investigators were told by the leader of the Damascus terrorists, when asked for an explanation of this complicated plot: "The Saudis do not wish the Hashemites to rule Jordan in peace." *

At this point, the history of Egypt and Jordan cannot be separated. Again Brigadier John Bagot Glubb is the witness that the Egyptians too dispatched many of their saboteurs via Jordan and for the same reason as the Saudis—they did not like the ruling family of Jordan and so they wanted to cause more trouble between her and the Israeli.

Glubb Pasha asserts that Jordan herself, while he was the head of the Arab Legion, was opposed to the infiltrators' terroristic acts. But, he admits, there were "free lance" Jordanians and there may have been others, too, closer to the government. Israel listed 160 violations of the cease-fire agreement in the five months up to the middle of September 1956. In the light of conditions prevailing on the "infiltration front" after the Suez campaign the Glubb thesis that Egypt and, to a lesser extent, Saudi Arabia were responsible for the acts of terror seems to be corroborated.

* Sir John Bagot Glubb, *A Soldier with the Arabs,* Harper, 1957, pp. 305-306.

One footnote is in place at this point of Middle East history. Relations among the Arab countries are subject to violent changes on short notice. One day the Saudis want the downfall of the Hashemites and another day they all participate in a brotherly feast. Without this qualification the record would appear too contradictory, completely lacking in consistency. It is contradictory and lacking in consistency, indeed.

The Explanation and the Aftermath

Israel's Sinai campaign against Egypt in the late autumn of 1956 was described in the chapter on the United Arab Republic. In this chapter a word of explanation seems to be due to explain Israel's quick victory in the desert—a country of two million people winning against a nation of twenty-four million. Another word of explanation is due about the results of the victory.

Brigadier General S. L. A. Marshall of the United States provided a professional estimate of the victory of the Israeli arms.* In three days the decision was won, the general noted, and on the fourth some of the brigades were already engaged in mopping-up operations some 200 miles beyond their assembly point. The limits of military daring were greatly extended by the Israeli army, according to Marshall, and that was why the Israeli army won. Its hitting forces in the Sinai campaign traveled farther, over more formidable terrain, and in less time than any other combat body in recorded history. Also, Israel's soldiers looked their best in those hours of the greatest combat difficulties, when enemy pressure was such that total disorganization might have ensued. The United States army would not have displayed the same combat mobility, in General Marshall's view. The difference may have been accounted for by different logistics.

To send the fighting forces directly against the decisive object was the Israeli's ruling combat principle, and then let the supplies follow. The Israeli army was thus a closely knit fighting force,

* "Why the Israeli Army Wins?" *Harper's Magazine,* October 1958.

and not just an aggregation of specialists; and supply shortages—inevitable in some cases—did not delay the battle. Nor was there any place for frills in that army. A bare-walled cubicle was the headquarters of the chief of staff. Occasionally the men saluted their officers, who were often called by their first names. The main body of the regular army was composed of draft inductees getting their two and a half years of steady training, and there were no volunteers. The troops themselves were clean but not neat in the old "spit and polish" way. In training, too, Israel placed little stress on the drill of the parade ground. The main aim was to teach the men to think clearly, observe keenly and then report accurately. The average age of the newly commissioned second lieutenants was nineteen, and all officers came from the ranks. The army had a high proportion of women in service and their presence in the combat zone itself had a high morale value. The women soldiers assigned to the combat units were well trained in the use of arms. When the soldiers were trapped in sudden fire, movement was considered more helpful than the foxhole. These soldiers truly believed in the dictum: in the attack risk, risk, and risk again!

President Nasser's claim that Israel's swift advance was a hollow victory because he had ordered his men out of the Sinai peninsula was not true and, making this claim, he discredited his own soldiers, some of whom fought gallantly though the command lacked initiative. By the same token, the Israeli record was not unblemished. Here and there a leader hesitated, attempting to combat from far in the rear and bending his ears more to the beat of peril than to the call of opportunity.

In sum, the picture that emerged from the Sinai campaign deserved close attention from the world's statesmen and soldiers because it demonstrated what enormous group strength could be generated by consummate daring. Also this picture emerged from the literature of the campaign: granting the use of "conventional weapons," as in this war, there appeared to be two main factors that accounted for Israel's stunning victory. One of them was the question of morale. The Israelis knew what they were fighting for, as in 1948. They had a graphic picture of the diplomatic constellation and were convinced that Israel's survival demanded that it be changed. The other one was that of technique. Modern weapons need literate people and a measure of technological knowledge, which Israel's armed forces possessed.

And the Aftermath....

The Sinai campaign was described as the "strangest war in history." Was it a war or was it a campaign of retaliation? "Whatever they call it," a keen observer recorded, "their [Israeli military leaders'] intention was clearly to call the Arab bluff after eight years of harassment, to destroy the biggest of their enemies' armies and to force the fall of the man who was building a ring of steel around them before he himself was ready to close in. The Israeli were contemplating such an attack since the fall of 1955, when Nasser made the arms deal with Russia. Because of British and American pressure and adverse international opinion they made no move. But when Nasser nationalized the Suez Canal in July 1956, Israel was certain of two things. Egypt had alienated Britain and France and, secondly, if Nasser got away with it, he would become so inflated a hero in the Arab world that the pressure on him to make war on Israel would be irresistible. Israel looked at the United States and saw Dulles retreating from high indignation against Nasser to irresolution and capitulation." *

On February 20, 1957, President Eisenhower declared in a nationwide broadcast that Israel should comply with the United Nations' plea to withdraw from Egypt. In the same radio broadcast he also stated: "Egypt by accepting the six principles adopted by the Security Council last October in relation to the Suez Canal, bound itself to free and open transit through the Canal without

* C. Sterling, "When Foreign Policy Fails," *The Reporter*, November 15, 1956.

332

discrimination and to the principle that the operation of the Canal would be insulated from the politics of any country. . . ."

The following day Premier Ben-Gurion stated to Israel's legislature (Knesset) that his country would be able to withdraw only after she had obtained firmer guarantees of security for her borders and shipping and he appealed to the United States as well as other United Nations members to offer such guarantees. World pressure on Israel continued, however, and on March 1, Foreign Minister Golda Meir announced her government's decision to withdraw from the occupied land. A near-crisis was precipitated by this move in Israel's Jerusalem where mass demonstrations strengthened strong political opposition to topple the government on this issue. Finally, the decision was made that United Nations Emergency Forces should be stationed in critical areas to prevent the two opposing sides from coming to grips. One of them was in the Gaza Strip, which had been an important launching point of the guerrillas. The other one was in the region of Sharm-el-Sheikh, where the Gulf of Aqaba fans out into the Red Sea. This force was to ensure free navigation into and out of the Gulf. On March 4, therefore, the Israeli troops withdrew from the occupied territories.

When the tumult and shouting subsided, the speculation started, engaged in by historians and the lay public. Had the Israeli troops on the one side and the British and French troops on the other had a day or two more time to move ahead, Egypt's strategic points might have been seized. Because of the topography of the country, everything in Egypt is concentrated in the great cities, the Delta and the narrow strip along the Nile. Because of that, the occupation of the key points of the country would not have presented unsurmountable handicaps. The effect of such a loss to Egypt might have proved catastrophic to her government. Egyptians are proverbially whimsical. One day they went so wild over General Naguib, their first President, that they almost killed him out of sheer affection. Then they forgot him. They also went wild over Nasser but, had it become evident to

333

them that he had lost the war, they might have literally torn him to pieces. Secretary of State Dulles probably saved Nasser's life and regime by calling a halt to the campaign before Egypt's day of wrath arrived.

What was the balance sheet of the historic ledger when the campaign was over? The presence of the United Nations Emergency Forces saw to it that Egyptian commandos did not harass Israel for years to come. The Gulf of Aqaba was fully opened to Israeli shipping and this enabled the country to look to the Far East for trade contacts. The Suez blockade was tacitly lifted for two years, not to be resumed until 1958. Also, Jordan, Lebanon and Iraq were now in a better position to resist Egypt's encroachments and the West was given a better opportunity to improve its political fences in the Middle East. The campaign gave an impetus to Israel further to open up the Negev. Attention was called to the fact that 60 per cent of Israel, her Negev south, contained but 5 per cent of her population. With the techniques of cultivation and development successfully employed in the north the Israeli felt that they would be capable of absorbing very large numbers of newcomers in the south. Some of them also felt that the country's problem in the next decades might well be a shortage of population and not land, as her main sources of prospective immigrants were in the Soviet bloc and North Africa. The emigration of Jews from both of these regions was prohibited.

And what was the result from the broader historic and global points of view?

Let us recall that in the campaign Egypt lost territory half as big as California. Israel's conquest of a large fortified area was at the cost of 150 dead and wounded. Britain and France, too, won every battle in the campaign. The British had lost 21 dead and 112 wounded, the French 20 dead and 100 wounded. Israel lost only one prisoner in the campaign and he was exchanged, along with three others taken in previous border raids, for 5,000 Egyptian prisoners. The balance sheet of the war was overwhelmingly in favor of these three countries. However, the balance sheet

334

of peace was just as overwhelmingly in favor of the defeated nation. Israel, too, learned that now small countries no longer possessed the right to take recourse to the arbitrament of arms even after all other measures had failed. She learned, if she looked into the seed of things, that the United Nations was as impotent to act as she herself. It was used merely as a forum by the two great World Powers—the United States and the Soviet Union—and their decision was final.

Simultaneously with these events the equanimity of the world was rocked by the uprising of the Hungarians. In their origins the two events were unrelated but their sequels formed parts of the same pattern. The campaign in Egypt was followed by the formulation of the Eisenhower Doctrine—as we have seen—to place the Middle East out of bounds for the Soviets. There was no Eisenhower Doctrine for Middle Europe, of which Hungary is a part. Thus the existence of two spheres of influence was recognized in Washington, the Middle East—American—no longer British and French, and the central part of Eastern Europe—the satellite belt—Soviet.

The Problem of Arab Refugees

The Arab refugee problem is a controversial issue which seems to arouse more emotion than logic. The question of how this issue arose transcends the framework of this book. Here the problem is briefly sketched and the possibilities of some solutions are outlined. This problem concerns not only Israel and her neighbors but the entire region.

Officially a Palestinian refugee is a "person whose normal residence was Palestine for a minimum period of two years preceding the outbreak of the conflict in 1948 and who, as a result of the conflict, has lost both his home and his means of livelihood." This is the definition of the United Nations and the conflict begins at this very point. The Israeli claim that a decade after the Palestinian war about half the people who dwelt in refugee

335

camps failed to satisfy the conditions mentioned in this definition. Many people died in the meantime, and many were born.
The dead were not reported, in numerous instances, so that their
food rations could be used by others. A large number of refugees,
according to the Israeli view, cannot be qualified as such because
they live in the former Palestine, which is now the Cis-Jordan
part of the Hashemite Kingdom, formerly Jordan, and have been
given Jordanian citizenship.

The United Nations Work and Relief Agency (UNWRA),
established in 1949 to provide immediate relief, and to co-operate with the interested governments in developing a long-range
program of assistance, reported the number of refugees in June
1957 as 933,556, distributed as follows: 221,058 in the Gaza
Strip; 517,388 in the Hashemite Kingdom of Jordan; 102,586 in
Lebanon; and 92,524 in Syria. Their greatest concentration per
square miles is in the Gaza Strip where they form 221.3 per cent
of the local population. In Jordan it is 56.3 per cent; in Lebanon
7.4 per cent and in Syria 2.4 per cent. Because of the lack of
co-operation by Arab country authorities there has never been a
comprehensive refugee census. Israel claims the best possible estimate would put their number at something close to 600,000.
Each year the number of "refugees" increases by about 22,000,
due in part to births but also to infiltration into the camps by
non-refugees. The United Nations stated why it was impossible
to have a reliable census of refugees: "To increase or to prevent
decreases in their ration issues, the refugees eagerly report births,
sometimes by passing a newborn infant from family to family
and reluctantly report deaths, resorting often to surreptitious
funerals to avoid giving up a ration card."

In Gaza, where the refugees have the highest concentration
per square mile, they are in a territory occupied by Egypt but
not officially part of that country. Arab refugees in the Gaza
Strip, for instance, cannot move freely into and out of Egypt.
This is partly in order to maintain the fiction that there is a
separate Palestinian administration which may eventually come

336

into its own. Also, this is to prevent some quarter of a million refugees flooding Egypt, where the population pressure on land resources is one of the highest in the world.

In Jordan the refugees were partly assimilated—for political reasons, in the main. Jordan was an artificial creation of the British, as we have seen. She has no natural frontiers, there had never been a country in that area, and most of her people seemed to consider themselves as Jordanians only for a brief time. The Hashemite Kingdom of the Jordan had a very small population. It was through the absorption of the refugees that Jordan's government wanted to establish an additional *raison d'être* and to increase the population.

In Lebanon there is a delicate balance between Christian and Muslim Arabs. The official assumption is that there are more of the former than of the latter and because of this the Christians occupy a privileged place in the country's political life. The absorption of the refugees, mainly Muslim, would upset the country's religious balance and accentuate tendencies to join one of the Muslim Arab neighbors.

It is notable that Syria has a very small percentage of refugees and Iraq hardly anything at all. Yet, it is these two countries which have surplus land that could be drawn into cultivation, so as to feed the refugees.

The United Nations special organ described refugee camp conditions: "About one-third of all the refugees are living in sixty organized camps that vary in size from a few hundred to over 20,000; the other two-thirds live scattered among towns and villages of the host countries. . . ."

In a decade the United Nations Work and Relief Agency spent about $300 million on behalf of the refugees. The United States supplied about 70 per cent of the agency's budget; Great Britain contributed 24 per cent and the rest of the world, except for the Soviet bloc, the remaining 6 per cent. The Arab countries themselves made very small contributions. Egypt had contributed, as of December 1957, 2.03 per cent; Syria 1.1 per cent; Jordan 0.8

per cent; Lebanon 0.6 per cent; Iraq 0.3 per cent and oil-rich Saudi Arabia 0.2 per cent. The Soviet bloc has contributed nothing to the agency's support. The living expenses of each refugee amount to about 7 to 8 cents a day, an inadequate sum. Yet, the Palestinian refugee is sometimes better off than the non-refugee Egyptian. Their incidence of illness and death rates is lower and most of the refugee children are schooled.

Though they were carefully conditioned by Arab propaganda to believe that they were suffering wretchedly at the hands of "imperialists and Zionists" the refugees gradually found themselves better off materially than they had been at home. They have a higher caloric ration (1,500–1,600) than some of the fellahin in Nasser's Egypt, better health and sanitation services than they had ever known in Palestine. . . . *

The General Assembly of the United Nations had authorized, on December 11, 1948, the creation of the Palestine Conciliation Commission for the purpose of bringing about a settlement of the Arab-Israeli conflict. Article 11 of the Assembly Resolution provided that "refugees wishing to return to their homes and live at peace with their neighbors should be permitted to do so at the earliest practicable date, and that compensation should be paid for the property of those not choosing to return. . . ."

Several attempts have been made to solve the refugee problem. The United Nations Work and Relief Agency removed several thousands of those who found outside occupations; other rehabilitation projects took additional thousands off relief permanently and some 100,000 for short periods. Israel instituted a Reuniting of Families project, involving another 48,500, by which separated family members were permitted to return to Israel and to obtain citizenship. Before a Special Committee of the General Assembly of the UN, Israel's Ambassador Abba Eban cited figures to show that Israel had integrated 48,500 of the returning Arabs into her economy. She also announced

* *Time,* December 2, 1957.

her readiness to compensate the Arabs for their abandoned property contingent upon the settlement of differences between her and the Arab states; the recognition of her internationally covenanted rights in the Suez Canal, and the termination of the economic boycott by the Arab countries.

Israel contends that the Arab countries have rendered impossible the reintegration of refugees in the new country even if space were available for them. By their constant insistence on the illegality of the existence of Israel, by their dwelling on the "second round"—after the first round of the 1948 Palestine war —which will cast the Jews into the sea, the Arab governments may have imbedded the seeds of hatred into Arab refugee hearts. In Israel they might form a permanent fifth column, bent only on expelling their neighbors.

Israel, on the other hand, points to the 430,000 Jewish refugees from Arab countries who, as a result of the Arab war against her, were forced to flee from their homes, abandoning large liquid and immobile assets. These refugees, given immediate citizenship, were absorbed at Israel's own expense. The Israelis claim in consequence that this was an exchange of population for the Arabs, brought about by war and partition.

An adviser on refugees to the World Council of Churches, Dr. Elfan Rees, stated:

The history of United Nations Work and Relief Agency has been a clinical study in frustration. No agency has been better led or more devotedly served, but the organized intransigence of the Arab States concerned has brought all its plans to naught. The net result is that relief is being provided in 1957 to refugees who could have been rehabilitated in 1951 with homes and jobs, without prejudice to their just claims.

Not only have the Arab States been of no help but they have placed obstacles in the way of the efforts of the United Nations and of other organizations, mainly religious. Lebanon and Syria required import permits for Agency supplies and have levied taxes on them. Jordan tried to control United Nations Work and Relief Agency personnel and restricted the Agency's right to import food for the refugees.

"We shall be most insistent on perpetuating the Palestinian problem," a Jordanian legislator stated, expressing the official view. "The Palestinian war continues by dint of the refugees only. Their existence leaves the problem open . . ." "The Arab League must continually demand the return of the refugees and strengthen in their minds the spirit of revenge. . . ." "The fact that Israel is trying to solve the refugee problem proves that she has an interest in solving it—and this alone is reason enough to rule out any such attempt by us."

The refugees are used both as a symbol and as a potential pressure group. They represent the Arab countries' undying hostility toward Israel, on the one hand. On the other, it is thought that their bitterness might contain explosive possibilities that would come in good stead to Israel's Arab neighbors in the case of a "second round."

King Hussein of Jordan told an American newspaperman (Associated Press, January 17, 1960): "Since 1948 Arab leaders have approached the Palestine problem in an irresponsible manner. They have not looked into the future. They have no plan or approach. They have used the Palestine people for selfish political purposes. This is ridiculous and I could say even criminal."

For about eight years these refugees had been exposed to the barrage of anti-Israeli propaganda. Also, they are worse off than most of the other refugees because they are packed together so closely in a desolate environment. Yet, what happened when Israeli forces moved in on the region where the refugee camps are situated? Their reception was good, even enthusiastic in some cases. True, when the Israeli troops moved out and the Egyptian government officials moved in, preceded by the United Nations forces, their reception was also good, and occasionally enthusiastic. These receptions may not have meant more than the weariness of the refugees. They wanted to be on the winning side, whether it was Israeli or fellow Arab. At any rate, there were no serious acts of sabotage in the Gaza Strip, nor desperate explosions of bitterness. Counting on the refugees as an effective pressure group may be another frustrating experience.

Occasionally, a public-spirited Arab, moved by the refugees' plight, takes matters in hand. This was done in the Jordan valley by a distinguished lawyer of Palestine, Musa el Alami, a refugee himself. In order to improve farming methods in the valley he launched an Arab Development Society with the aid of a grant obtained from the Ford Foundation. Under his leadership about twenty-five wells were dug not far from the river, involving some 2,000 new arable acres. This work was accompanied by developments of many other kinds: clinics, modern plumbing, roads. Then, on December 18, 1955, some thirty thousand refugees carrying torches marched out of nearby camps into the project and wrecked it. An investigation disclosed that for three days before the riot, the demagogues had incited the refugees to destroy the place, claiming that Musa el Alami was an agent of the West and that his project was a symbol of Western imperialism. Musa el Alami happened to be away at the time or else they might have killed him, too. "Whatever gives the refugees hope is treason," a leader of the rioters said.

Who Has the Answer?

Speaking about the refugee problem, Secretary of State Dulles stated: "These uprooted people should through resettlement and, to such an extent as may be feasible, repatriation, be enabled to resume a life of dignity and self-respect. . . . Compensation is due from Israel. . . . There might be an international loan to enable Israel to pay."

A congressional investigating committee headed by Representatives L. H. Smith and W. L. Prouty produced what is known as the Smith-Prouty Report:

Responsibility for the administration of the program should be transferred to the Arab States and should be distributed in such a way as to provide an incentive to the Arab governments to open their doors to the refugees and to assimilate them. . . . The United States should announce that it will contribute no further assistance to the refugees as such after a specified future date. This would put the refugees and the Arab States on notice that the status quo cannot be maintained indefinitely. We should give help to the host countries in developing their resources so that a substantially larger population can make a living. . . .*

Minnesota Senator Hubert H. Humphrey said:

The resettlement of the Arab refugees in Arab lands is the only effective and realistic way of solving the Arab refugee problem. . . . Half of the refugees are now under fifteen years. . . . This means that despite the clamor of professional refugee leaders for a return to Palestine and the insistence of the Arab governments on repatriation to their former homes, half of the refugees have in fact no roots in Palestine at all. They were either less than five years old when they left that country or were born in the refugee camps in the Arab States. To return them now to an alien society they have been taught to despise would be as self-defeating and unsatisfactory as abandoning them to mature in the appalling atmosphere of hopelessness which now pervades the refugee camps. The destiny of these young Arabs clearly lies in an opportunity for a productive and self-reliant life in an Arab environment and culture.

The Chairman for International Economic Growth, Eric Johnston, has been campaigning for a specific solution. The Arab refugees, he has pointed out, exploited by unscrupulous politicians, have become the focal point of tension. They need to be resettled and recompensed for their losses.

* L. H. Smith and W. L. Prouty, "The Arab Refugees and other Problems in the Near East," U.S. Government Printing Office, 1954, House Report No. 1250, 83rd Congress, 2nd Session.

342

In the last decade, we, in the United States, have spent almost $200,000,000 for their subsistence. Soviet Russia has put up not one ruble. . . . I propose that the United States, beginning now, offer to contribute $3 for every $1 from the Soviet Union to the international UN fund for a massive effort to settle the refugee question. Out of this fund a repayable loan should be made to Israel to compensate for the losses that have been suffered by Arab refugees from that country. . . . But there is another element that embitters relations and tears at the vitals of the Middle East. This is the notion, whipped up by Arab propagandists, that the Arab States will one day obliterate Israel from the scene. The UN must make it indisputably clear that Israel is here to stay as a sovereign State and that the world will not tolerate her destruction or dismemberment by force or otherwise.

Going beyond this, the view has been gaining ground that the solution of the refugee problem is feasible only within the framework of the solution of the problem of the Middle East. Some of the Great Powers have made several attempts to offer solutions—the United States always in the van. However, they have never come to grips with the basic fact that the great problems of the region are indivisible. The Soviet Union can no longer be left out of account, as Mr. Johnston has made clear. Only a massive international program, possibly under the auspices of the United Nations as a co-ordinating agency, can do justice to this task. But it, too, is at the heart of the problem and piddling little solutions, such as those that have been offered so far mainly, will never do.

The Problem of More Land

And I am come down to deliver them out of the hand of the Egyptians, and to bring them up out of that land unto a good land and a large one, unto a land flowing with milk and honey. . . . *

Before the First World War the Palestinian reality was stone upon stone, desolation upon desolation, with only occasional patches of land. It appeared hopeless to try to turn the wilder-

* Exodus, 3:8.

ness into fertility. That could be done only by a miracle—the miracle of faith that could make the desert bloom like a rose.

Though sparsely settled, Palestine was then overpopulated per cultivated acre. Had a scientific survey been taken under the Ottoman Empire it probably would have discouraged investment in Palestine's barren soil. Only years later did scholarly explorers, venturing into sun-flamed southern Negev, find that its central plateau once had been tilled by patriarchs and, later, by the farmers of Nabataea. There was no more rain in the area in those days, millennia ago, than there is now. But where the twentieth century's winter rains scour barren hills and scurry off to sea the patriarchs and Nabataeans had known how to channel the rain down hillsides to cultivate valley land. If primitive people with their simple tools could tend vineyards, how much more could modern technology accomplish? In the light of this discovery, it was revealed that even after its population had trebled in a single decade the Holy Land was still underpopulated.

From Polish counting houses the new settlers had come, and from Lithuanian peddlers' stalls, from Rumanian offices and Galician stores. Their Gentile neighbors had looked down upon them because their hands lacked cunning and did not know how to hoe a row. In Palestine, however, they learned how to drain off marshes, to loosen boulders, implant the seeds of trees and, after a cruel interval of waiting, the desert did begin to bloom like a rose. Palestine's native population, which also had looked down upon the Jews, then began to copy them. Still, when Israel was created people said that she was an absurdity, nay, a monstrosity, and that she could not sustain all the newcomers.

This was the age of Big Machines and of Large Industries. But Israel learned that before the industrial plants there was the soil and that faith could loosen stones. Indeed, the boulders were removed and there was the soil. But this was the Middle East where there were clouds in the skies, but there was no rainfall for months. There was, however, the river Jordan whose sources tapped the water resources of the Hermon. The United States

had been successful with "integrated river systems," irrigating greedy land with water from another region. Perhaps the system would work for Israel, too.

There was Walter Clay Lowdermilk, formerly of the United States Soil Conservation Service, who had a plan. An irrigation canal was to link north and south, channeling Jordan river water into the arid regions, and this, in turn, was to be linked to the Mediterranean–Dead Sea Hydroelectric Power project. The Dead Sea lies nearly 1,300 feet below sea level and this drop was to be utilized for the generation of water power by the channeling of Mediterranean waters into the Dead Sea through tunnels. Because of the attitude of most of the Arab neighbors this plan could not be carried into effect. King Abdullah of Jordan made a small beginning with a feature of the plan in the spring of 1949 when he inaugurated the Wadi el Arab irrigation project at Shuna near the Jordan River. Since the Jordan and Yarmuk rivers run through Israel and Jordan, both governments' consent was necessary before the plan could be implemented. Israel announced her readiness to enter into an agreement with Jordan for the development of the region. But Jordan did not respond, presumably because of Arab League pressure.*

The total amount of water available annually in Israel is estimated at 2,000 million cubic meters, half of which consists of springs and rivers, while the rest is mainly ground water, with some storm runoff and returns from irrigation and other uses. Under Israel's development plan, the principal water scheme is

* An anticipation of the Lowdermilk plan was recorded in the diaries of the father of modern Zionism, Dr. Theodor Herzl, in the following entry: "August 23, 1856. Baden. I had a long talk with the electrical engineer Kremenzky. [He said that] large chemical industries could be erected on the banks of the very salty Dead Sea. The present sweet water streams would be drained off and used as potable water. This, in turn would be replaced from the Mediterranean by means of a canal which would have to be partly a tunnel because of the hills (an object of world-wide interest) and the difference between the levels of the two (waterfalls) would provide many thousands of horsepower for the machines. . . ." (Author's translation from the German original text.) Theodor Herzl, *Tagebücher*, Erstes Band, Zweite Auflage. Berlin: Jüdischer Verlag, 1934, p. 523.

the Jordan-Negev project, which aims at diverting 320 cubic meters of the available Jordan river waters, through a 250-kilometer conduit, to the Negev. This conduit traverses the country from north to south, and links the various regional water systems. The two large ones are the Western-Galilee-Kishon River project, begun in 1950 and designed to provide 180 million cubic meters a year, and the Yarkon-Negev project, brought into operation in 1955, which is a part of the flow of the Yarkon River to the Negev at the rate of 100 million cubic meters a year. A projected pipeline will carry another 100 million cubic meters of Yarkon waters to Tel-Aviv and the Negev. It had been estimated that all this work would cost some $150 million and take several years to complete. On the tenth anniversary of the establishment of the state about 60 per cent of the estimated water resources had been brought into use and, in another decade, the entire project should be completed. Thus in nine years the area under cultivation had been increased fourfold, and amounted to a third of the cultivated land.

Another plan, even more ambitious than this project, was worked out under the auspices of Eric Johnston on behalf of President Eisenhower. This scheme envisaged the co-operation of several neighboring states to draw upon the integrated resources of a much larger area, which contained not only the Jordan, but also Lebanon's Litani River, the Tigris, Euphrates and part of the Nile. The operative area of this plan embraced some 800 million acres, of which about 50 million could be regarded as presently arable and only 23 million of which is actually under cultivation. Properly harnessed, the five rivers could provide enough water to irrigate about one-third again of the present cultivated area. The addition of this acreage would provide a solid economic base for about ten million people. The United States offered $200 million to finance the Jordan valley section of the project.

Arab veto stayed the implementation of this beneficial project

346

and, thus, it has not materialized even though its realization could have raised living standards all around. What went wrong?

The answer, I think, lies in these factors [Eric Johnston wrote], the basic instability of the region; the intensity of inter-Arab mistrust and rivalries; the Arabs' emotional rejection of Israel and the whole pattern of political insecurity and social ferment that has made the region a hotbed of trouble.

In this charged atmosphere the Arab nations have ignored a simple fact, fundamental to the river development in the Middle East or anywhere else. This is the fact that rivers ignore political boundaries, that watersheds are not defined by political lines. Instead of attacking the rivers on a regional basis, watershed by watershed, each country has preferred to go it alone on whatever portion of a river happens to lie within or along its borders. The result has been a tragic waste of the waters of the region. As we proved in the Tennessee Valley, there is a right way and a wrong way to develop a river system for the benefit of man. The Arab States, up to now, have done it the wrong way.*

Israel was ready to engage in a major development project by piping water from the Sea of Galilee in the north of the country, to irrigate parts of the Negev in the south, her government announced late in 1959. The execution of this project was to take several years. Simultaneously, it was also announced by the government in Jerusalem that Israel would not exceed her allotment of water under the Johnston Plan. The representatives of Jordan, Lebanon and the United Arab Republic thereupon met in Cairo in order to counteract this proposed measure. They threatened to dam up the sources of the river Jordan. In answer to this, Foreign Minister Golda Meier declared that it was for Israel alone to decide what she was going to do within her own borders. "Today it was the water that was involved," the Foreign Minister continued, "tomorrow it might be some other aspect of development. It would be much better all around if the Arab rulers,

* Eric Johnston, "A Key to the Future of the Mideast," *The New York Times Magazine,* October 19, 1958.

instead of trying to cramp Israel's development, evinced some interest in developing their own countries. Fruitful co-operation between them and Israel might then follow."

To make more water available Israel decided, at the same time, to build at Eilat, on the Gulf of Aqaba, the first of a series of plants to desalt sea water by freezing and then melting it. She was to do this in partnership with a large American concern. American experts estimated that the cost of desalted water would equal approximately the cost of well water in the United States.

Expanding Frontiers

Israel has frequently expressed her wish to enter into relations with the Arab states which, she believes, would be fruitful for all those concerned. Other economically underdeveloped nations have noted the advantages they could derive by developing trade relations and technical co-operation with the new state. Indeed, for several of them Israel has represented an ideal combination. Here was a small country—one of the smallest—with certain skills of the technically most advanced Great Powers. The economically backward nations were apprehensive about entering into a teacher-pupil relation with the Great Powers. Previous experience had illustrated that the latter often acted in the grand manner and could seldom forbear from taking advantage of their strength with the result that small states with which they entered into relations easily slid into satellite roles. No such danger threatened small nations when entering into relations with Israel. There they encountered an ideal combination: technical knowledge and small-power status. Also Israeli technicians and advisers work at lower costs. They can put themselves more easily into the place of economically backward nations. Their plans are practical, not grandiose in the sense that they are beyond the reach of poor countries.

Several Asian and African countries have found it to their advantage to enter into close economic relations with Israel. One of

348

them is Burma which, situated in the southeast Asian rice bowl, seeks to raise its living standards in a variety of ways. Farming is to be improved; public utilities are to be established; light industries are to be set up. From the outset Burma has been interested in the co-operative system—the middle way, neither capitalism nor communism, and is not ashamed to admit that her goal is the type of state—the welfare state—in which all citizens are provided with at least the simple necessities of life, if handicapped by sickness or age. The Burmese have a picturesque name for it—*Pyidawtha,* The Happy Land.

So, Burmans traveled to Israel to study her farming system and Israeli technicians went to Burma to teach the skills to the local population. Major water supply and irrigation projects for Burma's dry zone are scheduled with the aid of Israeli advisers; teams from Israel have shown that many field crops could be grown more profitably in Burma than had been the case before; and specialists from Israel have helped in the establishment of a rubber-tire plant.

Other Asian and African countries have sent teams of trainees to Israel, among these Japanese scientists doing advanced research at Israel's Weizmann Institute, students from India, Liberia, Thailand and Ethiopia, from the new Federation of Mali in West Africa (the Republics of Senegal and the Sudan of the French Communauté), and several other countries. Subjects of study include co-operative villages, industrial management, medicine, economic and other humanities and natural sciences.

Particularly close relations have developed between Ghana, the former West African Gold Coast, and Israel. Israeli technicians to Ghana include financial advisers assisting in the establishment of a co-operative bank, instructors in mechanized farming, teachers in the newly established Nautical College and a delegation to help establish a school of aviation and an air force. The Ghana National Construction Company was created with the co-operation of Solel Boneh, the Israeli Federation of Labor's great industrial development firm; and the Israeli-Ghana

349

shipping company, the Black Star Line, was established with the co-operation of the Zim Navigation Company, Israel's shipping company.

Israel's trade with Asian and African companies now includes the export of motor cars, refrigerators and farm equipment to places like Mozambique, a Portuguese African possession; phosphates to Japan and equipment for public works and residential quarters to Turkey. To reinforce economic ties, Israel has established embassies and consulates in a large number of Asian and African countries, such as Liberia, Guinea and Ghana. In addition, the former Premier and Minister of Foreign Affairs of Israel, Moshe Sharett, went on an important good-will mission to the Far East in 1957-1958, and early in 1958 Foreign Minister Golda Meir visited Nigeria, Ghana and the "great African bulge" where she was warmly received. She followed this up with a mission to South America the following year.

Nigeria, the most populous of all African countries, manifested great interest in Israeli institutions and trade, in preparation for her independence in 1960. Political leaders and prominent journalists of Nigeria paid visits to Israel, becoming acquainted with her institutions and ways of life. The press of Nigeria paid close attention to Israel's development, which was to serve as a model in the task of nation building.

From the Israeli point of view these relations were significant. Through them she broke out of the encirclement of her Arab neighbors and established herself as an important member of the international community. The neighbors told the world that Israel was a menace, while Israel proved to the world that she was an asset. Thus she made herself useful to the economically backward part of the world; indeed, made herself indispensable in the very Afro-Asian group within which the Arab Legion sought to acquire a dominating influence.

From the point of view of the economically backward countries Israel appeared to be indispensable. Their case was stated by the

350

Director of the Public Works Department of the Republic of Vietnam, Pham Minh Dwong:

"I spent two months in the United States on a study tour. I went to many towns. At the end they asked me what I thought of America and I answered that it was wonderful! Fabulous! Fantastic! Then they asked me what I had learned and I said: Nothing! You see, America is too big for us. The smallest project I saw cost millions. Israel is closer to the problem we are up against." *

The Hardships of Transition

Jewish immigrants seeking entry into Israel had to be admitted. Some of them felt their lives endangered in their home countries and where else were they to go but Israel? Though many countries were full of good intentions toward the tragic case of Jews, they had no place for them. The classical land of immigration, the United States, had a quota law which was very unfavorable to countries of Eastern Europe and Asia. Had Israel's gates been closed to the Jews, all the gates would have been shut in their faces. What would then have been the justification of Israel's existence?

However, in order to keep the gates open vast sums were needed. Most of the immigrants had backgrounds which called for retraining in their new homes. Every immigrant required food which had to be imported or coaxed out of a recalcitrant soil. Since it was impossible to import food from just across the frontier where it was available, it had to be transported across the seas, from many thousands of miles away. Israel had to work harder, and needed help, at least during the period of transition.

The productivity of the Israeli worker improved, in spite of all the handicaps and, by 1958, the output of the country's manufacturing and extractive industries advanced at the rate of 12 per

* Y. Leo Kohn, "Israel and the New Nation States of Asia and Africa," *The Annals of the American Academy of Political and Social Science,* July 1959, Vol. 324, p. 101, quoting Kermit Lansner, general editor of *Newsweek.*

cent a year, a remarkable achievement. Exceptionally large rises were registered in the extractive industries—phosphates, bromides and potash. An increase in the demand for durable goods and construction materials contributed to the expansion of output in those areas. A rise in exports of about forty per cent was noted in the 1957–1958 period over the previous years, mainly in woolen yarns, apparel, cement, cardboard and rubber tires. While the productivity and output in the manufacturing industries varied, the largest increases were shown in the electrical appliances and a sluggish one in some other fields, such as leather products.

Because of Israel's unusual situation, the preponderance of imports over exports continued, fluctuating between $200 million in 1954, to nearly $300 million five years later. The average annual trade gap in the first decade of the country's existence was $300 million, but during that same time Israel had trebled—and, largely, settled—her population. The United States helped generously under her treaty of friendship, commerce and navigation with Israel. During the decade Israel received about $3 billion in foreign aid, partly governmental, partly private. This was considered good investment not merely from the humanitarian point of view but also from that of international trade—opening up great economic possibilities in the Middle East. However, the full unfolding of all these advantages had to wait upon the establishment of normal peacetime relations in the region.

Let Bygones ...

The orgy of frenzied murder in which the Nazi cannibals had indulged exacted a toll of many millions of lives and the surviving Jews in the formerly German-occupied territories found themselves despoiled of their belongings. No accounting has ever been made or can be made of the material damage sustained by the Jews because of the Hitlerite genocide.

At the end of the war, unconditional surrender and Allied

352

occupation took the place of a German government. Then, after several years, two separate governments were established, only one of which was recognized by the Western world—the *Bundesrepublik,* the Federal Republic. The other one, set up by the Soviets and recognized by them and their satellites, was grandiloquently called *Deutsche Demokratische Republik*—the German Democratic Republic.

Hundreds of thousands of Jews were trekking to Israel—survivors of Europe's charnel houses and of Arab hostility. In the meantime, the Federal Republic experienced an "economic miracle," with record-breaking production, capital-building, national income. Included in the assets with whose aid the Federal Republic started climbing the economic peaks were the funds the Nazis had extracted from the Jews. Most of the victims were dead. The Federal Republic, now integrated in the defense system of the West and sharing its ideology, felt it was its duty to help Israel's task of nation building. Germany's Soviet zone, the D.D.R., on the other hand, refused to countenance any claims. A reparation agreement was reached, therefore, in 1952 between the government of Chancellor Konrad Adenauer of the Federal Republic and the Israeli administration under which the former undertook to pay the latter $750 million over a period of twelve years. Payment was to be made mainly in goods Israel needed, such as chemical products and iron. An additional 450 Deutsche mark (about $112 million) was to be paid by the German government for the support of organizations throughout the world which could provide evidence that they were backing Jewish war victims through material, educational and social aid.

This arrangement was protested by the Arab countries, which did not want any help extended to Israel for the settlement of immigrants. By strengthening Israel's economy, they charged, the Bonn government was helping it to prepare a "new war of aggression." This they considered an abandonment of German neutrality in favor of "belligerency." The Arab governments threatened Germany with concerted boycott. Though the Federal Republic entertained close business relations with the Middle Eastern Arab countries, and its stakes in the region were large, the German government stood its ground and its payments of reparations to Israel continued. The Arabs did not carry out their threat.

In the task of nation building, Israel was aided greatly by German payments. While the Nazis' unspeakable crimes were not forgotten, a line was drawn between them and the postwar German regime, a member of the North Atlantic Treaty Organization. "We shall be risking our lives in the literal meaning of the word," Prime Minister Ben-Gurion stated, "unless everything possible is done on our part to encourage friendship and assistance from those countries that are able and willing to help us."

In line with this policy, Israel signed a contract in the summer of 1959 for the delivery of 250,000 grenade launchers (devices for service rifles to fire grenades) to the *Bundesrepublik*. The left-wing opposition, *Ahdut Ha'avoda* and *Mapam* raised a protest in the Jerusalem Knesset which the Premier answered by explaining that it was Israel's duty to cultivate good relations with West Germany, an important member of the world community, whereas it would serve nobody's interest to treat her democratic regime as if it were Nazi. "In matters of international relations," the Prime Minister added, "we ask ourselves the simple question: What is good for Israel? And if it is good for her, all my Jewish feelings and instinct, all my honor as a Jew and man, tell me: Do what is good for Israel and what is needed for her security. And if the martyrs from the holocaust could speak from their graves, they would tell us to be strong and of good courage."

War or Peace

On the seventh anniversary of the ousting of King Farouk of Egypt, on July 23, 1959, the United Arab Republic displayed its tanks, cannons and soldiers in a three-hour parade down Cairo's Nile Corniche, while nearly 200 Soviet-made MIG jets and light bombers flew overhead. Speaking in the presence of President

Nasser, Field Marshal Abdel Hakim Amer, Vice-President of the country and Minister of War, declared: "If Israel attacks us at any point of our border, she must face total war." Even stronger were the words President Nasser himself used three days later at Alexandria on the third anniversary of Egypt's nationalization of the Suez Canal. "Israel is a crime," he declared, "established by treachery and imperialism. . . . This time we will exterminate her. . . ."

More objective observers were of a different opinion about the relative strengths of the two countries. Wrote *The Times* (London), a ponderously mature newspaper, in a sober appraisal of the two countries' forces: "Israel cannot be pushed into the sea."

On Israel's eleventh birthday an estimated crowd of half a million spectators lined Tel-Aviv's streets to watch marching units of the army, navy and border police. They, too, saw a large number of military planes, many of them jets, fly down the route of the parade. Both they and the interceptors were, no doubt, capable of matching the performance of the Soviet-supplied Arab aircraft. The important comparison, however, was not so much the strengths of the armed forces. Far more important was the mood of the country, its belief in itself and in the ability to solve its problems.

Many problems were yet to be solved in Israel, linked with the task of creating a new country in a hostile environment, peopled with immigrants, mainly, from all parts of the world and with the most varied backgrounds. Some immigrants still had no assurance of full employment, and some were inadequately housed. Then there were the other persistent problems, such as the gap between exports and imports, which was still great. Nevertheless, it was found at this hour of stock-taking that in the preceding year alone more than twenty thousand workers had been added to the labor force and Israel's total industrial output was four times as large as eleven years before. In agriculture cultivated farm land had been increased from 400,000 to more than a million acres. The country was a going concern, and more. It was also a model

355

emulated by nations many times its size. Asian and African countries were looking to Israel for help and inspiration. And all this had been accomplished in a nation which was the very model of democracy, in a country which drew the vast majority of its citizens from autocracies. The melting pot, or, as the Israeli like to put it, the pressure cooker was at work.

Watchman, What of the Night?

These were the travails of nation building. Especially difficult had been the conduct of international relations. Different people saw it in different lights. *The Economist* of London enumerated in the spring of 1959 what Israel has got and what she had to go without. From France she gets credits, jets and sympathy, this respected weekly wrote; from Germany generous reparations, warships from Britain and generous help from the United States. "All this is welcome and necessary but does not alter the fact of Israel's basic isolation—Israel is the world's loneliest nation."

Far more optimistic looked the situation to the Israeli themselves. "We are confident," said Prime Minister Ben-Gurion, "that sooner or later a true alliance between equals will arise between the Jewish people in its own land and the free and independent Arab peoples in their countries." Until that day came, the Premier said, Israel would seek no vengeance against her hostile neighbors nor bear them grudges.

Israel was not alone because many Asian and African countries looked to her for technical assistance and inspiration. Has the world ever seen the like of this—the small guiding the big— Israel with her population of two million being visited by the representatives of Nigeria, with her nearly forty million inhabitants, wanting to learn, to be inspired.

But Israel was situated in the Middle East and her fate would be decided there. Her enemies said that eventually she would be pushed into the sea as the Crusaders' countries had been in the Middle Ages. The Crusaders, too, had only a small strip of land along the coast, not the hinterland, where death and destruction lurked.

Israel was recognized by all the major countries, was a member of the United Nations, and was a respected guide of nations and territories many, many times her size. What were the causes of Arab hostility—the basic, not the superficial ones? Time is the great healer. The belligerents of war often become allies in peace. There are examples of this all over the world, throughout history —Germany, Japan, many other countries after World War II. Memories cannot be too long in human relations or else soon there would be no humanity. So, the question has to be repeated: Why the apocalyptic hostility?

The basic cause of the hostility of the Arab leaders to Israel [a thoughtful American observer noted], is fear of the impact of her social experiment on their own people. The progress that has been made within a relatively short period by the Arab community in Israel is of particular significance in this context. The treatment on the basis of equality of both Jewish and Arab workers in matters of wages and union rights, the introduction of free compulsory elementary education for both boys and girls in Arab schools and the health services provided by the state have enabled the Arab community of Israel to achieve a standard of living which can only be envied by the Arab masses elsewhere. . . . Arab rulers are less eager to engage in peaceful competition with Israel in raising living standards than to divert attention from pressing social needs by militaristic adventures and arms purchases, justified by pointing to the Zionist danger. Eventually, however, Arab leadership will have to come to grips with the real problems of their nations—pitiable wages, disease and illiteracy. When that happens, Israel feels, peace will have come to the Middle East.*

Another reason for enmity toward Israel on the part of Arab leaders seems to be strangely involved with their hostility toward one another. There is a competition within the Arab world, as we have seen, for leadership. We have also seen that the rivalry be-

* A. C. Liveran, "Israel in the Middle East," *Current History*, November 1957.

tween Egypt and Iraq, the ancient Mesopotamia, "land of the two rivers," is as old as written history. Rivalry between the valleys of the Tigris and Euphrates, on the one side, and the valley of the Nile, has been chronic and has been one of the reasons why these regions have so often been overwhelmed by outside forces. So long as such rivalry exists the two antagonists fight one another, not only directly, but through a third party. Today this party is Israel. Each of the Arab antagonists must outdo the other to prove that it hates Israel more than does the other. Presumably, the contest is won by the greater hater. The greater the antagonism among the Arabs themselves the louder must the voices of Cairo and Baghdad rant against Israel.

It is therefore in the interest of Israel and of peace that the Arab countries' living standards should rise and the rivalry between them abate. The higher their own standards the less they need to engage in tactics in order to divert attention from their failures. When the Arab antagonists can succeed in demonstrating superiority in peace their need to wage campaigns against Israel will decrease.

Forces are at work already to prepare the ground for an *entente* between Israel and the Arab states. This view was expressed, among others, by Israel's former Prime Minister Moshe Sharett,* who said that things did not remain as "rigid and forbidding" as they appeared on the surface, even though the Soviet Union was extending a "most effective encouragement to the intransigence of Arab anti-peace policy." The facts of Israel's continued existence and the consolidation of her position were penetrating ever deeper into the political consciousness of the people around her. In the weaker Arab countries which refused to relinquish their independence to the "lust of expansion of Big Brother [Nasser]" people began to appreciate the salutary role played by Israel as a barrier to the realization of such designs.

The former Premier did not see Israel as "lonely." On the

* In an address at the meeting of the Socialist International at Hamburg, summer, 1959.

contrary, he saw her linked with a network of friendly relations to several African and Asian nations. When these countries found it worth while to co-operate with Israel in economic development and social progress, why should Israel's immediate neighbors continue to deny themselves the chance of working with her, especially since their own needs of development and progress were similar? The former Premier saw the message of Israel's achievements piercing through the walls of hatred and, in the Arab lands, reaching the ears of the common man, anxious for better living conditions, improved public services and higher personal dignity. Certainly, the message was making a strong appeal to constructively minded members of the educated classes among the Arabs. The imperative need, according to the Israeli statesman, was to build an internationally solid consensus in favor of a freely negotiated peace.

Signs of a "thaw" on the part of thoughtful Arabs, especially in Jordan, have been noted also by members of the diplomatic corps, who believe that many Arabs are growing weary of the existing situation and that, some day in the not too distant future, there may be a crack in the wall. Sustained hatred gets wearisome and loses its potency after a while. Time is on their side, the Israeli believe, and even the more pessimistic among them like to feel that an eventual combination of dawning realism and boredom among the Arabs will produce the beginning of peace.

In the case of the Middle East, the much-used expression states a well-tried axiom: all countries of the region are "in the same boat." It would be in the interest of all the inhabitants of the area, Arabs and Israeli included, to participate in a massive process of reconstruction and development with the object of raising living standards. A Middle East Development program, sponsored by the United States, was the suggestion of Aneurin Bevan, "Secretary of State for Foreign Affairs" in the "shadow cabinet" of British Labour and treasurer of the party.

Thus, it is agreed, the solution of these Middle East problems cannot be achieved through the mere display of armed force. The

359

area is a vacuum, of course, which both the United States and the Soviet Union have been trying to fill. The United States' attempts—Baghdad Pact and Eisenhower Doctrine—have been failures. The Suez campaign solved no problems; the arbitrament of arms has been tried and found wanting. When the Soviets tried to strengthen Egypt, their protégé, she turned against them eventually. The results of their subsequent attempt to strengthen Iraq are not hard to foresee. Naïve, indeed, is the person who believes in gratitude in the field of diplomacy.

It would seem to be far more realistic of the two super powers to concentrate their efforts and their funds in constructive investments, to help raise the peoples' living standards in the Middle East. Israel has provided the proof that she wants to take a constructive part in building up the creative potential of the region.

Epilogue

IT is no longer necessary to stress the importance of the Middle East today. Across it the Russians have been trying to break down the barriers separating them from the outside world in an attempt to reach warm waters—their historical warm-water thirst. What does the Soviet Union want there? Is it security or expansion? It may be impossible to give the answer since the two of them are related, especially within the framework of Soviet policy.

For about two centuries it has been a basic Western policy to contain Russia for fear that monumental size coupled with favorable strategic location might result in a preponderance of power. This containment was effected most of the time by Britain operating under special conditions. She had no mass army but only a professional one which was necessarily small and therefore its distribution required the establishment of priorities. Through long practice, Britain established a rule of law—the rule of protocol—within which each country could move freely. Only when one of them threatened to upset the balance of power did Britain remove the velvet gloves.

The task of the global policeman has now been assumed by the United States. She has a mass army that can be assigned to various parts of the globe. But she lacks the experience institutionalized in diplomatic protocol. Therefore there is much groping in the dark and reckless talk in which people indulge who have found that the masses are easier to attract if the voice is edged with spite. So they talk and write recklessly. The same people—and the writer speaks from personal experience—often sought to con- vince America in the interwar period that this country did not belong to the same planet as the old world. Do we not have every- thing we need? Why, then, bother with the rest of the world? The cycle has now turned a full circle.

Free-world leadership has been assigned to the United States by the influential European "club." Most of Asia and Africa have yet been keeping aloof. They are far from being as influential as the European club, but they are far more numerous—at least twenty times as numerous. We have been fairly lucky with NATO, whose members are also those of the European club; but not very lucky with other parts of the world, especially the Middle East. We sponsored the Baghdad Pact which, eventually, had to do without Baghdad, and proclaimed the Eisenhower Doctrine, which was a cry in the wilderness. Turkey, Iran and, farther east, Paki- stan, followed America but the core of the Middle East did not. Their former masters were Britain and France and these two countries were America's closest associates. Thus, Britain and France would be smuggled back into the Middle East under Amer- ica's protective mantle—so thought the Middle Eastern countries.

Alliances need strong anchoring places and these are the estab- lished social forces. In large parts of the area these social forces are autocratic and antiquated. It would be suicidal to foster dis- content against them, but it is also suicidal to accept them because they belong only to the fleeting moment. Here, then, has been one of those problems that can never be solved. Changes have been needed in many parts of the region but forces to bring them about are not tolerated. The road has thus been open to underground organizations—the Communists. Leading the crusade against the revolutionary forces, the United States has gained the reputation of being the leader of a latter-day Holy Alliance.

America has been suffering also from another handicap in the region. It is an area where technical skills are scarce. The United States has them in abundance and is eager to share them with others. This helps the spirit of missionary dedication prevalent among Americans. It also creates good will and eventually it may prepare the ground for missile-launching sites. Middle Easterners have the impression that for every American doing constructive work, there are two others watching whom he associates with and what publications he reads. Increasingly, the technical missionaries of the United States have been those who knew their specialty but nothing else besides. People who think about social problems are considered risks. They talk and—worst of all—write and—still worse—they are not satisfied with everything they see. The suspicion surrounding the technical experts makes them retire into themselves and they are thus cut off from their environment. The "silent American" does not belong to the world of the people he wants to help. During the reign of *Pax Britannica* the British learned to make a distinction between mature thought and subversion. Some of their greatest Prime Ministers were iconoclasts.

These and other factors have been instrumental in opening the Middle Eastern gates to the Soviets. What do their leaders want to do there; what does Khrushchev want? Are they or is he the man who will push the fatal button? History should have taught us long ago that individual people are the instruments of those dark forces whose heavings and tossings we occasionally detect in the eruptions of group actions. In historical perspective Napoleon, for instance, was also an instrument, and not the great motive force. He represented one of history's great attempts at European integration, an urgent need in his day and an urgent need today.

It is the same with the Soviets' Khrushchev. He has told the world many things which may be contradicted by history's inexorable forces. The absolute master is not he but the interaction of those forces and their consequences. Those forces consist also of the impact of other nations, personal and group interests, traditions, fears—motivated and unmotivated, emotions, mistakes—

363

sometimes ludicrous but more often tragic. In Russia's penetration of the Middle East, Khrushchev is not the final arbiter.

This is shown also by the fact that Soviet Russia, in this respect, too, has followed the pattern of Czarist diplomacy. There is the problem—Russia's landlocked condition, coupled with her gigantic strength. There is also the fear of encirclement. Nowhere is this more obvious than in the Middle East, adjacent to the Soviets for thousands of miles and their natural gate to the seas. Yet, the West feels today as it has felt for many decades that Russia's claims, no matter what their legitimacy, cannot be recognized. A strong geographic position coupled with the Soviets' tremendous size would inevitably produce a massive power that would enhance Russia's strength immeasurably. Hence the policy of containment in this region which, however, has been unsuccessful so far.

One of the reasons of this failure may be due to mutual suspicion among the Western allies themselves. For several years now a little "cold war" has been raging between members of the Western alliance, sometimes a two-cornered fight, sometimes a three-cornered one—the United States vs. Britain and France; then Britain and France against the United States; and then again America, Britain and France against one another separately.

Let the reader recall the muted accusations members of the Western alliance have hurled against one another in the Middle East. In the beginning there was the oil and most of it belonged to Britain. Then the United States wanted to join the petroleum club and today most of the oil belongs to her. Let the reader recall the charges leveled by France against both the United States and Britain, in the Middle East. She was the dominant power in the coreland of the region, Lebanon and Syria, and then, according to French accusations, along came her two "friends," America and England, and ousted her from the region after the Second World War. Let the reader recall the story of the Buraimi Oasis in the depths of the great Arab desert, waged with the weapons of America on the one side and Britain on the other, in the hands of native soldiers. As the last illustration let the reader recall what happened in the autumn of 1956, at the time of the Suez campaign, with the United States an antagonist to Britain and France.

The United States also entertains grievances against her allies in this region: the resistance to the participation of American oil at the outset; British policy in Palestine; the endangering of the status quo in Suez, and other instances. One of the reasons Western policy has not been successful in the area is because of the "cold war" among the Western allies. Let them conclude peace and the climate of opinion may then become more favorable for concerted action in this strategic region.

America, as the leader of the Western alliance, has been bending to every passing breeze in this region. President Truman brought a State Department secret into the open when he stated that within that body there have been both pro-Israel and pro-Arab factions, feuding among themselves and thus paralyzing American policy. Let, then, American diplomats conclude peace among themselves so that a constructive and consistent policy may be applied in the region.

There are vast American investments in the Middle East. Up to 1957 direct petroleum investments in that region amounted to $1,777 million. We have seen that the area is floating on a sea of oil—about 75 per cent of the known reserves. Large investments have large lobbies, which conduct their own foreign policies. They have joined those who believe that Israel is a disturbing force in the region. They do not realize that Israel is also a stabilizing force. Instead of trying to bring Israel and the Arab countries closer together they have been pandering to the Arab potentates. They do not seem to realize that the Arab rulers need them no less—perhaps more—than they need the Arab rulers. What would happen if the oil companies were to withdraw from these regions? The case of Iran provided the answer. When Iraq went revolutionary and turned away from the West, she did not turn away from the Iraq Petroleum Company. Had she done so she would have become bankrupt. The extraction of oil needs the stability created by peaceful conditions. Oil diplomacy could help in bringing these about.

The Soviet Union is directly adjacent to the Middle East and it would be unrealistic to assume that it could afford the West's taking the region over. Sooner or later a Middle East settlement would have to be reached. The Soviets can no longer be left out of account. This is one of those areas of the world in which even the most highly developed nation is economically underdeveloped. Some of them have to spend about half of their national budgets on armaments. They cannot afford it. If the enemy is communism, it must be fought with higher living standards. Jet bombers have never been too good defenses against ideologies. Keeping military budgets high, these nations have to keep living standards low. Communism sneaks into countries by springing across the low-living-standard fence. Decreasing armament expenditures, these countries would be in a position to increase calories for their peoples. Well-fed people do not start revolutions. The Middle East is thus ready-made for a reduction of armaments under the auspices of the Great Powers acting through the United Nations.

Many of the countries composing the region are not natural units. One of them, Jordan, had to be created in order to pay off a debt owed by the British to the Hashemite family, whose assistance they had during World War I. The other countries were created under the stress of international pressures: the French insisted on having Syria and Lebanon. Economic integration corresponds to the needs of the age. The European common market has shown the way. There is just as much need, if not more, for a Middle Eastern common market. Development funds are needed in this underdeveloped area. A fraction of the sums the Great Powers spend on unproductive armaments could release many productive forces in this key region.

Sooner or later the time is bound to come when the world's major nations will realize that their own survival depends on the survival of the hungry nations. An anomalous situation prevails at present. Some of these major nations are already producing so much that they must devise various projects to enable prospective customers to buy from them; the United States is the most prominent example of this type of country. Some people do not seem to realize that the United States *had* to appropriate billions of dollars to help foreign countries. Directly or indirectly that money went into the purchase of American goods without which the United States might have ended in bankruptcy.

Finally, the Arab-Israeli problem will have to be settled. Many attempts have been made but they were all piecemeal and not integrated. Settlement will be more likely to be effected after the steps outlined before have been taken. All the interested nations and all the Great Powers will have to have a hand in this settlement. The "war" between the Arabs and Israel is an anachronism. Among the Arabs there are sensible people, too, who know that the next constructive step is the conclusion of peace. They need trade with Israel, and they need her transportation facilities. They cannot afford the high armament costs the present situation entails. Nor can they afford to let their people sit on a powder keg.

There was a time when the Middle East made the most substantial contribution to the body of knowledge of the Western world. Then, for centuries, it was stagnating. Its Golden Age may never be recaptured but there is every reason to hope that its countries will make great contributions to the world in the region where man's conscience first began to dawn.

Appendix

COUNTRIES OF THE MIDDLE EAST

COUNTRY	AREA (*Sq. mi.*)	POPULATION (*Estimated*)	CAPITAL	FORM OF GOVERN-MENT
Egypt *	386,198	23,240,000	Cairo	Republic
Iran	636,000	21,146,000	Tehran	Monarchy
Iraq	116,600	5,200,000	Baghdad	Republic
Israel	7,800	2,000,000	Jerusalem	Republic
Jordan	34,750	1,500,000	Amman	Monarchy
Lebanon	3,400	1,500,000	Beirut	Republic
Saudi Arabia	597,000	6,500,000	Riyadh	Monarchy
Sudan	967,500	8,971,000	Khartoun	Republic
Syria *	171,104	3,906,000	Damascus	Republic
Turkey	296,185	24,111,000	Ankara	Republic
Yemen *	75,000	4,500,000	San'a	Monarchy

In addition, the following areas on the fringes of the Arabian Peninsula which are not independent countries but exist under special treaty relationships with Great Britain—*Aden Protectorate:* 112,000 square miles, population 800,000; *Kuwait:* 5,800 square miles, population 207,000; *Sheikhdom of Qatar* (on the Persian Gulf): 8,000 square miles, population 40,000; *Bahrein Islands* (in the Persian Gulf, off the coast of Saudi Arabia): 213 square miles, population 120,000; *Trucial States* (on the Gulf of Oman): 32,300 square miles, population 60,000-80,000; *Sultanate of Muscat and Oman* (in the southeast portion of the Arabian Peninsula): 82,000 square miles, population 550,000. Adjoining the Aden Protectorate is the British Crown Colony of *Aden;* it has an area of 75 square miles and a population of 140,000. (All population figures are recent estimates.)

* Egypt and Syria are members of the *United Arab Republic.* Together with the Kingdom of Yemen, they form the *United Arab States.*

INDEX

371